The Prehistory of the Crusades

The Prehistory of the Crusades

Missionary War and the Baltic Crusades

Burnam W. Reynolds

Bloomsbury Academic
An imprint of Bloomsbury Publishing Plc

B L O O M S B U R Y
LONDON · OXFORD · NEW YORK · NEW DELHI · SYDNEY

Bloomsbury Academic
An imprint of Bloomsbury Publishing Plc

50 Bedford Square
London
WC1B 3DP
UK

1385 Broadway
New York
NY 10018
USA

www.bloomsbury.com

BLOOMSBURY and the Diana logo are trademarks of Bloomsbury Publishing Plc

First published 2016

© Burnam W. Reynolds, 2016

Burnam W. Reynolds has asserted his right under the Copyright, Designs and Patents Act, 1988, to be identified as Author of this work.

All rights reserved. No part of this publication may be reproduced or transmitted in any form or by any means, electronic or mechanical, including photocopying, recording, or any information storage or retrieval system, without prior permission in writing from the publishers.

No responsibility for loss caused to any individual or organization acting on or refraining from action as a result of the material in this publication can be accepted by Bloomsbury or the author.

British Library Cataloguing-in-Publication Data
A catalogue record for this book is available from the British Library.

ISBN: HB: 978-1-4411-5560-3
PB: 978-1-4411-4389-1
ePDF: 978-1-4411-5039-4
ePub: 978-1-4411-5008-0

Library of Congress Cataloging-in-Publication Data
Names: Reynolds, Burnam W., author.
Title: The prehistory of the Crusades : missionary war and the Baltic Crusades / Burnam W. Reynolds.
Description: London ; New York : Bloomsbury Academic, 2016. | Includes bibliographical references and index.
Identifiers: LCCN 2015048002 (print) | LCCN 2016010476 (ebook) | ISBN 9781441155603 (hardback) | ISBN 9781441143891 (paperback) | ISBN 9781441150394 (epdf) | ISBN 9781441150080 (epub)
Subjects: LCSH: Crusades. | Baltic States–History. | Missions–Baltic States–History–To 1500. | Culture conflict–Baltic States–History–To 1500. | BISAC: HISTORY / Medieval.
Classification: LCC D162.2 .R49 2016 (print) | LCC D162.2 (ebook) | DDC 947.9/02–dc23
LC record available at http://lccn.loc.gov/2015048002

Cover design: Clare Turner
Cover image: Battle near Tannenberg 1410 / Geiger © akg-images

Typeset by Deanta Global Publishing Services, Chennai, India

CONTENTS

List of Illustrations vii
Acknowledgments viii

Introduction 1

PART ONE   The Problem 9

1   Frankfurt, 1147: The Baltic Crusades begin 11
2   A peculiar institution 28

PART TWO   The Method 41

3   The crusade studies revolution 43
4   The uses of prehistory 53

PART THREE   The Application 67

5   "Missionary war": Preaching with a tongue of iron 69
6   Baptism by treaty 97
7   The ministry of shields and swords 120
8   A new kind of pilgrim 142

9 Christian on Christian violence 158
10 The legacy of the Baltic Crusades 179

Notes 195
Glossary of People and Terms 232
Bibliography 242
Index 262

LIST OF ILLUSTRATIONS

Figure 1   The *Kaiserdom*, Frankfurt, Germany. Wikimedia Commons, courtesy of rupp.de. 15

Figure 2   The *Aula Palatina*, Trier, Germany. Photo by the author. 77

Figure 3   Heavenfield battle site, near Newcastle, UK. Photo by the author. 84

Figure 4   Charlemagne's chapel at Aachen, Germany. Photo by the author. 92

Figure 5   The Mary Window at Marienberg Castle, Malbork, Poland. Photo by the author. 137

Figure 6   Church of the True Cross, Segovia, Spain. Photo by the author. 150

Figure 7   Church of the True Cross, Segovia, ground view. Photo by the author. 152

Figure 8   Moat at Marienburg Castle, Malbork, Poland. Photo by the author. 164

ACKNOWLEDGMENTS

The writing of a book on even one facet of the Baltic Crusades proved to be a larger undertaking than I had originally anticipated. It was not, however, an experience such as George Orwell once described when he wrote: "Writing a book is a horrible, exhausting struggle, like a long bout of some painful illness. One would never undertake such a thing if one were not driven on by some demon whom one can neither resist nor understand." This strikes me as a much-overplayed version of the medieval Irish scribal complaint that in writing "three fingers do the work, but the whole body labors."

Such sentiments, while seductive on those bad days that inevitably arise, overlook the positive benefits of producing a book: the opportunity to discover and then share with the public new information and interpretations. That is a real privilege well worth the cost. I more nearly agree with Edward Gibbon, who admitted upon the completion of his masterpiece on the fall of Rome, that "a sober melancholy was spread over my mind by the idea that I had taken my everlasting leave of an old and agreeable companion."[1] I come away from this experience much the better for it. But the writing of this book was not entirely a solo endeavor as there are many who contributed wisdom, encouragement, and, above all, patience to the task. I must thank these active players, even as I fear I may omit many.

I owe many thanks to Michael Greenwood who suggested this book and helped to shepherd the proposal through the vetting process. Also, Emma Goode who has patiently, very patiently, overseen the book to completion. I must also thank Ian Buck, Production Manager for Bloomsbury and Grishma Fredric of Deanta Global for conducting the book safely through the electronic thickets of production.

I am also indebted to my home institution, Asbury University, and its provost, Dr. Jon Kulaga, who provided financial assistance for my research in Germany and Poland. I must also acknowledge Wendy Jones, our departmental administrative assistant, who was always ready to solve some of the technical problems that arose in this project. Rasa Mazeika, the noted scholar of the medieval Baltic, also provided wise counsel on some key points in the manuscript's argument. Any variances from her wisdom in my finished product are mine alone.

And I must give my deepest thanks to my family, in particular my greatest inspiration, my wife Machel, and my children, Maura, Joshua, and Andrew who have always provided encouragement as well as the occasionally needed spur to keep the project going.

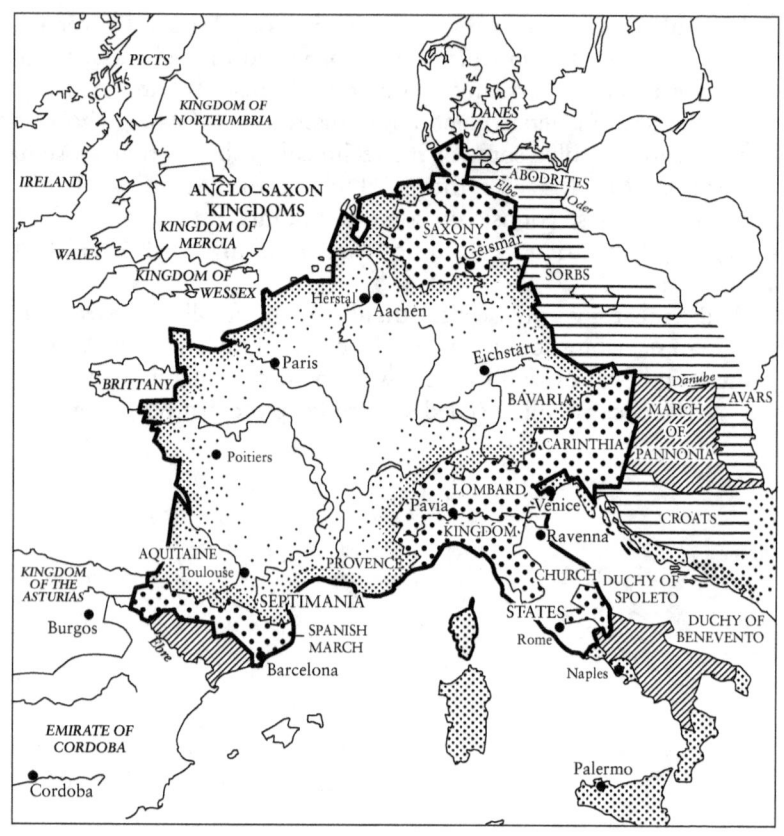

MAP 1 *The Carolingian Empire after the Conquest of Saxony.*

MAP 2 *The Baltic at the time of the Wendish Crusade, 1147.*

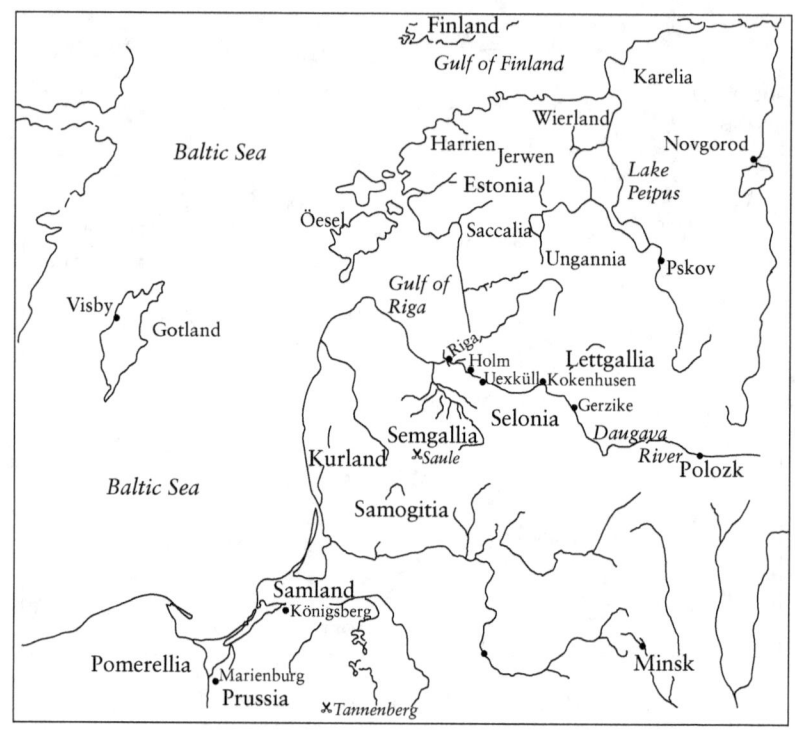

MAP 3 *The Baltic lands and peoples during the Crusade era.*

Introduction

The Crusades continue to exercise an enduring fascination, even centuries after their conclusion. As Christopher Tyerman has noted, they retain "an attractive tang of relevance," and therefore "seem approachable to modern observers, whether delighted, intrigued or appalled."[1] International events of the past decade have only reinforced this fascination. Apparently they retain their "attractive tang" for both the West and the Muslim world. The insistent use of the terms "crusade" and "crusaders" by terrorists has "plastered (them) across the world's front pages" and generated many new course offerings and seminars on the Crusades.[2] Multiple movies and historical video presentations have employed some of the finest scholars on this topic, often, it must be said sadly, telling the story of these formative events in a way that departs from the expressed opinions of the very experts that give these projects their credibility. Even with these perhaps inevitable flaws, the public seemed for a time to have an insatiable appetite for all things crusader, especially anything relating to the Knights Templar. This "crusade fever" does seem to break occasionally, but it may be that it merely subsides, like malarial attacks, only to flare up again after the next series of terrorist threats.

Yet whatever the current motivation, when the subject of the Crusades comes up, typically one thinks of the bitter, multigenerational conflict in the Holy Land between Christian and Muslim forces. The term conjures up images of the epic conquest of Jerusalem by the First Crusade in July 1099, and the subsequent romanticized figures of men such as Richard Coeur-de-Lion, Saladin, and St. Louis. These scenarios are often implicitly cast as a clash of civilizations. Yet there were other theaters of war under the umbrella term "crusade." There were other clashes of civilizations and cultures far removed from the eastern Mediterranean, and this change in locale often produced dramatic alterations in the intent and practice of crusading as well. One of these theaters lay along the shores of the Baltic Sea in northern Europe: the Baltic Crusades.

While the exact qualification of these Baltic Crusades as authentic crusades remains a matter of scholarly dispute in some circles, it is true that the participants and the Popes who authorized the campaigns were not in doubt as to the legitimacy of the enterprise.[3] Yet the change of venue from the Holy Land to the Baltic and the exchange of Muslim opponents in favor of pagan Baltic and Slavic tribes make these crusades novel. An integral part of the novelty, and perhaps a driving force for the entire undertaking, was the notion that these military invasions would convert the target peoples to Christianity. This "missionary war" emphasis gave a distinctive cast to the ebb and flow of this version of holy war and produced several odd extrapolations of religious practice.[4]

These Baltic Crusades, with their peculiar orientation toward missionary war, have long seemed an anomaly within the field of crusade studies. The lack of Jerusalem as a target, no Muslim opponents, and the emphasis on conversion and mass baptism seem to mark them out as an unfortunate corruption of crusading proper, particularly since they emerged after the First Crusade. Crusade scholars have found them curious and have often dismissed them as glorified border wars under the pretense of crusade. Standard medieval history textbooks have traditionally omitted any mention of these Baltic Crusades, an understandable decision for those works titled "A Brief History of the Middle Ages," but a culpable one for the more complete accounts.[5] How can the story of Eastern Europe be known fully without an account of the campaigns that brought these lands and peoples into the narrative? Further, popular histories have sometimes resorted to caricature to convey the sense of the quarter-millennium-long, violent campaigns of the Baltic Crusades. When describing the warrior-bishops who often directed this "sword-point conversion to Christianity," Simon Winder limned a stock character that verges on the satirical.

> This was the beginning of the great age of that long-lasting German phenomenon the "fighting bishop," a scarlet-faced predator who, dabbing the meat juices from his chin, was as happy grabbing his chain-mace and stoving in some pagan chief as putting on a mitre and attending vespers.[6]

Perhaps some of this reflexive aversion to the Baltic Crusades and the idea of "missionary war" is due to a deeply held view on war and religion. Whether or not there is awareness of the nineteenth-century Prussian war theorist, Carl von Clausewitz, most people seem to subscribe, albeit unconsciously, to his definition of war as "an act of violence intended to compel our opponent to fulfill our will."[7] When placed alongside the belief that it is against the nature of religion to force religion, the two precepts seem irreconcilable. Yet at various times and in various cultures war and religion have joined in powerful tandem. The Crusades stand as a clear example of this power. However, the Baltic Crusades, with their frank objective of expanding the faith, seem to stand out, if not apart, from crusading generally. The crusades to the Holy Land came rather late to the notion of converting their opponents, as St. Francis' attempts during the Fifth Crusade in the early thirteenth-century attest. The Baltic crusaders were not shy about making the connection between crusading and conversion some seventy years earlier. The priest Henry, author of *The Livonian Chronicle* and an actual participant in the military activities of the 1220s, summed up the Baltic Crusade's purpose:

> Their (the crusaders) business was holy, for they, when called, came to baptize the pagans and to plant the Lord's vineyard—and planted it with their blood.[8]

Yet for all the controversy, the Baltic Crusades have, although grudgingly, come to shelter nicely under the rubric of Crusade and like their more studied cousins aimed at the Holy Land, they have a long antecedence, or prehistory. The differentiating characteristics of these campaigns of conquest and Christianization did not simply materialize *de novo*, but were in many ways the end result of generations of theoretical and practical development.

William Stubbs, the noted nineteenth-century historian of the English Constitution as well as the bishop of Oxford, once observed that virtually all important current issues have their antecedence in the early medieval period.[9] While that sweeping viewpoint tends toward hyperbole, a better case might be made for locating the Crusades' origins in earlier portions of the Middle Ages. This, if true, however, presents a daunting challenge. There are so many components to crusading, whether economic, social, religious, technological, political, symbolic, etc., that bewilderment is more likely than enlightenment. While the whole question of the prehistory of the Crusades is in need of reexamination, the Baltic Crusades, owing to their sequential placement after official crusading had begun, offer a suitably delimited subject for study. Much that these crusades featured were already in place and rationalized. The vast expanse of features comprising the origins of crusading in general can await a future analysis in other volumes on crusade prehistory. I must agree with the approach taken by Sverre Bagge in his examination of medieval German historiography: "I have preferred a limited number of spotlights over a large landscape to an attempt to lessen the darkness over the whole field."[10]

The practices peculiar to the Baltic Crusades, the "spotlights" we shall ignite, seem discrete enough to allow for a closer look at their origins. However, though these practices are singularly identifiable, their ramifications are quite numerous. The various lines of development that eventually were woven together to form the Crusades made a type of institutional whole cloth. As one pulls a line out for examination, there is also a need to examine the points at which each one interweaves with others. This makes it very difficult to study in isolation the prehistory of one thread, without straying into a multiple thread count. I have opted to restrict my examination to those collateral issues that derive directly from a particular aspect of a particular set of crusades. However restricted, this study will not answer sufficiently all the questions generated by the topics examined. Indeed there will be far more questions raised than answers given. The great Belgian medievalist Henri Pirenne once said that the most blessed historian is not the one who answers questions, but the one who raises new inquiries. I take refuge in that thought.

One is obliged to follow the advice given to the singular scholar Peter Brown upon his decision to pursue a medieval history dissertation topic at Oxford. The young Brown was asked, "Have you got a bishop?" in an effort to make him seriously consider a focal point for his labors.[11] It seemed that a narrowing of research to a particular bishop would provide a platform for a more expanded understanding of the Middle Ages. That Brown did indeed "choose a bishop" is demonstrated by his subsequent biographical gem on Augustine of Hippo.[12] This study will not concentrate on a bishop—although a suitable candidate might be Albert of Buxhövden whose martial activities animated so much of the Baltic Crusades—faced with the difficulties involved in pursuing an open-ended prehistory of the Crusades, I have been constrained to take the advice given to Professor Brown and "pick a crusade" from among the multiple enterprises available. But I have discovered that even a further narrowing of scope is necessary. Thus the controversial hallmark of the Baltic Crusades—the use of what has been called appropriately "missionary war"—seems a suitable prism through which these generations-long, seemingly "eternal" crusades might be viewed. Missionary war has a *terminus ante quem*, an inception moment, in the astonishing conversion of the Roman Emperor Constantine. Prior to that, Christian warfare was virtually unthinkable. The charge of being an argument *ad novitam*, what David Hackett Fischer described years ago as "the unfortunate habit, which historians have formed and which the public has encouraged, of assuming that special significance attaches to a subject if it can be proved to be chronologically first in some respect"[13] should not pertain to this present study. In the case of missionary war, a point of origin can be determined. I do not argue for "special significance" but only that the course charted by this novel move ultimately led to a finished product in the Baltic Crusades. One cannot appreciate that finished product without understanding how it came to be.

Even with these narrowings in place, missionary war as practiced in the Baltic Crusades created a variety of associated practices that also must be examined. It seems a daunting paradox that the more one restricts the scope of this inquiry the broader it becomes. The implications for all the other components of crusading must be contextualized and sometimes recontextualized through this new angle of vision.

Therefore the principal axis of this work must revolve around two points: prehistory and the notion of "missionary war," a term coined by Carl Erdmann more than eighty years ago. Like a Venn diagram, these two concepts intersect, sometimes directly and sometimes in the subsets they spin off. The avowed objective of the Baltic Crusade, to convert pagan populations, created a series of issues such as the efficacy of conquest in defending and spreading the faith, the validity of mass conversion and the frequent apostasy that followed, the role of negotiated tribute in Christianization, and the use or abuse of local cultural mores. All these problems did not arise suddenly, but had a traceable prehistory, often of great antiquity.

The angle of vision taken will necessarily be one of an eastward gaze. For it was the western, Christian portion of Europe that expanded eastward to claim and reclaim adjacent lands and peoples in an ever-extending arc. Implicit in this perspective is a heavy focus on western ideology and the institutions that it produced. However, it is also necessary to recognize both the impact of such western views on the peoples they encountered as well as the similarities between these seemingly disparate societies. The door will be seen to swing both ways. Crusading will change its intended target even while it is modified by the conditional peculiarities of the act itself.

Of course one approaching the Baltic Crusades will, to use the felicitous phrase of Lucien Febvre, employ their own *outillage moral*, or "moral equipment."[14] The preexisting set of values that comprise this *outillage* will often govern whether one condemns or exonerates both the premise for the Baltic enterprise and its implementation. It is, basically, the same problem for historical research in general: there will be a precondition that establishes the questions asked and, unfortunately, often the answers obtained. As my principal muse for the early Middle Ages, Gregory of Tours, noted, writing history can be deceptively arduous because of this precondition:

> Writing history seems a difficult job in the first place because what you put down has to correspond exactly to the facts; and secondly because if you permit yourself to criticize any wrongdoing, most of your readers think that you are being malevolent, or even envious.[15]

Acknowledging these problems, however, does mitigate somewhat the controlling power of the *outillage*. The objective is to grasp, as much as possible, the *outillage* of the actual participants in the Baltic Crusades, both crusader and pagan. This is not to excuse, but to understand the way this equipment was put into use. But the issue goes beyond an attempt to diminish present biases in favor of a more accurate assessment of motivation. There may well be a *outillage methodique*, or "methodological equipment," that also shapes the questions asked and influences the answers obtained. My approach, derived from work in the history of early medieval Europe and influenced by taxonomical divisions used in the field of prehistory, provides my own *outillage* as I approach this study. This may prove to be as subject to error as any other approach, but its novelty may serve to either inspire or provoke productive alternatives.

To that end, I have decided to divide the work into three sections. The first addresses the problem that the Baltic Crusades present the investigator. This starts with an overview from the Crusades' beginnings at Frankfurt in 1147 and extends on into the subsequent quarter of a millennium of their development. Next is a survey of the peculiarities of the Baltic Crusades and the role of those features in setting a new course for crusading in general. The second section deals with the methods used to analyze these campaigns, beginning with a look at how crusade studies has developed over the past generation and whether or not the Baltic efforts actually qualify as true crusades. Then a chapter deals with the uses of prehistory in understanding the Baltic Crusades and lays out a useful taxonomy for organizing that prehistory. Section three follows with an analysis of the application of these analytical methods on the question of missionary war and the various extrapolative issues that come from it: war as a missionary tool, forced conversion, baptism by treaty, a reinterpretation of pilgrimage, the jarring presence of Christian on Christian war, the legacy of these crusades for future generations, and the like.

As this book is intended for a broad audience, I have chosen to include multiple quotes with the belief that using the words of the participants in this historical drama conveys the flavor of the times more accurately. In so doing, I use English translations to ease the reader's path to understanding, except when the translation leaves out or substantially modifies the impact of the passage. These quotations are, of course, referenced in the notes so that those whose curiosity has been piqued from the ideas presented here may find avenues to further their knowledge. The selection and use of sources has relied heavily on the wisdom expounded by Richard Fletcher, who advised:

> We must not shirk enquiry, of course. But it so soon becomes mired and snagged by worries about the status of the evidence (authorial sources, methods, intentions, topoi, etc.) and by vain attempts to find a means of distinguishing between the genuine—or even the "genuine"—and the conventional or the assumed.

At a certain point one just has to take the plunge, without any concomitant incitement to others to take it too.[16]

Given the potentially rancorous arguments for or against the Baltic Crusades as they are depicted in the sources, it is fair to say that I have indeed taken the plunge. I hope the reader will join me, if not in agreement, at least in curiosity. At the least we may understand a bit more of the tides of beliefs and practices that carried crusading and missionary war across the turbulent Baltic to their vexed destination.

PART ONE

The Problem

1

Frankfurt, 1147: The Baltic Crusades begin

In early March 1147, as the ice began to melt and winter promised to loosen its grip, the nobles of Christian Germany were on the move. Riding their palfreys and leading their prized warhorses, their retinues and baggage trains streamed like rivulets across the thawing landscape toward a confluence at Frankfurt on the Main River. There, atop a low hillock on an island formed by the arms of the river, stood an old church. The *Salvatorkirche*, in the blended Latin and Germanic of the time the "Church of the Savior," was built at the command of Louis "the German" (r. 843–76), a late Carolingian monarch, nearly three centuries before.[1] Now the nobles would meet there at the behest of their current king, Conrad III (r. 1138–52).[2]

Frankfurt was a familiar meeting place for such gatherings, or Diets. Less than five years earlier, it had seen the brokering of a fragile peace that ended a vicious civil war in the land.[3] Now that peace was in grave danger of coming apart at the hands of Germany's fractious nobility and their chronic territorial disputes. Yet this Diet was summoned for a quite different purpose. The beginning of the penitential season of Lent coincided with Conrad's response to the crisis that had sent shock waves through all of Europe.

That crisis had unfolded thousands of miles away north of the fabled Euphrates River. At Christmastime in 1144, the atabeg of Mosul, Imad ad-Din Zengi had marshaled enough allies in the fragmented political world of Islam to form an army capable of reversing the gains of the First Crusade.[4] Luring the Christian Count of Edessa away from his defensive position, Zengi had laid siege to the city, undermined the walls and entered it on December 24. The last holdouts surrendered on January 5, 1145, and the Crusader County of Edessa effectively ceased to exist. While this would certainly rank as a major setback in the centuries-long warfare between the Christian West and the Muslim East, the fall of Edessa seemed to do even more. It reached into the very souls of western Europeans.

Edessa, alternately under Christian Armenian and Muslim Turkish rule during much of the eleventh century, had been taken by the forces of Baldwin of Boulogne in a most treacherous fashion as part of the quickly mythologized First Crusade.[5] Baldwin had tricked the Armenian ruler, Thoros, into designating him as heir and then promptly had the gullible prince killed. Now, some forty-six years later, the County of Edessa had emerged as one of the "Crusader states" and few remembered, or cared, how the territory had been obtained. But almost everyone in Christendom did care very deeply that it had now been lost. Zengi's conquest not only meant the loss of Edessa, but also signaled a growing threat from Islam.

Since most crusaders, those who survived the journey and the combat, returned home at the end of their mission, the Crusader states were chronically short of defenders.[6] While there was an intermittent stream of new warriors coming from Europe quite apart from the official numbered crusades, the Christian enclaves had to depend upon local support, called "Turcopoles" or "Syrians," for sufficient troops to maintain their hold on the territory.[7] The main defensive advantage for the Crusader states was the disunity of the various Muslim governments in the region. Thus when Zengi created a movement offering to consolidate Muslim armies, the fear was that all the Crusader states might fall like dominoes. The possibility that Islam could recoup its losses, including the Holy City of Jerusalem, seemed imminent.

The answer to this crisis was obvious: the reignition of the crusade spirit that had led to the great victories of nearly fifty years before. If another *motio valida*, as the groundswell of public support had been called, could be generated, Zengi's victory would be reversed easily. There had been around 200,000 participants in the First Crusade and there was a strong feeling that another such response could not only regain Edessa, but extend Christian reconquest of the Holy Land in significant ways. It was to this end that Pope Eugenius III

(r. 1145–53) issued the bull *Quantum praedecessores* on December 1, 1145,[8] citing the need for a crusade and challenging the nobles of France and Italy to measure up to their ancestors' First Crusade performance. Eugenius' use of an appeal to ancestral pride while calling for a crusade continued a practice that had by then become common. Even Urban II, in his speech at the Council of Clermont in 1095, had made the same kind of appeal, praising—according to Robert of Rheims, a chronicler of the First Crusade—Charlemagne for having "destroyed the kingdom of the pagans" and urging the assembled nobles thus: "Oh, most valiant soldiers and descendants of invincible ancestors, be not degenerate, but recall the value of your progenitors."[9] The use of an appeal to ancestral pride was a predictable component in the challenge to crusade by the 1140s.

However, this challenge was not received enthusiastically in a Europe widely infected with civil war. It took all the diplomatic skills and personal charisma of the Pope and his former mentor, the celebrated St. Bernard of Clairvaux (1090–1153), to persuade sufficiently powerful feudal lords to take the cross.

The initial target of the crusade call was Louis VII (r. 1137–80) of France. France had been the hotbed of early crusading, so much so that the Muslims forever after called crusaders *Franji*, or "Franks."[10] Louis' kingdom could reasonably be expected to provide immediate and numerous candidates for this new enterprise. No monarch had as yet committed to crusading, but Louis was apparently quite enthusiastic about the idea. Perhaps wishing to atone for his massacre of more than a thousand people in a church burning at Vitry,[11] Louis appears to have taken the cross at his Christmas court in December 1145. His lead was not, however, followed by his nobles, who may or may not have heard of the various exemptions and protections offered by *Quantum praedecessores*, issued only days before. It would take nearly four months of further domestic diplomacy to convince the French nobility to follow their king.

Finally, at the Burgundian town of Vézelay, during Holy Week 1146, the preaching of St. Bernard and the slowly building fervor for crusading erupted in a frenzy of support. It was said that so many rushed to take the cross that Bernard ran out of his prepared cloth insignias and was forced to rip up his own clothes to make new ones.[12] But even this frenzy of support was not enough. Pope Eugenius, at this point basically shut up by opponents in Rome, authorized Bernard to preach in Flanders, formerly a hotbed of First Crusade support, as well as in Germany.¹³ While the preaching at Flanders proved less than fruitful, Germany promised to supply not only many warriors, but also another royal participant of the highest order: Conrad III. If the crusade could recruit both Louis VII of France and Conrad III, who was the *de facto* emperor, it would seem to guarantee success.

Thus it was that St. Bernard appeared at Conrad's Christmas court at Speyer in 1146, prepared to enlist the king of the Germans. Like Louis, Conrad was subject to persuasion. What better place and time to take the cross than the annual crowning ceremony at Christmastime? The tradition of holding a Christmas court had become linked with the reaffirmation of the coronation oath in which the monarch reminded himself and his people of the traditional constraints of governing. Conrad had apparently taken a trip to the Holy Land years before becoming king, and was thus quite well acquainted with the perilous predicament of the Crusader states.¹⁴ Despite this predisposition to the cause, Conrad had been a bit reluctant to join the enterprise when first approached by Bernard in mid-November.

His concerns were well founded. The sputtering civil war between Conrad's house, the Hohenstaufen, and the other major dynasty in Germany, the Welfs, always bubbled just beneath the surface. The peace that was holding the warring parties apart was like a basted seam on a garment, subject to coming loose at the slightest pressure. Should the king journey east, with the extended absence this involved as well as the very real possibility of death either by combat or the uncertainties of travel, the kingdom would be in imminent danger of fracture. Further complicating the issue was the fact that Conrad's likely successor, his son Henry Berengar, was only ten years old and thus not at the traditional age of majority of fourteen.¹⁵ Obviously, there were many securities that must be put in place before the King could depart.

Yet Conrad did take the cross on December 28, after a moving and pointed sermon from Bernard, and many of his leading nobles from western Germany joined in. A more widespread positive response, in particular a positive response from the fractious eastern Saxon magnates, was needed to establish the dynastic security measures required to safeguard Conrad's kingdom in his absence. Therefore the call went out for a Diet to be convened more than fifty miles to the north, at Frankfurt, in March 1147.

FIGURE 1 *The Kaiserdom, Frankfurt, Germany. This fourteenth-century church sits on the site of the original one called Salvatorkirche ("Savior's Church"), which hosted the Diet of Frankfurt in March 1147. It was here the Wendish Crusade was proclaimed, beginning what would become the Baltic Crusades. (Wikimedia Commons, courtesy of rupp.de)*

It was for this purpose that the nobles of Germany gathered at the Church of the Savior. The assembly must have presented a glittering spectacle, with all the trappings and finery attendant to the nobles' station in society. While the ornamentation associated with heraldry had not reached the levels it would attain in the coming centuries, in 1147 it was noticeable enough to cause concern for some. Pope Eugenius took note of the tendency to emphasize material things at the expense of spiritual matters in his papal bull *Quantum praedecessores I*, when he warned anyone going on crusade "not to care for precious clothes or elegant appearance or dogs or hawks or other things that are the signs of lasciviousness" and to "pay no attention to multicolored clothes or minivers or gilded or silvered arms,"[16] instead telling them to concentrate on the issue of subduing the infidels. The tension between the customary material desires of the world and the spiritual side of crusading would be a constant in the coming Baltic Crusades.

It is difficult to ascertain exactly how many of the feudal aristocracy were in attendance, largely because there exists no full account of the proceedings. Even though the eminent historian Otto of Freising, the half-brother of Conrad III, was not only present at Frankfurt, but also accompanied Conrad on the ensuing crusade to the Holy Land, one has to piece together the roster of participants. Otto only tersely records that "Conrad, the king of the Romans, called together the princes at Frankfurt . . . for the holding of a general diet."[17]

As sketchy as the records are, those known to be in attendance represent a worthy sampling of the leading nobility of twelfth-century Germany. Joining Conrad at Frankfurt was the eighteen-year-old Henry "the Lion," Duke of Saxony, and his ally, the nineteen-year-old Count of Holstein Adolf II of Schauenburg. Also present was Conrad of Zähringen, now nearing sixty, but firmly in control of his ducal holdings of Burgundy (not the French territory, but a portion of modern-day Switzerland and the Black Forest). These magnates had a history of opposition to Conrad's government and needed to be pacified before any crusade could be launched. But a strong supporter of Conrad's Hohenstaufen cause was also present, Albert of Ballenstedt, nicknamed "The Bear," a veteran campaigner in his late forties who would ultimately expand his northern border territories, called the Nordmark, and turn them into the Margraviate of Brandenburg, the ancestor of the Kingdom of Prussia.

Those church leaders present were overshadowed by the famous Bernard of Clairvaux, nicknamed *doctor mellifluus*, or "honey-tongued teacher." So great was Bernard's fame as he progressed north from France that word of his miraculous healings caused him to be mobbed by enthusiastic supporters upon his arrival at Frankfurt. He was only saved from physical damage at the hands of his admirers by the quick thinking of King Conrad himself, who swept the slightly built Bernard up in his arms and rushed him to safety.[18] Other notable churchmen in attendance included Peter the Venerable, abbot of the famed monastic house of Cluny; Conrad's younger half-brother, Otto, bishop of Freising; and the eminent Anselm, bishop of the border see of Havelberg, who would subsequently be designated papal representative for the upcoming crusade in the north.

Frederick of Swabia, Conrad's nephew, who would later become famous as the Emperor Frederick "Barbarossa," was also present along with Conrad "The Great," Margrave of Meissen, and the Count Palatine Hermann. How many of the lesser nobles were present is not known, but the scene was set for making an effective call to the German lords, both secular and ecclesiastical, to set out on the crusade at hand. All that was needed to nullify the threat of renewed civil war was for Bernard to work his oratorical magic on the assembly and explain the sufficient papal guarantees. Otto of Freising later reflected on how things changed after the Diet in Frankfurt: "Suddenly almost the entire West became so still that not only the waging of war but even the carrying of arms in public was considered wrong."[19] All petty disagreements ceased and the warring factions, as of one accord, turned their military might toward the Holy Land.

King Conrad arrived on March 11 and there seems to have been—there is a paucity of records—significant business transacted on Thursday, March 13. The date was more than a happenstance, in that Conrad had been crowned king at Aachen exactly nine years before by Cardinal Theodwin of Santa Rufina, who now was in attendance at Frankfurt as the papal representative.[20] The delicate diplomatic negotiations that were necessary to secure the kingdom while on crusade would be strengthened by the anniversary commemoration of Conrad's coronation and the presence of the same luminous prelate that had inaugurated his reign.

Those diplomatic negotiations revolved around the long-standing Welf and Hohenstaufen power struggle. This rivalry had reached critical mass upon the death of Emperor Henry V in 1125. The constant struggles between the royal house and the nobility of Germany had coalesced into these two major factions.[21] Against the backdrop of sputtering civil war an uneasy truce was brokered in 1142, but the Welf-Hohenstaufen rivalry would provide an impetus to the early Baltic Crusades as well as form a constant, kaleidoscopic backdrop to territorial ambitions in northern Europe for quite some time.[22]

It was in this atmosphere of tension and distrust that the preaching of the Second Crusade reached Frankfurt in March 1147. The tension and distrust was exacerbated by the fact that the Welf-Hohenstaufen conflict not only involved Saxony and Bavaria, but also included the on-again, off-again expansions east of the Elbe River into the land of the Slavs. Should any sizable portion of either faction depart for the Holy Land, the other side could reasonably be expected to seize the opportunity to infringe on the present, and perhaps future, territorial holdings of their opponents. But that was not the immediate prospect. A crusade to the Holy Land would siphon off most, if not all, of the warring, contentious nobles of Germany and thus bring a type of peace to the land. Crusades were often framed as "healing" excursions that took the disruptive nobles and their combat retinues out of European internecine war to a more productive war on behalf of the faith in the far *outremer* or "overseas" shores. All that remained at Frankfurt was to secure the succession, in the eventuality that Conrad would not return from the proposed crusade, and allow the mellifluous Bernard of Clairvaux to work his recruitment magic on the assembled nobility.

The first part of the agenda seems to have gone smoothly. The German magnates agreed to designate young Henry Berengar as coruler in Conrad's absence as "Henry VI" and placed him under the tutelage of Archbishop Henry of Mainz and Abbot Wibald of Corvey.[23] The second, and by far the most important part, did not go as expected. The objective was to persuade large numbers of German nobles to take the cross, so that an overwhelming military force would flow from both France and Germany to certain victory in the Holy Land. But the blandishments of St. Bernard, rhetorically elegant as they no doubt were, appear to have been received in an entirely different manner by the German nobles. They seem to have liked the idea of crusade, but with a novel target in mind. Against all expectations, the Saxon nobles passed on a crusade to the Holy Land and demanded that they be authorized to crusade against the pagan tribes east of the Elbe River—a multiple peoples commonly lumped under the name "Wends."

Given the lack of information on this decision, we cannot know if they were aware of the implications of this move. Can this proposed campaign truly be called a crusade? If so, how can we apply the mechanisms of crusading, as established in the First Crusade? If the religious rites of the pagans were to be "wiped out," as Bernard would later urge, Christianity was to be the obvious replacement. Does that make these wars a missionary effort? The sources are as maddeningly vague on who it was who suggested this Wendish Crusade as they are on the reasoning behind it but the eventual makeup of the enterprise was heavy with Saxon nobles. All Helmold of Bosau would say, writing some twenty years after the event, was that "the initiators of the expedition . . . deemed it advisable to design one part of the army for the eastern regions."[24] One is tempted to see the "young lions," those Welf princes in their late teens, Adolf of Holstein and Henry "the Lion" of Saxony, as instigators of the move. Both had inherited their lands as small children, been protected by regencies against rapacious opponents, and now, as young adults, longed to expand their territories eastward. In fact, Adolf had, at the tender age of thirteen, founded a trading post on the Baltic just east of the Elbe that would become the massively powerful commercial hub known as Lübeck. If these aggressive young princes did lead the charge for a Wendish Crusade, it would explain why Hohenstaufen supporters such as Albert "the Bear" also participated. Their participation would ensure that no one side gained the upper hand in adding territories; for Albert, who had recently been driven away from the Duchy of Saxony, the crusade would possibly allow him to add to his holdings in the northeast, the Nordmark.

Whatever the motivation, the German participation in the Second Crusade would indeed include a major force destined for the Holy Land, led by King Conrad himself; however, it would also feature a large military operation to the pagan lands northeast of settled, Christian Saxony. Crusade historians have seen this venture into the pagan lands as setting a dangerous precedent. The chronic shortage of crusaders in the Holy Land would now be worsened by the diversion of large numbers of potential crusaders to a project far from Palestine.[25] Was it a sincere desire to expand the church or a desire to expand their own power and wealth that moved the Saxon instigators of the Wendish Crusade? This would be a question that would linger throughout the coming quarter of a millennium and bedevils scholars even today. A contemporary Danish historian, Sven Aggessen, would note that the "proud Teutons (Saxons) . . . were never content with their own boundaries."[26] Given this, the campaign east of the Elbe River would seem to be nothing more than a continuation of the normal practice of land acquisition under the novel rubric of crusade.

We have no account of whether there was heated discussion about this. Bernard had been tasked, after receiving special permission and authorization from Pope Eugenius III, to preach and recruit in Germany for the Holy Land objective. No mention had been made, or perhaps even imagined, of a secondary front against the Slavs. Surely Bernard must have been resistant to the idea. Yet it appears that the saintly Cistercian doctor did agree with the proposition at the Diet, only afterward to seek papal approval. Nearly a month later, on April 11, the pope issued a revised, and apparently updated, version of *Divina dispensatione*, his original description of crusading status, in which he granted the Wendish crusaders the same privileges as those destined for the Holy Land.[27] Bernard had apparently convinced his old pupil that the opening of a second crusading front was in the best interest of the church. Since military operations were already underway in Spain, that theater of war was also included in what had suddenly become a multiregional endeavor.[28] It was as if each portion of Christendom that shared a border with a hostile foe was authorized to attack under the papal rubric of crusade. No longer would the crusade be confined to the Holy Land; it now would be directed against non-Muslims too.

There were, however, some issues to work out concerning the target of this new crusading effort. The Baltic and Elbe western Slavic peoples, known collectively as "Wends," had been in constant contact with the German people for centuries, often as allies, sometimes as coreligionists, and frequently as enemies. As early as c. 800 AD, the *Royal Frankish Annals* record that the Abodrites, a major tribal grouping among the Wends, were called into service to support Charlemagne's war against the rebellious, and as yet pagan, Saxons because they "have always aided the Franks, ever since the Franks accepted them as their allies."[29] As with most tribally organized peoples, there were numerous small subgroups that tended to coalesce into larger, more manageable, affiliations. The three major ones were the aforementioned Abodrites, located east of the Elbe up to the Baltic coast in Mecklenburg, the Wilzes, further south to the Spree River yet still east of the Elbe, and the Sorbs, even further south toward Meissen. Beyond the territory of the Wends was a vast expanse of pagan tribes, what Robert Bartlett has called "an arc of non-literate polytheism that stretched from the borders of Saxony to the Arctic Circle."[30] It represented "the most enduring bastion of European paganism,"[31] presenting Christendom with a sequential roster of potential conquests once crusading was authorized. The Holsatians were present in the west, and there were also the Rugians, Semgallians, Livs, Letts, Esths, and many more eastward all the way to Finland; once crusading began, it would be hard to know where it should end. Even the Christianized Russians might feel the wrath of a crusading army.

This undertaking represented a strange version of crusade. Lacking a transcript of the discussion, we must rely on the letters of St. Bernard, written in the aftermath of the Diet of Frankfurt and the subsequent *Divina dispensatione II*, for details on the purpose of the Wendish Crusade. Bernard, apart from making general arguments in favor of the crusade—of note, his calling the time in which he lived the *tempus acceptibile*, or the appropriate eschatological moment for wresting the once Christian lands back from the pagan enemies of Christ[32]—appears keen to see crusading as a way to redirect, if not stop altogether, the Western penchant for civil war. In a contemporary letter to the English lords, he criticized them for their infighting. "For how long will your men continue to shed Christian blood; for how long will they continue to fight amongst themselves?"[33] It would be far better to fight on behalf of the church than against fellow Christian lords. This was an important point to make in war-torn Europe generally, but especially in the fractious Holy Roman Empire.

For objectives specific to the Wendish Crusade one must turn to Bernard's letter addressed "to all the faithful," not just the Germans, in which he spells out the rationale for this novel enterprise.[34] While he notes the need for Christians to take "vengeance on the pagans" and to reclaim formerly Christian lands, he believes conversion to be the prime objective of the proposed crusade: "But the evil one feared far more the damage he would incur from the conversion of the pagans." The answer for this was to launch a crusade into pagan lands not only to reclaim lost territories, but also to forcibly bring the target people to Christianity. Bernard drove the message home with the most problematic statement of the Wendish Crusade: that war against the pagans should continue "until such a time as, by God's help, they shall be either converted or wiped out" (*donec auxiliante Deo aut ritus ipse aut natio deleatur*).[35] Bernard also made sure his readers understood that this was not simply his interpretation of the situation, although he was authorized to preach this crusade, but the official decree of the Holy Roman Empire. With "the council of the king, bishops, and princes who had come together at Frankfurt, the might of Christians was armed against" these "wicked pagan sons." Bernard cast his net wide by emphasizing that any military candidate who had "not yet taken the Cross for Jerusalem may know that they will obtain the same spiritual privileges by undertaking this expedition." To drive the point home that this was no mere border raid made temporarily holy, he "utterly" forbade any truce or tribute settlement with the pagans, short of total victory for the Cross.[36] As a parting instruction, he urged that a copy of this letter "should be carried everywhere and that the bishops and priests should proclaim it to the people of God." The crusading army's departure date—this was to be the day of the Feast of the Apostles Peter and Paul, in June 1147—was appended to establish a concrete timetable for the expedition. The redoubtable Anselm of Havelberg, keen to recover his Episcopal city, was installed as papal legate for the campaign.[37] All was in place for a smooth launch of this new crusading venture.

It cannot be said that the enterprise went well. The prince of the Abodrites, Niklot (c.1090–1160), who had ruled the Slavic confederation since 1131, got wind of the impending campaign and sent an urgent appeal to Count Adolf of Holstein, an erstwhile ally. Finding that Adolf had aligned himself with the crusaders, Niklot rather ominously told the Count that "thus far I have stayed the hands of the Slavs from troubling you; now, at length, I will withdraw my hand and leave you to your own devices."[38] Making good on his threat, Niklot launched a preemptive strike on Lübeck. As a staunch pagan, he felt betrayed by his former Christian allies, particularly Adolf of Holstein, who now suddenly seemed to regard him as a suitably evil target for religious aggression. Since Adolf had founded Lübeck under a rapprochement with Niklot, the new trading city seemed the obvious choice for a retaliatory target. At dawn on June 26, 1147, as the crusading armies were forming up farther south in Saxony, Niklot's fleet caught the citizens of Lübeck drunk "with many a potation" and destroyed their ships which were "heavily laden with merchandise."[39] From there the Abodrites devastated the whole surrounding province of Wagria, paying special attention to the settlers from Westphalia, Holland, and "other foreign peoples" that Adolf had imported to work the land. But Niklot was aware that retaliation would be swift; he had fortified the town of Dobin as a refuge when he first heard of the proposed crusade. It would be a prepared and determined enemy that the Wendish Crusade would face in the lands beyond the Elbe.

The Crusade lasted for one campaigning season. The Christian army, augmented by a contingent of Danes, besieged both Dobin and the other key Abodrite stronghold of Demmin, but could take neither. After a detour to attack the city of Stettin (Szczecin) the crusade descended to the level of a fiasco. Stettin was a Christian city, a fact only made apparent to the crusaders when the citizens posted crosses on their walls and sent their bishop, Albert, out to talk to the besieging army.[40] Apparently the crusading fervor melted away amid this embarrassment and the dawning conviction that the damage being done during the campaign was ultimately going to cost the crusaders more than the Slavs. Helmold tells us that the crusading force decided that "the land we are devastating (is) our land, and the people we are fighting (are) our people."[41] At length, the stalemate was broken with an agreement that the Slavs would accept baptism, albeit later events would show the Slavs' faith to be quite ephemeral. The crusaders, now effectively bought off, straggled home.

This Wendish Crusade would seem to be no more than a failed experiment; a blip on the screen of history except for the precedent it set. For this was to be no one-time affair, but rather the beginning of an era. Once these military forays to the east had been blessed by the rubric of crusade, the limits to such endeavors seemed boundless. The failure of the crusade of 1147 did not deter the Saxon and Danish nobility from continuing their efforts in the coming years. Valdemar "the Great" of Denmark, who emerged from a three-way civil war to become king in 1157, killed Niklot in battle in 1160 and completed the conquest of the Wends in 1168 by taking their stronghold of Arkona and destroying their principal shrine to their god Svantovit in a most colorful way. The crusader king had the huge wooden idol "brought forth; a noose was put around its neck and it was dragged around the Danish forces before it was cut into firewood and burned."[42] At this point the Wends became Christian. Valdemar even struck coins with a palm branch on one side, the traditional symbol of a crusading pilgrim, and a cross on the other.[43] The imagery was unmistakable and the crusading march eastward continued. As the years rolled by, Christian German and Danish knights pressed ever forward against a wide variety of pagan opponents in what would be known as "the Baltic Crusades."

The difficulty in ensuring a steady supply of crusaders was largely addressed when the aggressive Albert von Buxhövden was appointed the first bishop of newly founded Riga, Latvia, in 1201. Having received a papal sanction for crusading, given in 1199 and reaffirmed by Pope Innocent III in 1201,[44] Bishop Albert wasted no time organizing a fighting force that could at once protect the new Christian mission in Livonia as well as gain new territory for the faith by the sword farther along the Baltic shoreline. Owing to the work of this warrior-prelate, the bishop of the Livonians for nearly thirty years, and aided by the political turmoil in Germany, annual recruitment of crusaders became commonplace. These *reisens* ("risings" or "setting out," similar to one of the Latin terms for crusading, *iter*, or "journey") consisted of short-term German crusaders who pressed forward for generations in what came to be so routine as to be called the "eternal Crusades."

The system even expanded into a year-round affair sometime around 1211–12, when the crusaders realized that campaigning in winter was possible. The relative shallowness of the Baltic Sea meant that it was warmer than expected during the summer sailing months and susceptible to freezing in the winter. William Urban describes the advantages of crusading in the winter: "In Livonia . . . winter was often more suitable for cavalry operations than summer. The swamps froze, the underbrush was less obstructive, and the natives had more difficulty hiding their tracks."[45] The freezing temperatures of winter created ice bridges over waterways causing "a better path over both land and sea."[46] It goes counter to most military histories to think of a campaign in deep winter, but it became a regular part of the Baltic Crusades. It must have been an impressive sight as Henry's *Livonian Chronicle* attests.

> As they trod on the ice with their horses and vehicles they made a noise like a great peal of thunder, with the clashing of arms, the shaking of the vehicles, and the movement and sound of men and horses falling and getting up again here and there over the ice, which was as smooth as glass because of the south winds and the rain water which had fallen at that time and the cold that followed.[47]

The *reisens* were then divided into two basic categories, the larger one in summer, called the *sommer-reysa*, and a smaller one in December and January—there were breaks for the feasts of Christmas and Epiphany—called the *winter-reysa*.[48] Apparently the winter campaign was a type of spoiling expedition designed to keep the pagan forces off balance while the summer one was designed for purposeful territorial gain. Both involved what one crusader called the *Tanz mit den Heiden*, or "dance with the heathen."[49] It is tempting to see this as a type of packaged, all-inclusive military and penitential adventure, but we must remember that it was a potentially lethal way to gain honor, fame, and forgiveness.

But the need for a permanent fighting force to supplement this seasonal flow of crusaders from Germany caused, in 1202, Bishop Albert to found the *Fratres militiae Christi Livoniae*, commonly called "The Swordbrothers" after their German nickname of *Schwertbrüder*. For more than thirty years, until their defeat at the hands of the pagan Samogitians and Semgallians in 1236, the Swordbrothers not only protected Christian lives and property in recently converted lands, but also actively campaigned to extend Christianity by the sword. Even after their defeat, the survivors were simply folded into another military order, the Teutonic Knights, who had migrated northward from the Holy Land crusading front to the Baltic, to continue their conquests. The cast of characters in the Baltic Crusade was now complete. The only question was just how long these "eternal crusades" would endure, and what impact they would make on the expanding borders of Christendom.

The Baltic Crusades exhibited an intensity and ferocity that could alternate between the tragic and the comical. On more than one occasion, as crusader ships disappeared over the horizon, the newly baptized Slavs would dive into the river to "wash off their baptism," saying, "scrubbing off the faith we have received, we send it after the withdrawing Saxons."[50] In 1206, Bishop Albert of Riga, when presented with the bloody head of a particularly troublesome pagan leader, "rejoiced and gave thanks to God, who through a few, wrought the salvation of His church."[51] When cautioned that the church might not approve of the violent tactics regularly employed in these campaigns, a crusader quipped that "the sword was Pope enough for them!"[52] Both Christian and pagan alike indulged in wanton bloodshed and in the taking of the opponent's women.[53] All in all, the Baltic Crusades seem to represent a grim chapter in the history of Christianization. But to decry their violent practices in what was generally a very violent era is to simultaneously ignore their eventual positive benefits and to close off any effort at understanding why they happened.

These crusades would mimic much that is associated with crusading proper, including papally sanctioned warfare as penance, and even the establishment of military orders such as the Swordbrothers and their later incarnation with the Teutonic Knights. But in several significant ways, the Baltic Crusades marked a real departure from the notions associated with crusading. Even the terms used to describe the crusading activities took on a different significance in this exotic arena of conflict. Baltic crusaders regularly were called "pilgrims" although there were no holy places to visit in their campaigns. Further, the crusaders often found themselves arrayed against opponents who were fellow Christians, not pagans. Riding above and through these oddities was the notion of missionary war. Rather than fighting simply to recover formerly Christian lands, the Baltic crusaders would be intent on the conversion of their opponents. This was to be accomplished by the application of military force, with victory sealed by treaties and requiring mass baptisms. These crusades certainly pose a problem for any easy, lapidary, classification of the phenomenon of crusading. While some attempts at conversion were undertaken in the Holy Land in the thirteenth century, most of these features of the Baltic Crusades were missing in the traditional theater of operations for crusades—the Levant.[54] Thus the origins and ramifications of what transpired at Frankfurt, and beyond, are necessary subjects of investigation and well deserve their rightful place in crusade studies. But as one embarks on that study, the long train of development that led to these peculiarities must be evaluated in order to reach a fuller understanding of the Baltic Crusades.

Questions for discussion

Why did the Saxon nobles want to crusade nearby and not in the Holy Land?

Why was it dangerous for Conrad III to leave his kingdom and go on a crusade? How was this danger resolved?

What caused the calling of a Diet at Frankfurt in March 1147?

What role did the Hohenstaufen-Welf rivalry play in beginning the Baltic Crusades?

Was Bernard of Clairvaux out of line to authorize the Wendish Crusade at Frankfurt?

What do you think Bernard of Clairvaux meant by "either the rites or the nation is to be wiped out"?

Why did the Wendish Crusade of 1147 fail?

How was the Wendish Crusade the beginning of many more to come?

2

A peculiar institution

When the meeting concluded on a day in March 1147 at the Church of the Savior, which was perched on a low island on the river at Frankfurt, the leaders of the expedition, later sources briefly note, felt it advisable that one-third of what would be the Second Crusade expedition should be directed toward the pagans living close by the German edge of Christendom. This rather laconic appraisal of the situation in the later sources gives one the impression that the Wendish Crusade, the prototype of the Baltic Crusades to follow, was fully within the understood boundaries of crusading in general. But that would be incorrect. The crusades east of the Elbe and along the Baltic were singularly different in many important aspects. The differences did not, however, lessen their impact in any way. A quarter of a millennium later a great sweep of territory would be added to Christendom. Marcia Colish has summed up the enabling changes that brought about this historic impact. "A reconceptualization of Crusade ideology was needed, and provided, to justify the invasion of regions which had never been in Christian hands."[1]

The label given to these efforts, "the Baltic Crusades" or "the Baltic Crusade," contains a misleading message. The campaigns included in the term Baltic Crusades are multiple and consist of several, and separate, efforts: the Wendish Crusade, the Prussian Crusade, the Livonian Crusade, the Samogitian Crusade, and the like. But through all these discrete conquests, a consistent theme remains: the use of warfare to expand the Christian world. A fundamental, perhaps *the* fundamental, reason for the Holy Land Crusades had been the reclamation of formerly Christian lands. In the case of the Baltic Crusades this was manifestly not the reason. Something new was born at Frankfurt, yet like most newborns, it had a suitable gestation period. This period of formation begs investigation.

However, as a subset of the often overlooked Second Crusade, the affairs at Frankfurt and the subsequent Baltic Crusades are doubly cursed with neglect. Since they represent a radical expansion of the crusading structure, they are difficult to fit into the standard interpretive template. Typically, many who are unsure as to how to categorize the Baltic Crusades either downplay their significance or omit altogether their very existence. Geoffrey Hindley's discussion of the Second Crusade recruitment efforts says not a word about Frankfurt and suggests that Conrad III's taking of the cross at Christmastime at Speyer represented the totality of German involvement,[2] while Rodney Stark calls the Wendish Crusade of 1147 a mere "sideshow."[3] Yet the Baltic Crusades proved to be a most fruitful "sideshow" that moved the notion of crusading in multiple new directions. What exactly was this movement, touched off almost casually at Frankfurt, but which stretched out for nearly three centuries? This has been a question difficult to answer and therefore productive of a wide variety of responses. It makes the Baltic Crusades a type of mirror reflecting the preoccupations of the viewer. Eva Eihmane has identified at least five different ways these crusades have been made to serve contemporary agendas, from being a vehicle for a superior culture, or conversely a "heroic" struggle for freedom, all the way to serving as an example of Marxian class oppression.[4] As has so often been the case with complex developments, the inception of the Baltic Crusades generated far more questions than answers. In order to catalog these changes, it is as important to say what they were not as to say what they were.

Most obviously the Baltic Crusades were not directed toward the Holy Land in general and Jerusalem in particular. William Urban notes that some have seen this distinction as a deficiency, noting that "until recently" crusade scholarship has focused exclusively on "only those expeditions to the Holy Land that ended in 1291."[5] As the avowed objective of the dissident Saxon nobles at Frankfurt was to crusade nearby, and indeed the "nearby" continued to move as a portable frontier for generations, the recovery of sacred sites in the Holy Land was distantly peripheral to the project. It seems that Christendom's border was the edge of an idea as much as an actual territorial marker.

Further, the Baltic Crusades were not directed against Muslim opponents but rather against pagan neighbors who were, as the kaleidoscopic political situation dictated, often allies and occasionally coreligionists. The initial opponents in the Wendish Crusade, the Abodrites, had been, as recently as in the period 1128–31, under the rule of the Christian Danish king Cnut, after he had imprisoned the two native contenders for power, Pribislav and Niklot.[6] Only when Cnut was assassinated did the Abodrites fall back under local control. This Niklot, who eventually gained control of the Abodrite lands, was the same leader who unwisely trusted in Count Adolf of Holstein's support in the run-up to the Crusade of 1147, and who responded to the Count's duplicity by attacking Lübeck. There was a long history of this type of on-again, off-again alliance. The Baltic Crusades were not from the outset a contest between rival monotheisms, such as in the Holy Land, but a revival of older, military struggles against polytheism.

In fact this mixed relationship may be seen as key to the whole enterprise. The difficulty lay in dealing with a partially Christianized land and people. The need to physically protect new converts from their still hostile neighbors produced a scenario wherein warfare became a necessary function of conversion. Henry's *Livonian Chronicle* makes it clear that the first mission to the Livs was given instructions on fort building and for acquiring and training garrisons to guard the forts. Bishop Meinhard of Uexküll, the predecessor to the martial Albert of Riga, "promised (the Livs) that forts would be built if they decided to become and to be considered the sons of God."[7] The Livs were quite "pleased . . . and they promised and confirmed by an oath that they would receive baptism."[8]

Since the Baltic Crusades were not directed against Muslims, many of their characteristics assume a wholly different shape. Even most of the crusading features they seem to share, at least superficially, with the expeditions to the Holy Land are, upon closer inspection, found to be different in motivation and often application as well. Take the point of view ascribed to Urban II in his call to crusade in 1095: the need to expand Christianity, or *dilatatio Christianitas*. That would seem to be completely congenial to the Baltic Crusade mandate to expand the faith eastward at the expense of the pagan tribes queued up along the coast. But the difference in the nature of the target populations requires making a distinction in our understanding of the crusading enterprise. The Baltic Crusades largely did not seek to expand Christianity by liberating a territory once Christian from their contemporary captors, as in the Holy Land, but rather attempted *dilatatio Christianitas* by reviving the practice of the faith in lapsed, apostate lands. These lands were deemed to be in need of a Christianizing mission for two reasons: the early successes in converting the populace left vulnerable enclaves of Christians needing military protection and that subsequent protection produced conversions that were dependent upon victory in war. As military control changed hands, as it surely did, the "conversion" was renounced, producing apostasy. Thus the Baltic Crusades were often an effort at re-institution and reclamation more than liberation. Indeed, in some cases the faith was a completely novel implant; a true application of "missionary war," but even this could be understood as being related to the need to protect recent converts.

This targeting of pagan peoples rather than adherents of a conquering alternative monotheism also figure in the discussion of the justification of crusading in general. The development of a crusade authorized against non-Muslim opponents and located far away from the Holy Land highlights a major distinctive of Baltic crusading: the difference between a hostile, alien polity imposed on the church, as in the Holy Land, and a native one, equally if not more hostile, but homegrown. This change in location pioneered a change in the nature of crusading—there were now subcategories: exogenic crusading, called *exterius*, was against Muslims and endogenic crusading, termed *interius*, was against the Baltic pagans. These designations went on to become part of general church terminology not only through the Baltic Crusades, but also through the reconquest efforts that were ongoing in the Iberian Peninsula, as well as through the eventual campaigns against heretics within Europe itself. This two-front view of crusading came to be categorized as *crux transmarina*, or "overseas crusading" against Muslims in the Holy Land, and *crux cismarina*, or "crusading on this side of the sea," to denote crusading activities close to or within the Christian homelands.[9] This has often been misunderstood. While the Baltic Crusades were categorized generally as *crux cismarina*, they were not fully "within Europe," as it existed in those days. While we see "Europe" in its later iteration, the medieval world saw it in its unexpanded, still developing form. The pagan lands along the Baltic were yet to be incorporated, so the crusade might accurately be classed as *crux transmarina*, particularly as the Baltic Sea played such a central role in the process.[10] In this way the affairs that began at Frankfurt in March 1147 inaugurated a process of legitimization that was not only novel, but also decisive for the future scope of the Crusades in general.

Facilitating this legitimization was the medieval penchant to describe all opponents of crusading as *pagani,* or "pagans."[11] The word originally meant the country folk dwelling in the *pagus*, or surrounding territory to the city, but it became a catchall phrase like "infidels" to describe any outside opponent to Christianity. In the indulgent decrees of a series of ninth-century popes, the term *pagani* was used to describe even Muslim opponents, a precedent followed by Eugenius III in his authorization of the Wendish Crusade of 1147.[12] This habit of seeing all opponents as *pagani* made it easier to classify the Baltic Crusades, targeting actual pagans, as true crusades, like the Holy Land variety aimed at Muslims. While the Baltic enterprise obviously was different, it would seem somewhat the same when overarching descriptors such as *pagani* were used to describe both their opponents. This makes the placement of the Baltic Crusades under the general crusade rubric much easier.

Nevertheless much of the rationale for the Baltic Crusades dealt with the reclamation of formerly Christian lands and peoples. Even though the latter stages of these "eternal" crusades featured campaigns against regions and tribes not Christian in the past, only a few without some earlier contact with Christian missionaries were the target territories in the first generations of the Baltic Crusades, and only a few were the peoples who had not at one time or another accepted a version of the faith. The boundaries between Christian and pagan lands, a type of conceptual frontier, was a permeable one, leading to a degree of familiarity born of commercial and interpersonal interaction between the two seemingly alien cultures. It also was productive of hostility. Christian missionaries and congregations were martyred occasionally, leading to, as Eric Christiansen has phrased it, the "belief that soil irrigated by martyrs' blood had been marked out for Christian rule, and that this blood cried out for vengeance."[13] Therefore the reclamation, apart from the physical reconquest of church property and administrative units, often was not a campaign to free Christians who had fallen under the rule of an alternative religion, whether monotheistic or polytheistic, but one of reclaiming lapsed Christians from their tribal apostasy and obtaining justice for those slain in the faith.

Such an assignment necessitated a change in motive and tactics for the Baltic version of crusade. The objective would be punishment, but also conversion—this could be a solidifying of wavering, even lapsed, faith or the introduction of Christianity among unreached peoples. Among the corrective measures would be the disentangling of actual Christian practice from pagan interpretations—a task that would remain long after the dust of battle had settled. For example, the pagan god Svantovit, worshiped at his cult center on the island of Rügen, is thought to be a syncretistic product of confused Christian principles and pagan beliefs.[14] As Friedrich Lotter has said, "It was the goal of converting the pagan Slavs that, above all, distinguished this operation from other wars of this epoch against heathens and even from other crusades."[15] Lotter might well have included "pagan Balts" in his observation as, once begun, the Baltic Crusades developed their own territorial momentum. This judgment accords well with the marching orders of the Baltic crusaders, as stated in Henry's *Livonian Chronicle*: "To baptize those who come voluntarily and humbly, to receive hostages and tribute, to free all the Christian captives, (and) to return with victory."[16] This apparently novel goal opens up a variety of questions as well as many practical dilemmas.

If conversion is the objective of crusading, how does the brutality of warfare fit into the equation? Is warfare permissible only in the just war sense of defense, or does warfare act as a tool for opening up a land to Christianity? Is warfare a means of disciplinary enforcement—keeping "Christians" Christian and punishing those who defect? The question of proper order looms large in this situation. Once again, Henry had no qualms about the correct role of combat, believing that the faith accompanied the sword. "And quite properly theological doctrine followed the wars, since at that same time, after all the above-mentioned wars, the whole of Livonia was converted and baptized."[17]

Further confusing the issue of war as a tool for conversion is the seductive shift from defensive to offensive warfare, as demonstrated by the efforts of Meinhard at Uexküll. This prelate found it impossible to defend existing Christian communities among the Livs as well as attract new adherents without a sufficient military defense force. His promise of fort building and his subsequent failure to defend the faithful seems to have led to his successor Albert's later full-throated involvement in crusade recruitment and campaigning. Even if offensive war were fully embraced, how might that bring about Christianization? Would it be somewhat like the Muslim *futuh* conquests, where the Islamic victories simply allowed their faith to percolate through the conquered territories, or would a Christian mechanism of conquest-conversion require an immediate adherence to the new, victorious faith?

If the latter, mass baptisms would not only be permissible, but necessary. It appears that this was the case. In this, the Baltic Crusades are quite unlike other ones, whether to the Holy Land, Spain, or elsewhere. Benjamin Kedar has shown that there were no mass baptisms in the Holy Land Crusades because the idea of converting the Muslim population to Christianity was something that was very slow to take hold.[18] But mass baptisms suggest a type of "conversion by treaty," wherein an entire people assent to the massive cultural shift of changing their religion solely because they have been subdued in war. Situational faith such as this can be renounced easily when the situation changes. This may explain the recurrent washing off of baptism in the Daugava River following successful uprisings by the Livs.[19]

Even those features that are considered standard for crusading often had a peculiarly Baltic application. Issues of papal authority, indulgences, penance and the like had already been established in the crusading context. What remained was to apply them to a new theater of operations. But the distinctiveness of this new theater of operations required some alterations to the basic features of crusading. For example, the "rolling front" nature of the yearly campaigns often proceeded without additional papal authorization, leading some to believe that it was only later in the Baltic Crusades that they were officially denoted as such. In this view, until well into the thirteenth century crusading "was driven by the local German powers" and these were the product of economic factors.[20] This overlooks the terminology of Eugenius III in his *Divina dispensatione II*, and does not credit the ongoing evolution of crusading, whether in Palestine or Livonia. German magnates were indeed instrumental in the inception of the Baltic Crusades, as was the "mellifluous doctor" St. Bernard, but the papacy repeatedly authorized crusading activity, before the pontificate of Honorius III, causing one scholar to label the Baltic the "*outremer* of the north."[21] The fact that the scope of the behaviors so authorized expanded, as did the theology supporting them, should not blind us to the existence of earlier official approval.

Another example of the peculiarities of the Baltic Crusades is the fact that crusaders were frequently called *peregrini*, or "pilgrims." This should not surprise us as the union of warfare and pilgrimage is seen generally as key to the inception of the Crusades. Traditionally the crusaders were to journey to a holy place, Jerusalem being the preferred destination, and receive penitential absolution for their martial efforts. Therefore many of the crusading host journeyed to the Holy Land, fought, and then received the palm branch emblematic of the completion of their pilgrimage, only to return home. In the Baltic Crusades, the Christian warriors are often called *peregrini*, but such a designation raises a question.[22] While most of the Baltic crusaders went east, fought, and returned to their homes, what holy place was their pilgrimage destination? Lacking a suitably beneficial pilgrimage objective, how did the warriors enhance their spiritual standing? Was it merely the act of fighting for the cross that sufficed as pilgrimage, or was it the conquest of pagan shrines and their subsequent reconsecration that acted as a sort of reverse *locus sanctorum*, in that the crusaders were making new holy places out of old pagan ones? It would seem that the notion of pilgrimage meant something quite different to crusaders along the Baltic littoral. The changes in practice that were produced by the change in location and opponent were several, and subtle.

While the permutations of these differences are many, and interwoven, the main points needing examination are the question of crusading motivation, the acceptability of warfare as a tool for conversion, the proper role of Christianization in the wake of such wars, and the impact of the union of church and state for both the pagans and the Christians. Thus, amid the multiple ways the Baltic Crusades differed from crusading in general, one distinctive commands special attention: "missionary war." The term was coined by Carl Erdmann as *missionskrieg* in his seminal 1935 study on the origins of crusading.[23]

This term may sound discordant to modern ears accustomed to thinking of missionary activity as focused on good deeds, such as construction of dwellings and infrastructure, supplementing local food supply, and care for orphans, as well as, equally, on the spread of the Christian faith, rather than on warfare. But the term "missionary war" is an accurate description of the activities of the Baltic Crusades. Once "missionary war" is identified and certified in the Baltic crusading, it may even explain the seeming barbarity of the enterprise, as exemplified by Albert of Riga's rejoicing over receiving the severed head of an opponent. The union of war with worship diminishes, or sometimes removes, constraints on violence. If violence is worship, then given that one cannot worship in excess, the temptation is to take violence to shocking extremes. The reluctance and doubt that constitute the traditional basis for the just war theory are replaced by a type of confidence in the efficacy of more savage forms of war. The fear that one may lose justness, or God's favor, by excessive barbarity no longer acts as a controlling and limiting agent.

In all these issues the prehistory, or the long antecedence building up to these events, must be evaluated. The Baltic Crusades were a new turn in the winding road of crusade development. Yet are these novel aspects legitimate additions to crusading or disqualifying aberrations? Adding to the uncertainty is the question of source reliability. Many of our sources on the Baltic Crusades were written by actual participants in those events. Henry's *Livonian Chronicle* was penned by a man who took part in the very campaigns he described. Likewise, the anonymous poet of the *Livonian Rhymed Chronicle* appears to have been present and involved in much of the action he immortalized, and was, at the least, an enthusiastic member of the Teutonic Knights. This apparent authenticity comes with a historical price. Did the sources gloss over some, or much, of the more incriminating parts of the narrative or were they guileless and unaware of how their actions might be construed by future generations? The practice of putting "spin" on events is not a modern invention.

Furthermore, these records would have necessarily been written some years after the events described. Henry's *Chronicle* finishes in 1227, yet covers events beginning in the early 1180s, just a few years before Henry's birth, while the *Livonian Rhymed Chronicle* covers the period 1143–1290, and was penned shortly after that last date.[24] In both these cases the historian is portraying events from long before his own era. Therefore the reader may suspect not just a creative interpretation of the recorded actions, but also the insertion of speeches and statements into the narrative based on what would naturally be a somewhat faulty recollection. While this is a fundamental problem with virtually all historical records, it is such a common problem in the medieval period as to rise to the level of a literary *topos*.[25] At the least, the descriptions of events more than a century earlier represent the received story at the time of the writing. So, factual inaccuracies of earlier occurrences may be factual representations of the contemporary view on these historical matters and as such are historical sources themselves. And yet, for all these problems, these are the sources we have. We must try to ascertain what seems trustworthy and ascribe a salubrious doubt to what does not. Such a procedure, unfortunately, leaves room for the manifestation of our preconceptions and preferences. For what seems trustworthy to us rests upon a foundation of our own making. This is particularly so when dealing with a topic as charged with feeling as crusading, especially one variant of that crusading as startling in its violence and zeal as the multi-century push along the Baltic.

As the Baltic Crusades therefore seem to introduce much that is new to the established model for crusading, the question remains as to whether the changes in particulars could create a change in kind. As Thomas Asbridge has concluded, "The Baltic arm of the Second Crusade was actually the result of the church superimposing the notion of crusading on top of a pre-existing conflict."[26] Of course it may be possible to argue that even the Crusades to the Holy Land were in some way the continuation of a multi-century, preexisting conflict as well. While Asbridge may be quite correct in part, there is a danger inherent in this point of view. To separate the Wendish Crusade and its continuation under the rubric "Baltic Crusades" from the whole of the Second Crusade by the inference that it was merely a corollary is the first and most important step toward disqualifying it as a "crusade." Giles Constable's conclusion that such a division is "in no way supported by the sources"[27] rightly calls this into question.

Were the Baltic Crusades actually "crusades" or some hybridization of crusading and border war acquisition? Were they a legitimate part of the phenomenon that was the Crusades, or an epiphenomenon laid over a previously existing structure? Many scholars see the Baltic Crusades as a pretextual sanctification of greed and violence. Typical of this opinion is the summary of Shami Ghosh: "It (the Baltic Crusades) was characterized by vicious warfare, economic exploitation and secular politics; and ... secular motives were just as important, if not more so, than religious ideals."[28]

Even though Ghosh allows room for religious motivation, largely leaving that to the individual crusader's conscience and not to the overall enterprise, he does believe that economics were the primary driver of the Baltic Crusades. Ghosh is assuredly not alone. Norman Housley has called the Baltic Crusades "a war of conquest, colonization and conversion."[29] Conversely, Eric Christiansen has condemned this type of judgment as "too easy," even labeling it "fraudulent."[30] While the Baltic crusaders were intent on reaping the fruits of their conquests, whether these were in the form of battlefield plunder or in the form of territorial control and the tax payments that it entailed, the use of religious war to accomplish this makes for debate and confusion. It has been common to view the Baltic Crusades as either actual crusades, or acquisitive border wars. A third optional point of view might be to see them as missionary wars, a developmental blending of the two. Ane Bysted seems to agree and has concluded that "they were missionary crusades and, as such, part of a new trend in the crusading movement."[31] Perhaps the confusion over the distinction between missionary war, crusading, and holy war in general explains the lack of crusade authorization that plagues the Baltic enterprise, as noted by Iben Fonnesberg-Schmidt.[32] She finds papal authorization in the Baltic to be inconsistent and, before Innocent III in 1215, not commensurate with papal sanctioning of the Holy Land expeditions, and concludes that "the development of a looser concept of the crusade, one that takes other forms of penitential warfare into account, might be fruitful."[33] Papal authorization may have been as open ended as the military campaigns it legitimatized.

So what were the Baltic Crusades? Were they border raids bent on spoils, actual sanctioned crusades, or the continuation of an older, holy war model, like Erdmann's *missionskrieg*? Were these campaigns truly "crusades" either in part or the whole? To answer these questions and pass a reasoned judgment on the Baltic Crusades, one must assay the state of discussion concerning the Crusades in general, and that has been an endeavor fruitful of much controversy.

Questions for discussion

Were the Baltic Crusades really "crusades"? If so, why? If not, why not?

Why have scholars been reluctant to classify the Baltic Crusades as crusades?

Can a campaign really be a "crusade" without targeting the Holy Land, or a Muslim opponent?

What are the peculiarities of the Baltic version of crusading?

PART TWO

The Method

3

The crusade studies revolution

Perhaps no topic in the study of the Middle Ages has been so recently reevaluated, and so productive of controversy, as the Crusades. The reappraisal, often involving the examination of new pieces of evidence, has been so pervasive as to deserve the term "revolution." On one level, it is not surprising that divergent interpretations have arisen about the Crusades since the chronological scope of this endeavor spans several centuries and, for some at least, multiple regions of Asia, Africa, and Europe. In fact, it is hard to identify any portion of medieval society that does not in some way touch upon the act of crusading. Noted military historian John France has spoken of "the centrality of the crusades and crusading to European medieval history" as producing a practical problem in that the wide-spreading subfields of study require knowledge of "an enormous range of different sources of different kinds."[1] This diversity has helped to propel crusade studies into prominence in that it has created a rather large tent under which all manner of disciplines can shelter. Christopher Tyerman has observed that a mere sampling of these disparate disciplines would stretch "from theology to archaeology, from liturgy to logistics, from institutions to mentalities, from the early middle ages to the sixteenth and seventeenth centuries."[2] The collective force of so many studies draws attention to the whole. However, anything of so wide a reach must surely spawn a variety of institutional and theoretical applications and, inevitably, controversies.

But if one takes an overview of this wide scholarly expanse, it seems apparent that the revolution in crusade studies is structured much like the just war theory. Scholars have long made the distinction between *ius in bello*, or how a just war is to be conducted, and *ius ad bellum*, or what constitutes a sufficiently acceptable basis for a just war.[3] In crusade studies, a similar division can be applied between studies that focus on the mechanics of crusading and those that deal with the qualities that make a crusade a legitimate one. The two categories frequently overlap, and one can construct a very artificial bright line between the two. Yet it is useful to subdivide the field for the purposes of analyzing crusades in general and the Baltic Crusades in particular.

Many of the new interpretations on the Crusades deal with correcting assessments of the actual practice of crusading, that is, they fall under the *ius in bello* category. The topics of this type of study are too numerous to catalog here, but a few examples might suffice to illustrate the point. The old "for faith and fiefs" view that rested on the notion that crusaders sought wealth in the Holy Land has been weakened, if not dispelled entirely, by the revelation that it took approximately six years of portable revenue to even go on a crusade. The collateral fact that potential crusaders had to mortgage their European holdings at unfavorable rates further undercuts the wealth-seeking objective of crusading. Most crusaders who survived the experience were bankrupted in the process. Additionally, the notion that crusading armies were comprised of younger sons who were left disinherited by the prevailing custom of primogeniture is corrected by information showing that the landed nobility provided the controlling portions of the Christian armies surging eastward. Thomas F. Madden has summed up the sea change in perspective by noting that "the Crusaders were predominately the first sons of Europe; wealthy, privileged, and pious."[4]

Recent analysis of the transportation factors involved in crusading, both naval and land based, has opened a window of understanding on the implementation of the Crusades.[5] This recent emphasis on naval support for crusading has great importance for the Baltic Crusades and their coastal orientation.[6] Studies concerning fortifications, weaponry, and battlefield tactics have further illuminated and explained the existence of this long projection of military power so distant from its European homeland.[7] All these lines of inquiry, and many more, are focused on the actual process of crusading.

But by far the most contentious portions of the Crusade revolution are those questions that deal with the *ius ad bellum* nature of crusading, particularly those concerning the authorization and legitimization of the enterprise. The points of disagreement are many, but derive generally from the question of definition: What is and what is not truly a crusade? The basic components of crusade such as papal instigation and supervision, crusade exemptions and indulgences, the Holy Land as the exclusive target, and even the moral justification of this variant of religious warfare, are subject to widely differing scholarly opinions. It is this second level of crusade studies, the *ius ad bellum* part, that most critically affects the status of the Baltic Crusades. The actual practices of crusading as realized on the Baltic frontier in terms of logistics, weaponry, and the like, while requiring adjustments for weather and topography, was not markedly different from the practices associated with the Holy Land crusades. The real divergence was not in practical application but in conceptualization: Can a campaign against pagans rather than Muslims in a territory far removed from the holy sites of Palestine qualify as a crusade?

This crusade revolution has produced a strange mix of clarity and confusion. Clarity in that many facets of the crusade enterprise is now illuminated properly, often for the first time. Confusion in that it seems the more we discover about the Crusades, the less unanimity there is on what exactly the thing was. As Norman Housley has summarized in his fine book, *Contesting the Crusades*, "The paradox of contemporary crusading studies (is) an unprecedented richness of research...set against a background of confusion in terms of definition which only seems to deepen the more we discover."[8] One is tempted to ask why this should be so. Perhaps Housley has the answer here as well: "More generally, historians have tended to focus on activities rather than patterns of thought."[9] Examinations of charters, mortgage deeds, logistical supply trains, weaponry, castellation, and the myriad of additional productive research topics have opened up a broad vista of understanding of the implementation of crusading, but have not touched fully on the motivations behind such a transformational endeavor. Scholars, to use Tyerman's assessment, "have not been led by theory"[10]—at least to the extent that they have focused almost exclusively on the practice of this multifaceted undertaking.

This crusade revolution can be seen as the revelation of new angles of vision, but it also includes, to a decisive degree, a battle for the very essence of "crusade." As an essence can be defined as that without which the thing ceases to be, the question for our purposes then becomes, "What is truly essential to make a crusade a crusade?" It is on this issue that most of the contention surrounding crusade studies swirls. Several different versions of "crusade essence" command allegiance from scholars across the discipline. Complicating the issue is the sense that "crusade" is a moving target, morphing in practice, and sometimes even in theory, in response to local conditions and the sheer passage of years. Giles Constable has noted that the failure to clarify exactly what a crusade was or was not led to a fluidity in both the practice and denomination of the enterprise—"its character changed over time."[11] Christopher Tyerman reacted to this growth process and its associated changeability in perhaps an overly serious way and once held that there was no crusading until the era of the Third Crusade in the 1180s.[12] Supporting this is the time lag between the emergence of crusading and its inclusion in canon law; it was not until the thirteenth century that it was treated fully there.[13] But the establishment of an accepted definition of crusade is essential to providing structure to the whole field of crusade studies, and particularly so when judging the seemingly quirky Baltic Crusades.

So what were the features necessary for a crusade to be a valid one? Some earlier efforts focused on what may be called the "ethic" of the crusade: components such as religious motivation, penitential rewards, an erosion, or even absence, of restraint in war, and the like.[14] One may argue about the applied accuracy of each of these components, particularly restraint in war. The medieval period already featured rather prominently an erosion of restraint against hostility toward the enemy as well as justification of extreme means to achieve objectives. This does, however, get at an essential gap in crusade analysis: the spirit that motivated the participants. There have been efforts to evaluate the religious fervor that moved large numbers of crusaders to action and simultaneously sustained their families back home as well as studies on the central role of Jerusalem in generating and validating the crusading ethos. Even with these attempts, there remains elusive and just out of sight of academic analysis the driving motion that caused these men to fight and die in such numbers.

Further complicating understanding is a type of cultural and ethnic preoccupation among those who investigate the Crusades. While crusading originated within the "heartlands" of Christendom, it is wise to remember that the target populations also had significant influence on the end product.[15] It is true that the Crusades were Western in origin and application; they were "done" by the West to their opponents, whether Muslim or pagan. It is also true that the decision to take the cross was a personal one leading scholars to rightfully delve into the motivations and sustainable religious intensity of the individual participants, whether royal, noble, or even the occasionally source-identified commoner. But this fascinating line of research may well crowd out the notion that the "other" of the crusading targets also deserve attention, particularly in the Baltic where the cultural influence seems to work as much pagan to Christian as Christian to pagan. This remains, however, an ethereal task to solidify intangible attitudes and properly describe their point of origin.

Perhaps this is why the principal focus remains on what can be seen and measured: the definition of crusade in terms of location and practice. Here Giles Constable has created a taxonomy that, as with all classification systems, may be subject to modification or reconfiguration, but remains useful all the same. Constable's taxonomy was in response to the explosion of crusade studies and reinterpretations that reached critical mass in the 1990s.[16] In Constable's view the spectrum of crusade studies may be divided into four groupings based on their differing requirements: The traditionalists see only those campaigns aimed at Jerusalem, or at least the Holy Land in general, as qualifying as true crusades, thus leaving activities in Spain, the Baltic, and other theaters of war outside the pale of crusading, while the pluralists open the category up to include the multiple fronts of combat between Muslim, Christian, and even pagans along the whole of the Mediterranean, Baltic as well as within Christian Europe proper. The determining factor was not the destination of crusading, but its inception in papal authorization. This elasticity has its critics. If crusading is that inclusive, is it a separate category at all? Constable also identified a third group, the popularists, who viewed crusading as largely a product of religious excitement; this definition would consider the Poor Peoples' Crusade and the Children's Crusade along with the commonly accepted ones as crusades. Lastly, there were those Constable termed generalists, who saw any religious war accompanied by either theological or ideological rationales as worthy of the title of crusade.[17]

Given this wide diversity, it may come as a bit of a surprise to see that there can still be some agreement on the basic elements of a crusade definition. While there are substantial, almost intractable, differences of opinion that remain, some of the general components of crusading pass muster among most crusade historians. A workable definition might be that of the doyen of contemporary crusade studies, Jonathan Riley-Smith, who defined crusade as "a holy war fought against those perceived to be the external or internal foes of Christendom for the recovery of Christian property or in defense of the Church or Christian people."[18] Riley-Smith later expanded his definition to include widely disparate geographical fronts, multiethnic and multireligious foes, and diverse motivations.[19] Housley sums it up stating, "the essential attribute of crusading, (is) the assumption of the cross with the intention of engaging in penitential combat, in response to a cause that was defined as holy by the pope and preached by the Church."[20]

What has this question of the true nature of crusade to do with our present study? In one sense, it may seem an obscure academic argument. The elasticity of the pluralist approach may even encourage jarring applications. Henri Daniel-Rops once called the Byzantine emperor Heraclius (r. 610–41 AD) "the first crusader" for his efforts in recovering Jerusalem from the Persians in 630 AD, and routinely referred to this campaign as "the First Crusade."[21] Alexander F. C. Webster has gone so far as to ascribe crusading structure to the years of Muslim conquest in the seventh and eighth centuries by calling a conquest a "crescade," making a historical pun on the cross' counterpoint, the Muslim crescent.[22] Despite this, the quest to ascertain the true nature of crusade is of paramount importance, particularly for our present study. For if crusade is limited to the Holy Land, then what happened in the Baltic lands was truly only a border war sheltering under the terminological cover of "crusade."

But if the idea of crusade is allowed to be broad in scope and not restricted to the campaigns to the Holy Land, the Baltic enterprise qualifies as a suitable topic for crusade study. Therefore, despite the logical attractions of the various views, all of which do justice in their own way to the varieties of holy war in the Middle Ages, I must agree with the pluralist structure in that it permits the Baltic Crusades to reside under the general rubric of crusade, thereby making this study possible. While the Baltic Crusades did not aim for Palestine, or generate an explosion of popular fervor, they were more than just religious wars of convenience. They were authorized by the pope, sometimes in an understood continuing way, promised penitential relief to the warriors, and sought to regain once-Christian territory as well as expanding the faith into unreached lands and peoples. It does seem, as Tyerman observed, to be "unnecessarily fussy to exclude from crusading history those who followed the precedent of 1095 . . . just because their stated goals did not coincide with those of the first crusaders."[23]

Indeed, much of the discussion about the legitimacy of the Baltic Crusades has focused on the question of whether the popes, from Gregory VII (r. 1073–85) and Urban II (r. 1088–99) to Eugenius III (r. 1145–53) and even Innocent III (r. 1198–1216), viewed crusading as extending beyond the operations in the Holy Land. This is an obviously correct line of investigation, but it is a limiting one. It makes the investigation of all the component developments that went before unnecessary.

An intriguing, and influential for our topic, line of dispute is the question of the beginning of the Crusades at the Council of Clermont in 1095. Traditionally, Pope Urban II's speech there on November 27 is seen as the moment when the crusading era began. If so, this effectively cuts the Crusades loose from what went before and has the double effect of limiting crusading to Urban's target: the Holy Land. Therefore, any work purporting to treat the prehistory of a "crusade" far distant from the eastern Mediterranean is by definition irrelevant.

The reconquest of Sicily in the period 1060–91, the campaign to retake the Spanish see of Tarragona in 1089, and the simultaneous granting of crusading protections to those fighting under the sign of the cross in Spain when the First Crusade was promulgated, all suggest that crusading was not confined to the Holy Land, nor suddenly born in 1095. There are those who insist on seeing the Crusades, as ignited at Clermont, as an enlarged continuation of long-existing struggles and institutions. Foremost in this camp is Paul Chevedden. Chevedden's position, based upon a close reading of contemporary Muslim sources, is that a form of crusading had been in effect prior to the Council of Clermont. He has stressed that crusading in the "crusade era" was a continuation of a centuries-long, intermittent, and multifront territorial struggle between the Christian West and the Muslim world.[24] In this, he is not alone. Paul M. Cobb, also using Islamic sources, but, curiously, not citing Chevedden's work, also does not believe that crusading began in 1095; for him, the First Crusade was "simply one outburst of European aggression that began decades earlier, in Spain and Sicily."[25]

Therefore both Chevedden and Cobb believe the reconquest of Sicily, authorized by Pope Nicholas II at the Synod of Melfi in 1059, as well as the efforts in Spain in the 1080s qualify as crusades despite them being before the official beginning at Clermont. In this they expand on the views of the first great American medievalist, Charles Homer Haskins, who as early as in 1915 called these campaigns "a sort of crusade before the Crusades."[26] As Chevedden is concerned with identifying the beginnings of what might be called "crusade," he spends little time plumbing the depths of earlier medieval theory and practice. In short, he pays little attention to the prehistory of the crusades because he sees their beginning earlier. There is not much need for a prehistory of something that has existed from the beginning. Yet, wherever one places the beginnings of crusading, the antecedents to that beginning need evaluation. While few would argue that crusading did not undergo developmental change as the centuries rolled on, the issue of the actual beginning, even in a type of prototypical format, of the endeavor is at the heart of establishing its prehistory.

This debate over the view that crusading was a continuation of long-standing warfare also has the effect of influencing attitudes on the later Baltic Crusades. Chevedden believes the focus on crusading as beginning at the Council of Clermont is a type of "big bang theory"[27] that confines all subsequent crusades in areas other than the Holy Land to being nothing more than "trivial and unimportant modifications of the original form of crusading embodied in the so-called 'First Crusade'."[28] The later and disparate versions of crusading are only legitimized by the degree to which they "endlessly reproduce" the form of the original.[29] The Baltic Crusades might well fall under the accepted practice of crusading developed by the twelfth century, but they suffer greatly when compared with the famous crusades directed at the Holy Land. The continued development of crusading theory and practice as seen on the Baltic front must be viewed as yet another phase of growth to an overall institution that did not remain static either in Palestine or in northern Europe. This viewpoint is common, even in the most recent accounts of crusading, as the Baltic campaign is dismissed by the assertion that "the traditional perspective informs their exploration of crusading phenomena in these other times and settings."[30] As Chevedden sees a longer line of development for crusading that precedes Pope Urban's star turn at Clermont, he likens crusading to a sequoia tree, holding that "Like the mighty sequoias, the Crusades grew from small beginnings,"[31] an obvious, and correct, acknowledgment of the role of crusading prehistory. Perhaps a better tree analogy might be a bamboo analogy. The sequoia could not fail to attract notice, even as a sapling, and thus force scholars to analyze and explain the earlier, prehistory phases of crusading. Whereas bamboo can grow for years underground, and thus out of sight, only to burst forth in a growth spurt above ground that might mislead one into seeing it as a sudden, "big bang" event.

Further enriching Chevedden's views on the origin of the Crusades is his decision to see crusading as a struggle that encompassed a wide expanse of geographic locales. He relies once again on an examination of contemporary Muslim sources that viewed the conflict between the two religiously based civilizations, whether in the Holy Land, Sicily, or Spain as being of one piece.[32] While warfare between Muslim and Christian forces would seem to hold little significance for the Baltic, the expansion of crusading to areas outside the Holy Land permits the possibility of considering campaigns against pagan peoples in Northern Europe as a type of crusade. This is what Giles Constable noticed when he reviewed the contemporary literature on the Wendish branch of the Second Crusade.[33] The issue might also be a manifestation of medieval thinking generally, as Ane Bysted has written concerning the Baltic Crusades: "Perhaps the crusades were not perceived as anything new. They were simply wars against the infidel which were pleasing to God, and which were already known from the Christian kings' attempts to convert their pagan neighbours to Christianity."[34] While this view acknowledges a type of prehistory to the Baltic Crusades, it still marks the Crusades as a radical new turn in the development of religious war. Unfortunately, this allows validation for those who see the Baltic Crusade as nothing more than a baptism of old territorial and cultural wars.

As useful as this discussion is for crusading studies in general, such a dispute does bypass the essential difference between crusading proper and the activities in the Baltic. These examinations generally focus on Muslim versus Christian scenarios, and therefore are not readily applicable to the Baltic Crusades. The two issues, whether crusading outside the Holy Land is authentic crusading, and whether crusading against pagans, either unconverted or apostate, is part of crusade proper seem to run on parallel, nonintersecting paths. These paths converge in the Baltic and their inception and growth is instructive for understanding the final product. To that end, an examination of their prehistory is in order.

Questions for discussion

What is a "crusade"? Which components are essential and which not?

Why have crusade scholars not tended to investigate the prehistory of the Crusades?

Is crusading an unfolding institution or something essentially complete from its first appearance?

How much can crusading change and still be "crusading"?

4

The uses of prehistory

Before evaluating the usefulness of "prehistory" for the Baltic Crusades, it is necessary to determine what is meant by the term. The accepted definition of "prehistory" depends generally on the definition of "history." If history is seen to be the recording and interpretation of events, then the term prehistory cannot apply to an institution like the Crusades, which emerged from a centuries-long literate and historical tradition. But if prehistory is used to describe the extended strands of development that preceded the inception of a movement, or an idea, then "prehistory" is indeed accurate. This is the application that is used in this study. The use of the term in this context is decidedly not new. The father of modern historical practice, Leopold von Ranke, used the term "the prehistory of the crusades" in his posthumously-published volume eight of his *Weltgeschichte*, or *World History*, in 1887.[1]

The examination of the prehistory of the Crusades serves to answer a perennial question of introductory history students, at least of those who are not mesmerized by the pageantry and drama of the events of the Council of Clermont and its generational aftermath: "Why did the Christian Europeans suddenly decide to invade the Holy Land?" Implicit in such a question is the notion of aggression. The West is seen to be a violent invader, lacking any justification for disrupting an eminently peaceful equilibrium between the Muslim East and Christian West. While the study of the prehistory of the Crusades may not relieve the West of the burden of aggression, it can offer context for their actions and place the Crusades in the proper order of events and developments that constitute the history of relations between these antipodal civilizations.

Somewhat surprisingly, the issue of prehistory has emerged as a growing perspective in modern scholarship. Volumes examining the prehistory of religion, globalization, and even language itself, to name only a few, have appeared on the market since the turn of the millennium.[2] Perhaps spurring this line of inquiry is our technologically exploding age, or simply a desire to address a feeling of incompleteness that the received institutional historical narrative engenders. When one studies a topic without proper attention to its prehistory, one is entering the discussion *in media res*. This is certainly true for that trans-epochal, multiethnic, geographically expansive phenomenon of the Crusades in general and the Baltic variety in particular. A benefit to using prehistory as a means of tracing the development of institutions is that it allows for the slow, almost imperceptible mutation and lamination of seemingly disparate ideas and practices into a finished product. The term "origins," all the historical rage in past decades, implies that one can trace development back to an archetypal entity that, while the first of its kind, still bears an indisputable resemblance to its later descendant. Therefore, in the case of crusades and crusading, something much like these later activities must be present very early in order to qualify as original. It may be better to look for separable threads that over time wove the fabric of crusading. Prehistory is an elastic enough classification to allow for this type of "not yet" development.

The ongoing Crusade revolution that includes ever-unfolding insights on the mechanics of crusading has the natural tendency to focus attention on the immediate rather than the distant past. New angles of vision on the composition, maintenance, and comportment of crusading forces as well as the initial political and diplomatic causation of the Crusades have the power to preoccupy. The *longue dureé* view that sees the Crusades in the context of a multi-century struggle gets lost in the fresh rush of interpretation concerning 1095 and thereafter. Chevedden has decried this tendency to ignore anything contributing to crusading that occurred before the Council of Clermont in November 1095 as a type of "big bang theory." If Urban's speech at the council was the split-second moment that began crusading, then examination of what came before is at best unnecessary and at worst a waste of time.

Therefore it has also been customary to study the distinguishing characteristics of the Baltic Crusades, those things that differentiated them from "traditional crusading," only as they developed in 1147 and subsequent years. In this approach these features become an almost genetic mutation of crusading proper, leading to the seemingly logical conclusion that these Baltic endeavors evolved into something other than actual crusading. Even those who acknowledge some prehistory for the Baltic Crusades sever the end product from its crusading origins, saying, "The Wendish Crusade thus had a prehistory in which the idea of crusading had no place."[3] While it is true that the Baltic Crusades began officially as an appendage of the Second Crusade, such a view tends to discourage analysis of the multiple developmental strands that made it possible to link the two. The prehistory of the Baltic Crusades will not be confined to events along the Baltic, but will extend to the centuries-long and sequential incorporation of pagan peoples into Christendom throughout Europe.

Conversely, one may take the approach that the singular attributes of the Baltic Crusades were possessed of an ancient, and full, prehistory. This view casts these crusades as a predictable product of centuries of development rather than as a sudden mutation of an established crusading norm. One view sees novelty, the other culmination. While the Baltic Crusades are inescapably different, that difference is more fully understood by a resort to a long look backward to the earlier encounters between the Christian and pagan sectors of Europe.

The term "prehistory of the Crusades" is an old one, albeit seemingly forgotten. The major exception to the general neglect of the concept is Carl Erdmann's 1935 work on *The Origin of the Idea of Crusade*.[4] Erdmann's untimely death ten years later prevented more volumes from this historian, whose book suggested many fruitful lines of inquiry. The door of prehistory once opened was not entered.

Such an approach featuring the prehistory of crusading has not received an enthusiastic welcome in certain scholarly circles. Many, seeing the Crusades as a wholly new phenomenon, feel it is a poor allocation of time and academic resources, or at best a distraction, to examine the centuries of development that preceded the emergence of full-blown crusading in the late eleventh century and thereafter. A typical example of this perspective is Joshua Prawer's reaction to the appearance, in 1959, of volume one of the magisterial *A History of the Crusades* under the general editorship of Kenneth M. Setton. Professor Prawer, a distinguished crusade scholar, critiqued the first volume, titled *The First Hundred Years* (1095–1189), as spending far too much time and attention on the prehistory of the Crusades. In frustration at this perceived misuse of resources, he asked the question:

> It seems to us, that the whole part of the work dealing with the "prehistory" of the Crusades is too far flung in space and time. . . . Is it really necessary to go back to the Visigoths to explain the Spanish background of the *Reconquista*? Has one to go back . . . to the Moslem invasions in the 7th century or the Norman capture of Sicily to connect Byzantine policy with the Crusades?[5]

Professor Prawer's evaluation is at once partly correct and partly incorrect. He is right to wonder about the limits of prehistory's reach backward, and equally right in wondering if anyone can treat all the streams of development that flow into the crusading floodtide. But his dismissive query, reminiscent of Tertullian's third-century plaint that resulted in the separation of classical learning from Christianity, "What has Athens to do with Jerusalem; what has the Academy to do with the Cross?"[6] has resulted in the severing of the topic at hand from its roots, leading to a self-inflicted limitation in understanding.

As with most issues in the historical realm, there are those who take a quite opposite view. Despite the lack of a full scholarly examination on the prehistory of the Crusades since Erdmann, there have been scattered calls for such work. Representative of this is James Waltz's review of Benjamin Kedar's seminal *Crusade and Mission*, appearing in *Speculum* in 1986. Unsurprisingly, Waltz found little to criticize in Kedar's fine work, but did lament the lack of an even deeper look backward into the prehistory of crusading views on missions.[7] He was reacting to the several tantalizing acknowledgments of a prehistory for crusading that Kedar left in his narrative. Addressing what could be classified as missionary war, he noted that "warfare and conversion were already linked in the reduction, about 973, of the Muslim stronghold of Fraxinetum on the coast of Provence." Regarding later missionary efforts in the north of Europe, Kedar hinted at the prehistory of the Baltic Crusades by stating that "missionaries there could have drawn upon experience gained while combating remnants of paganism among adjacent, previously Christianized tribes."[8]

The implicit, almost cryptic, nature of these snippets of prehistory begs a closer look at the prehistory of crusades.

In recent years, a slow awareness of the necessity to explore the origins of crusading has developed; yet this awareness is still insufficient to fully accredit the centuries of growth that produced this transformative phenomenon. Exceptions occasionally are to be found in studies at a remove from crusading proper. Richard Fletcher, writing in his magisterial *The Barbarian Conversion*, perhaps credited the prehistory of the Crusades overmuch when he described it as of long duration: "It has long been recognized that the origins of the idea of crusade need to be sought far back in the recesses of the eleventh and the tenth centuries, and indeed beyond."[9] Further, the respected crusade scholar Jean Flori seems to support Chevedden when he says that "the ideology of crusade did not suddenly appear with Pope Urban II's appeal at Clermont in November 1095," further noting that "it resulted from a slow evolution."[10]

Outside of Erdmann, and these tantalizing hints, the roster of those studying the prehistory of the Crusades is meager. Indeed, much of this muted call for an examination of the prehistory of the Crusades has been implicitly rather than explicitly expressed in the new works of the revolution in crusade studies. A good example of this is found in the work on the First Crusade by the renowned military historian, John France. While crediting Urban II with "novelty" in calling for an expedition to the East, France believes it was based on "component elements . . . already known to (Urban's) audience." France writes that "historians have come to believe that the crusade was the culmination of a series of impulses by which the church sought to reconcile the heroic and militant ideas of knighthood—chivalry in its crudest sense—with Christian ideology."[11] When the components of crusading are "already known" and represent a "culmination" one has but to wonder about their prehistory, and its process of development.

Perhaps some of the reluctance to investigate the prehistory of the Crusades derives from the scholarly angle of vision of the historians involved. Most understandably locate significance in their home era. Crusade scholars generally come to the topic from their study of the high Middle Ages (c. 1000–1300 AD). Thus, the necessary preconditions for crusading that existed in the centuries before the eleventh century receive somewhat short attention, if any.

Marcus Bull, writing in *The Oxford Illustrated History of the Crusades*, has discounted efforts to trace crusade prehistory back to Carolingian times by saying that the sources on which these efforts rely on are "heavily mythologized."[12] An example of myth-making is found in Notker the Stammerer's *Life of Charlemagne*, written some sixty years after the great emperor's death. Notker put forward the preposterous idea that the Caliph Harun al-Rashid had so esteemed Charlemagne that he granted the Holy Land to the Frankish ruler and voluntarily took the role of governing that land as his representative.[13] The gift of an elephant, which was what Harun actually sent Charlemagne, does not equal the governmental transfer of large tracts of land. Yet, while it is undeniably true that myth quickly surrounded the Carolingian age, useful kernels of truth could also be found in these myths. Matthew Gabriele has provided a distinction between the uses of history and *muthos*, or myth, for the medieval world. He sees history and myth as "not oppositional," but as "two modes of discourse constantly locked in a struggle over the meaning of the past."[14] As one of the few contemporary scholars acknowledging the importance of the prehistory of the crusading era, Gabriele goes on to note: "The Middle Ages placed little emphasis on the objective reconstruction of past events. Instead, recollection was an interpretative act, a selective process that chose what was thought to be valuable and worthy of remembrance."[15]

Given this perspective, it is neither profitable nor wise to dismiss the prehistory of the Crusades as "mythologized." The mythology is as much a significant part of the later record as the factual details of standard history, and of as long duration. Writing in the 1060s, the annalist of St. Amand opined that Charlemagne was "the emperor (*imperator*) . . . who acquired territory (*regnum*) all the way to Jerusalem."[16] Those details, factual or not as they may be, will profit from a salubrious backward view as well as an examination of how these earlier events worked their way into the received narrative. One example of a received narrative, among many, can be seen in Helmold of Bosau's *Chronicle of the Slavs*, written in about 1170, when Helmold praises Charlemagne as the one who stood out among "all the zealous propagators of the Christian religion who through the merit of their faith have . . . labored for God in the northern parts." He further claimed that "by the sword he (Charlemagne) overcame the most fierce and rebellious Saxon folk and subjected it to the laws of Christendom."[17] This martial encomium echoes that of Adam of Bremen but is not an exact copy, indicating that a received wisdom concerning Christianizing warfare percolated through the centuries. The earlier, perhaps mythologized yet still operative, understandings are key to a grasp of the Baltic Crusades. Further, as Hamilton Gibb once opined, it is good "for the specialist to wander occasionally far enough from home to obtain a fresh perspective of the landscape which bounds his daily labours."[18] That can be a suggestion to journey away from the chronological home base of normal scholarly activities to investigate the conceptual homeland, equally chronological, of the events and institutions at hand.

One who studies the earlier medieval period might be more capable of seeing these early planted seeds as well as the slow accretion of theory and practice that makes up their growth as the prehistory of the Crusades. While no serious student of the Middle Ages would denigrate the early centuries of this millennium-long era by labeling it "the Dark Ages," there remains a certain persistence among the public in using this term. As Christopher Dawson lamented more than fifty years ago, some of this persistence is related to our general cultural bent toward secularism. The era will by definition seem one "given up to unintelligible disputes on incomprehensible dogmas or to savage wars that have no economic or political justification."[19] While Dawson references an attitude that calls to mind Matthew Arnold and his poetic "ignorant armies clashing by night" on "a darkling plain,"[20] the contrast is too starkly drawn to reflect today's scholarly reality. Yet it is precisely at the intersection of "savage wars" and conversion that our present study is situated.

An added complication is the fact that prehistory is a seductive construct that can lead one ever backward into the indistinct mists of history. Jacob Burckhardt in the 1860s showed how a whole range of practices could fall under the rubric of the Italian Renaissance, touching off a trend among historians to find ever earlier "renaissances"; this trend began with Charles Homer Haskins' *Renaissance of the Twelfth Century* and included works uncovering "renaissances" of a Carolingian and Ottonian nature.[21] The Crusades, however, are not so burdened. There is a *terminus post quem*, a point in time beyond which their prehistory cannot go: the Constantinian revolution of the early fourth century. When the Roman emperor Constantine (r. 306–37 AD) won his civil war and set about to merge the Christian religion and the military mechanisms of the Roman state, the first seeds of what would one day be the Crusades were sown. Erdmann understood this and included a treatment of Constantine's policies in his groundbreaking *The Origin of the Idea of Crusade*.[22]

While there is a point beyond which the general prehistory of the Crusades cannot extend, the daunting fact is that there are almost endless lines of development that can be subjected to a prehistory examination. Fortunately, the fact that the Baltic Crusades came after the establishment of normative crusade institutions such as papal authorization, indulgences, penitential benefits, and the like, meant that a crusading context already existed. What remained was to apply them to a new theater of operations. The distinctiveness of this new theater of operations forces a more limited examination of Baltic crusading prehistory, as only those novel features of the enterprise need occupy us here. Therefore, the Baltic Crusades offer a topic with a ready-made circumference of study. But that circumference is surprisingly large in that established crusade institutions applied in the Baltic context either spun off novel issues or morphed into something sufficiently different so as to require attention.

Further, there is a certain sequential nature to the prehistory of the Baltic Crusades. For example, just as the Saxons experienced conquest and conversion in tandem and in equal measure at the hands of the Carolingian Franks, so did the Wends experience conquest and conversion at the hands of the Saxons. This sequencing continued farther eastward in a type of replicating pattern. As such, the mechanisms in play in Charlemagne's day, and even earlier, provide a prototype for the coming centuries. It is indeed difficult to understand the intentions and behaviors of the Baltic *reisens*, as the crusaders's annual campaigns eastward against the pagans were called, without a look backward at the reservoir of historical precedent that nourished them.

Since much of the rhetoric concerning crusading is couched in terms of the recovery of lost Christian lands, as wars of reclamation, the issue of the elapsed time between the original loss and its recovery must be addressed. This is a topic that needs further examination for the era of the Crusades in general, but the ebb and flow of territorial control from Christian to pagan hands makes this a viable point for the Baltic Crusades as well. Since some of the lands formerly populated by Christian outposts and fellowships and then reclaimed by the crusaders had been under pagan rule for generations, thus becoming a type of *stare decisis*, or settled situation, at what point does correcting these ancient grievances produce only fresh ones? On what basis did the Baltic crusaders predicate the reclamation of land lost long before, and what are the lines of development that allowed that? Once again, a close study of the prehistory of the Baltic Crusades can supply the answer.

Such a study can correct assumptions concerning motivation. For example, there is a certain presumption of aggression attached to correcting long-standing grievances. If cities, lands, and peoples have been in pagan hands for decades, or in some cases for centuries, is a form of inverse possession at play? Anyone attempting to restore the lands to Christian rule appears as an impulsively hostile aggressor bent on shattering the peace. Disturbing such an old status quo cannot fail to seem disruptive. Even if the original grievance is valid, the correction is not, and a customary wrong may become right by the simple expedient of the passage of time.

This issue is at the heart of crusading in general and the Baltic Crusades in particular. It forms the very foundation of crusading and as such has been so pervasive as to be invisible to scholarly evaluation. Yet for Christianity, justice operates outside of time. Martin Heinzelmann has noted that early medieval hagiographers spoke of the "life of the saints" rather than the "lives of the saints" because they all partook of one trans-temporal existence.[23] The wandering Irish provocateur and monastic founder Columbanus lectured a pope that "error is of long standing, but truth has always stood longer, and is its refutation."[24] If truth and rightness stand apart from considerations of time, then grievances, no matter how old, must be corrected. Crusading, quite obviously, was based firmly on the need to correct the existing situation in favor of truth and rightness. This is a notion much abounding in the crusade era. Thus Urban II, only three years before the Council of Clermont, could remind the Count of Flanders that long usage does not confer legitimacy. Quoting the third-century Christian author Tertullian, the pope stressed that just because something has been in the possession of a person or people for a long time, it cannot be said that the possession of that thing is lawful. "Thy Creator hath said: My name is Truth, not . . . My name is custom."[25] Had he wanted, Urban could have given a fuller account of Tertullian's text in "On the Veiling of Virgins," including the assertion that "truth, on which no one can impose prescription—no space of times" transcends "any and all erroneous customs."[26] Timeless truth must always correct the customary error. Thus crusaders of all stripes could quote Psalm 79, from the early tenth century BC, as fully appropriate for their actions in the later Middle Ages: "O God, the nations have invaded your inheritance. . . . Pour out your wrath on the nations that do not acknowledge you, on the kingdoms that do not call on your name."[27]

It may be that the grievances that seem so old, and thus past their expiry date, to us seemed less so to warriors involved in this ongoing series of reconquests that swept the Mediterranean from west to east and even spilled over into the northern pagan lands of the Baltic seacoast. Little consideration of the expiration of justness is needed when the next objective is seen as merely a part of a continuum of conflict that stretches back to the astonishing century of Muslim conquest from the 630s to the 730s AD. The campaigns become simply rings in a chain, to use Erdmann's metaphor.[28] Continuation works against any notions of expiration and the study of the prehistory of crusading can place this in its proper context.

While the prehistory of the Crusades sheds light on disparate concepts and practices, "rings in the chain" that eventually blended to form crusading proper, it can do more. Occasionally it provides a chilling connection across the centuries. A good example is the vexed quotation from Bernard of Clairvaux penned during the run-up to the Wendish Crusade of 1147: "With God's help, either the rite or the people will be exterminated." This has been the subject of much historical interpretation, but it finds an exact counterpart nearly four centuries earlier in *The Frankish Annals*. Here the anonymous author, writing in the context of Charlemagne's decision to begin campaigns against the pagan Saxons in 772 AD, foreshadows Bernard almost word for word, making the Frankish king vow "to persist in this war until they were either defeated and forced to accept the Christian religion or entirely exterminated."[29] The verbs for exterminate, *deleatur* for Bernard and *tollerentur* for the Carolingian author, are different but the objective is the same. Treating Bernard's statement as a novelty, or the Baltic Crusades in general as a novelty, ignores the long centuries of development that produced them both.

It is not enough to advocate for a study of the prehistory of the Crusades, nor is it enough to identify the discrete elements of the Baltic Crusades that are suitable for such a study. There must be an orderly approach to the often bewildering chronology of those components under consideration. Erdmann did a masterful job of identifying the various lines of conceptual development that led to, as his title proclaimed, the origin of the idea of crusade. Erdmann might have been expected to feature the Baltic Crusades in that his father lost his professorial post at the University of Dorpat (now Tartu) during an upsurge of Estonian national feeling against Germans. This bit of personal history was a direct rebuke to the Baltic Crusades, as the Estonians were reasserting their cultural independence against the very Germanization that the Crusades had established.[30]

Despite his brilliance in navigating the origins of crusading theory, it is, however, often somewhat difficult to follow Erdmann's chronological maneuvering as he blithely leaps back and forth through the centuries. While he treats fully the origins of papal banners, used to signify official approval of holy war, by focusing on Constantine's fourth-century use of the *labarum*, the Christian symbol formed by the Greek letters *chi* and *rho* for "Christos," he follows this chapter with a discussion of the late tenth- and early eleventh-century Peace of God and Truce of God movements. Next comes a chapter on Charlemagne's eighth- and ninth-century efforts against the pagan Saxons. Yet, two chapters later, in a somewhat a-chronological way, he once again picks up the story of papal banners with an analysis of the *vexillum sancti Petri*, the actual papal banners of St. Peter used by Pope Gregory VII (r. 1073–85). This nimble approach that sees him shuttling back and forth across the centuries, has the added problem of blurring the sequential unfolding of the very ideas and practices he describes. This chronological confusion is a product of the wide variety of developmental crusade strands that eventually join to form the finished product.

However, Erdmann's approach is easier to criticize than to improve. Marshaling these disparate lines into a coherent sequence is a daunting task indeed. In fact, it may be the very nature of the enterprise, the "nature of the beast," that makes this interweave hard to disentangle. Yet it is certainly necessary to follow each strand of crusade origins from inception to fruition, and to do so requires sturdier chronological scaffolding.

Perhaps a useful construct for analyzing the prehistory of the Crusades might be to borrow the taxonomy of the field of prehistory studies. The Stone Age has long been seen to be comprised of Paleolithic, Mesolithic, and Neolithic eras—"Old," "Middle," and "New" Stone Age designations useful in identifying the measurable stages of technological and organizational growth. These designations can be helpful in the study of the prehistory of the Crusades in general and the Baltic variant in particular.[31] Such terms as "paleo-," "meso-," and "neo-prehistory" have the utility of clearly marking the stages of development in the components that eventually emerged in Baltic crusading. In this way, while moving back and forth through the centuries a general framework of reference can allow the reader to place the developments in an easily understood order. This approach is not as novel as it may seem. I am in very good company in seeing a tripartite developmental scheme in a medieval topic. The pioneer of medieval frontier studies, C. J. Bishko, used just such an approach in his application of the Turner frontier thesis to the expansion of medieval Europe, seeing early, high, and later medieval developmental stages to the concept of the frontier.[32]

The chronology might vary somewhat, but the treatment involving a paleo-, meso-, and neo-structure remains similarly useful.

One must be cautious about becoming a prisoner of the methodology—any taxonomy runs the risk of being overly brittle. People, events, and even concepts often pass a permeable barrier that defies easy compartmentalization. Likewise, even the seemingly firm boundaries of classification can overlap and even intertwine, and concepts often form a type of Venn diagram rather than a linear progression. But seeing the prehistory of the Baltic Crusades, or crusading in general, as undergoing several discrete stages, whether labeled paleo, meso, or neo, can at least instruct us on the fact that crusading did not spring "full-blown from the brow of Jove," as Constable has famously noted. Once again, Christopher Dawson has a wise suggestion. Noting that modern scientists see the value in the study of remote prehistoric man, Dawson wondered if it were not even more important to focus on "those immediate ancestors whose influence still directly moulds our lives and determines the very language that we speak and the names of the places in which we live."[33] That admonition can be applied effectively to the Crusades. While we should not, as Marc Bloch warned long ago, "confuse ancestry with explanation,"[34] we will be hard-pressed to come to an accurate explanation without an understanding of the ancestry of the Crusades.

As we undertake this exploration of the prehistory of the Baltic Crusades we must address a major complaint about the enterprise. Crusades in general, and the Baltic variant in particular, have come in for criticism for the violent behavior patterns that were employed in the execution of the undertaking. The Baltic Crusades often lack even the fig leaf of justice that may be associated with the Holy Land Crusades given the elements of retribution and reconquest of improperly seized, formerly Christian lands that applied in the case of the latter. The Holy Land Crusades enjoyed a certain righteousness in that there was an effort to protect pilgrims and reclaim land once taken by the sword with the selfsame violence. Since the Holy Land was wrested from Christian control in the seventh century at the point of the sword, there is a symmetry in its reconquest via the same weapon. The Baltic campaigns are often not able to blunt the frequently harsh criticisms aimed at them by using this claim. The behaviors practiced in these campaigns have been almost unanimously viewed as wrong because of their apparent complete neglect of Christian principles, whether concerning atrocity or venality. But the matter is one of finding a reason for these activities, not an excuse for them. This is where the prehistory of the Baltic Crusades can illuminate the progression of rationalization that led to such practices now seen as exotic and repulsive in our contemporary view. Placing these events in context in no way excuses or softens their impact, but rather acts as a monitory study that may help to forestall current or future tendencies toward similar approaches.

When considering the prehistory of our topic, we must evaluate what missionary war is, or is not, as well as the acceptability of war as a vehicle for religious expansion. Then the various outworkings of this concept as it applied in the Baltic must be addressed: the adoption of pagan war practices, the use of religion as a treaty provision with all the changeability that implies, and the sacralization of the landscape for pilgrimage purposes that followed. As with crusading in general, at the heart of this web of behaviors and practices is the use of warfare to accomplish religious ends. The investigation of the peculiar application of this in the Baltic Crusades is our next task.

Questions for discussion

What is "prehistory" in the context of the Crusades?
Why is it important to study the prehistory of the Crusades?
How far back can the prehistory of the Crusades go?

Why do scholars frequently treat the Crusades as suddenly beginning in the late eleventh century?

What are the difficulties in invesitigating the prehistory of the Crusades?

Is correcting an old wrong only productive of more problems?

How did crusaders justify reclaiming land that had been in non-Christian hands for generations or even centuries?

Is a developmental stage approach useful in organizing the prehistory of the Baltic Crusades? Does such an approach always fit?

PART THREE

The Application

5

"Missionary war": Preaching with a tongue of iron

Sprinkled liberally through the chronicles of the Baltic Crusades is the frank admission that warfare was not a "necessary evil" but a major, if not the major, instrument of conversion. What is found in these chronicles is not just Christian approval of war, under certain carefully circumscribed conditions, but discussions on the Christian use of war. Typical of this sentiment is the passage in Henry's *Livonian Chronicle*, written in the late 1220s, in which he concluded, in a chillingly matter-of-fact tone, that the enemy could not "keep the Christian voices from preaching the Word of God; indeed through the increase of the faith they saw that in preaching and fighting they were daily growing stronger."[1] So that no one would mistake the linkage, Henry reflected on the recent conversion of Livonia as the logical result of this "preaching and fighting," *preliando quam predicando*: "Certainly, through the many wars that followed, the pagans were to be converted."[2]

The persistence of this approach and its presence outside of this one source is further attested by the many passages in the later *Livonian Rhymed Chronicle* that feature the grandmaster of the Teutonic Knights, Andreas von Stierland, praying fervently that God would make him "free of worry" and "grant me and the other Christians success in conquering the ancestral lands of the heathens."[3] The campaigns and sorties that flowed from this view, often announced to an enthusiastic audience, had a peculiar union of divine assistance with the most brutal of behaviors: "They (the crusaders) told their people that they wished to make a raid, and, with God's assistance, create widows and orphans."[4] After such a raid into pagan Samogitia, "the Christians filled their hands with booty, and then devastated the land with fire," returning home to Riga where they "immediately praised God in heaven for having defended Christendom with this expedition."[5] This was no spiritualization of warfare, nor a Joshua or Gideon scenario where God granted supernatural victory to a watching army, an "inactive spectator," as in the legendary "Alleluia Victory" in fifth-century Britain.[6] These Baltic victories were won by "spilling their blood for God"[7] in the most earthy and gory way.

The Baltic Crusades that spanned some two-and-a-half centuries have been called "the most protracted effort to force infidels into the font in medieval history."[8] The violent attempts at conversion that accompanied, and in many cases motivated, these crusades have proved to be at best an uncomfortable puzzle to scholars and at worst a repulsive one. The modern perspective, trained to think of religion as a personal and voluntary choice, finds little reason to credit an approach that emphasizes violence and conquest as a means of conversion. Thus Francis Dvornik, the great scholar of Slavic Europe, saw a link between the Saxon crusaders' culture and the medieval perception of Christianity in general, saying "all Europe in those days was prepared to consider aggression as justifiable proselytizing zeal."[9] This is a modernized version of Heinrich Heine's dramatic view of the relationship between Germanic culture and Christianity. Heine, writing in the 1830s, famously opined that Christianity had lessened Germanic love of war but "should that subduing talisman, the cross, be shattered . . . that insane berserk rage . . . will once more burst into flame."[10] It may not be necessary, in Baltic crusading terms, to "shatter" the talisman of the cross, rather merely to employ it.

While scholars such as Dvornik are right to assume a sort of "pay it forward" tendency in the conversion of European tribes by force, their approach highlights the essential puzzle in this saga: How and why was warfare seen as a viable tool for spreading the faith? The ferocity of the campaigns in the Baltic Crusades seems to be the worst realization of the old descriptive phrase that appeared in the ninth-century *Life of St. Liborius*. Christian warriors, it was said, were to "open the gates of faith" by "preaching with a tongue of iron,"[11] a reference that seemed to foreshadow Otto von Bismarck's description of the nineteenth-century war of German unification as one of "blood and iron." War, with all its brutal excess, had become the means of propagation of the faith for the Baltic crusaders. It is no surprise that Erdmann would call this *missionskrieg*, or "missionary war,"[12] and would consider it a major antecedent in the prehistory of the Crusades. As the creator of the term, Erdmann was perceptive enough to note its difference from the Muslim practice of *fath*, or warfare creating religious "opening." He did, however, wrongly believe that *fath* was "the direct imposition of the faith" rather than the conquest of a government that allowed a slow permeation of Islam into the subject territory.[13]

But before examining the origins of missionary war, it might be instructive to note a common misapprehension that has risen to the level of received knowledge in many contemporary circles: the firm belief that monotheism, much more than paganism, created intolerance and, consequently, violence. The argument turns on the fact that monotheists, whether Jewish, Christian, or Muslim, are exclusive—and exclusivity is by definition intolerant.[14] Of course such an interpretive view simultaneously ignores any record of coexistence between monotheists and polytheists while highlighting the episodic conflicts between the two. Complicating the issue is the "god versus God" nature of the struggles. The two sides apparently viewed these bloody contests quite differently: "polytheists rarely envisioned the victory of one set of beliefs over another."[15] Since the monotheistic Christians saw battlefield victory as a type of zero-sum proposition while the pagans apparently did not, there seems to be a certain inevitability in this rush to violence. One would be shocked if peace were to break out between these groups. This predetermined violence largely rests on identity since monotheists as monotheists must, by definition, be intolerant and violently so. Current scholarship has not been free of this view when dealing with the Baltic Crusades, even blaming the negative effects on monotheism. Given Christianity's universalist approach, which "could not accept that some societies might have their own 'truths'," this view promoted an "aggressive attitude toward pagan neighbors" that validated conquest and territorial expansion.[16]

Recently, however, a deeper look at interreligious violence has made its appearance. Brent D. Shaw, in his fine study on Christian-pagan conflict in late antique North Africa, has argued that "identity, in itself, is not an adequate approach to the problem. In the sectarian confrontations of the long fourth century, the reported incidents of violence rarely, if ever, emerged from identity alone."[17] There must be, he contends, some triggering event that would terminate what were long and productive periods of *convivencia* between the two disparate religious communities.[18] H. A. Drake has noted that in such cases "peace is as much a part of the story as violence itself."[19] A line of distinction must be drawn between the identities of the opposing forces and the actual *casus belli*. While there might be a type of matrix of belligerence that persists between the two sides, it needed a point of ignition to bring about actual violence.[20] In a similar way, crusading was in the air along the Baltic Sea but needed an activating agent or event to bring it into play. It was not automatic as the hopeful, yet tragically optimistic, story of Bishop Berthold attests. None of this is to deny the possibility of conflict between religions, nor even to mitigate the seeming inevitability of such violence, but to look for its immediate cause, or the trigger that would ignite this peculiar form of religious war.

According to the sources this is not difficult to ascertain; however, the reliability of the sources is in doubt. The question will always remain: Are such triggers, as described in our sources, mere pretexts or legitimate causes for violence? In medieval terms, the "superior" or ultimate cause for missionary war would be the Great Commission, the spreading of Christianity to all "nations."[21] It must be noted, however, that this commission was, prior to the fourth century, largely carried out in a peaceful manner. But universalism can fit a multitude of vehicles, whether peaceful or violent. The "inferior" or immediate cause for missionary war would be to defend against attacks on the fledgling church and its new converts. When Bishop Meinhard was expelled from his diocese by pagan pressure, he repaired to Pope Celestine II (r. 1191–98 AD) to ask for assistance. The pope ruled that those previously baptized should "not be deserted" and granted "the remission of all sins to all those who would take the cross and go to restore the newly-founded church."[22] The Livonians rightly expected retaliation and "feared and suspected that a Christian army would come upon them."[23] This began a sad pattern of conversion followed by attacks on the newborn church from their pagan neighbors. When attacks against the church continued past Meinhard's death, the next bishop, Berthold, tried a new approach. He opted to "test his fortune" without an army only to find that war was the medium of exchange in his mission field. He got a reaffirmation of crusading privileges from Celestine "as he had to his predecessor" (Meinhard), *et suo dirigens predecessori*, and the use of war to defend the Baltic church became a permanent recourse.[24]

So what does the term "missionary war" actually signify? Is it an accurate one to apply to the military adventures on the Baltic seacoast? If one views the term as descriptive of a war to convert a pagan people, the term is quite appropriate. In this view, the war itself is a form of missionary action even if repulsively violent. But if one sees this form of war as a defensive one, designed to protect previous missionary efforts, then the term misleads. The question turns on the issue of whether war itself is the agent of conversion, or if it is an agent of the preservation of conversions already accomplished. It is not as if the sources chronicle a Christian army invading, without sufficient provocation, a nearby pagan territory. In fact the sources seem to indicate, beginning in the centuries before the Baltic Crusades right on through the last iteration of "missionary war," that the military campaigns were designed to defend and protect the nascent churches in these regions from destruction at the hands of hostile pagan neighbors. Seen in that light, missionary war takes on a different, and perhaps more justifiable, character. When deciding on the descriptive validity of the term "missionary war" for what transpired in the Baltic, it is necessary to differentiate between process and product. Missionary war designed to bring people to the faith is quite different from missionary war to protect Christian populations. This distinction in process may have been obscured by the end product. When the dust of battle settled and the blood dried upon the ground, vast swathes of territory were Christian, at least in an official sense. It is only natural to survey this end result and assume the crusaders were mission-minded in their combat. Conversion may have been only a by-product of this undertaking, with baptism being used as a seal of military victory, rather than as the expressed objective.

It is true, and understandable, that defensive justifications are often lost in the violent borrowing of pagan practices by the "Christian" forces, but the original impetus for the war remains. The fact that every advance in Christian territory required further defensive protection against the next pagan foe makes this argument sound like the defense against the criticism directed at ancient Rome—that it conquered the world in self-defense. But one wonders what would have happened if, when the first pagan tribe beyond the Christian frontier saw its initial converts, there had been no attacks on the infant church. Would, or did, the Christian chroniclers and apologists create the justification for further war by exaggerating conflicts between the two faith systems, Christian and pagan? Or was there an actual triggering event, a violent pagan reaction to Christianity and the apparent cultural submission to the invading forces that came along with the change that was being imposed? Absent the pagan side of the story and left with Christian histories, we can only assume that the "missionary wars" of the Baltic Crusades were largely in response to attacks by pagans on the church, a position that puts the Baltic Crusades as following from the same rationale given for the Crusades proper.

This issue brings to the front two points that must be addressed: first, the debt that missionary war may owe to the defensive justifications found in the just war theory, and secondly, the seductively irresistible slide from defensive to offensive war that accompanied the use of defensive force. In this instance the use of descriptive language becomes critical. Kurt Villads Jensen has pointed out that

> medieval language was, in many respects, much more sophisticated than modern man tends to realize at first glance.... Every word and every sentence had four *sensus*, that is four different understandings, even though all of them pointed to the same meaning.... It might be natural for us today to assume that a word can have only one meaning, and that it cannot mean one thing and its opposite at the same time.[25]

His conclusion is that *defensio* "in medieval sources meant defense, which in practice could often mean attack."[26]

It is not, however, accurate to assume that these developments were either sudden or novel, nor is it enough to trace their inception only as far back as the wars of Charlemagne against the Saxons. The use of military force to protect or extend the boundaries of Christendom, both theological and territorial, has deep roots that stretch back long before the First Crusade or its later Baltic descendant. An examination of these roots can illuminate the activities of the quarter-millennium conflict that was the Baltic Crusades. But the presupposition exists that "preaching with a tongue of iron" was not always the acceptable mode of Christianization. Some train of events, or course of evolution, must have taken place to create the notion of "missionary war."

Two major issues must be addressed in the study of the prehistory of "missionary war." First, the approval of Christian warfare participation, whether for a variety of justifiable reasons such as self-defense, rescuing victims of slaughter, preventing greater evil, etc., needs to be in force. If true pacifism rules the Christian world, then the idea of "missionary war" is unthinkable. Warfare must be acceptable in certain circumstances before it can be used in such a seemingly wanton way. Secondly, once war is one of the possible options in the right situation, the question of its suitability for spreading the faith must be determined. These are formidable conceptual and theological hurdles to clear, yet in time these barriers were topped.

The received wisdom on the early Christian movement is that it was almost completely pacifistic in its view on war. The Apostle Paul's statement in II Corinthians 10:3-4 seems to express the majority opinion: "For though we live in the world, we do not wage war as the world does. The weapons we fight with are not the weapons of the world."[27] While there are multiple theologians from Origen to Tertullian who weighed in against participation in combat, pacifism was a bit more apparent than real in the early church.[28] The Christian community existed outside and in many ways apart from the Roman state. It was fairly described "as a persecuted minority given no status by, and indebted for no duties to, the civil order."[29] This type of parallel existence meant that the major objections to military service were based on individual religious scruples such as unwillingness to pray to the pagan gods and the emperor. The military induction ceremony, the *sacramentum*, was suffused with pagan religious ethos and seems to have presented at least as great a barrier to service as did the notion of violent warfare. That would explain the occasional, and seemingly anomalous, presence of some Christians in Roman combat roles—the fabled "Thundering Legion," for instance—as well as why the persecuting Emperor Diocletian (r. 284–305 AD) made the army his first target in purging the empire of Christians.[30] Thus, military involvement was based more on individual conviction and participation rather than church policy. It is, as Louis J. Swift has pointed out, simplistic to categorize the period before the reign of the Emperor Constantine as fully pacifistic and the post-Constantinian era as non-pacifistic.[31]

Unanimity was not a significant trait of the early church whether in theology, as the Pauline epistles testify, or in opinions about war. Constantine's "conversion" would change all this, not so much in its novelty, but in its shifting of emphasis in favor of approved war. This view avoids the temptation, in Swift's words, "to see this change as an abandonment of principles and the adoption of a policy of expediency after the interests of the Church and state had become synonymous."[32] It represented a shift rather than a reversal of the church's thinking. With changes in time and circumstance, the "weapons of the world" would be employed—enthusiastically and to great effect.

When Constantine, the victor in the Roman civil war of 306–12 AD, proudly proclaimed himself a Christian, regardless of whatever may have been his doctrinal deficiencies, the old model of the Christian community existing in a parallel space apart from the government was altered forever. Constantine's association with Christianity has been rightly called a "revolution," and it provides the *terminus ante quem* for examining "missionary war." At first Constantine merely allowed Christianity an approved status within the empire and stopped the active persecution of believers. However, he did consider himself to be a Christian and in a system that viewed disagreement with the emperor as *laesae maiestatis*, or "treason," it became increasingly uncomfortable for pagans to mount opposition to this new faith. In due time the empire itself became a Christian state worthy of defense, at least in the minds of those who were inclined to see the newly converted emperor as an *isapostle*, or a "new apostle." Therefore Constantine's conversion created a need for a rapprochement between the generally pacifistic Christian community and the basic needs of military defense. While war remained an evil, it would occasionally, under the right qualifications and constraints, be a necessary evil to protect the newly Christianized state.

It was to this end that the Christian just war theory was begun to be formulated, first by Ambrose (339–97 AD), bishop of Milan, and then elaborated by his prized convert Augustine (354–430 AD).[33] This theory of war permission was based on the two notions that, given the fallen state of the world, wars would sometimes be necessary to protect the innocent and that those engaging in these wars would of necessity do evil, but only to prevent a greater evil. This package also was predicated on doubt. There was not the certainty that would inform a holy war. The just warrior could

"MISSIONARY WAR": PREACHING WITH A TONGUE OF IRON 77

FIGURE 2 *The* Aula Palatina, *Trier, Germany. This mighty audience hall, or basilica, was used by Constantine to receive dignitaries and conduct imperial business while in residence at the western border capital of Augusta Trevivorum (Trier). Sometime around 315* AD, *after Constantine's acceptance of Christianity, he allowed this structure to be used as a church, illustrating the union of church and state that he envisioned. This building later became the site of the first trial for heresy as Priscillian was accused and condemned here in 385* AD. *(Photo by the author)*

err in judging a war's cause to be acceptable and also could lose justness by prosecuting the war in an unjust manner.

All this was to produce a sense of circumspection rather than bellicose license in the just war theory. No one could be completely certain that God would approve of either the reasons for the war or its actual implementation. Whether this circumspection actually came into play has remained an item of academic discussion and dispute to this day. It seems only natural that an exception, once allowed, can easily morph into a rule and many subsequent wars have been justified whether truly just or not. But these limitations in war permission, at least in theory, acted as a check on unfettered violence.

The emergence of Christian just war stands as the paleo-prehistory stage in the creation of "missionary war." If war could be used, albeit hedged in by restrictions, by Christian governments and warriors, how might it be used by the church for the spreading of the faith? This would become particularly problematic if there should be a blurring of the lines of demarcation between secular and church governments, as occurred in the coming centuries of the medieval period. R. A. Markus believes the just war theory is a quite malleable thing that "will encourage one set of attitudes in a society in which war is unthinkable . . . and quite different attitudes where it is readily accepted as normal." It would tend to make "the unthinkable thinkable" or "the unquestioned questionable."[34] He concluded that "in a world in which war and Christianity were both normal, they could coalesce readily."[35]

However, many see no connection between this early permission of warfare for Christians and later occurrences of approved war in the Middle Ages. While objections tend to fall into distinct categories, such as the lack of a state for authorization, the just war tradition of protection of society in general rather than the promulgation of a religious ideal, and the reluctance of just warriors as compared to the violently enthusiastic war-making of crusaders, the main objection seems to be that of authorization.[36] Just war depends on the existence of a state authority, what Augustine called *auctoritas*, to initiate a just campaign. The Roman Empire certainly fit this requirement as a state entity, but the barbarian kingdoms that followed the fall of the Western Empire did not. However, it is entirely reasonable that certain components of the just war theory did survive the fall of Rome. As Augustine himself reassured his readership in the years after his publication of *The City of God* in 426, the empire might fall but the church would not. There may no longer be a Roman state to authorize just wars but other portions of the theory could still have a useful existence beyond the fall of Rome. Forming a foundation for any of these surviving components would be the simple fact that a tradition of allowable Christian participation in war had been established.

But the importation of elements of the just war theory into the Middle Ages proper may go beyond the mere permission to fight under certain circumstances. There is another implicit trait that makes just war an ancestor to the Crusades. Apart from the often noted status of just war as the first version of Christian war approval, it has a structural affinity to crusading as well. The just war deals with corporate approval of violence. The individual just warrior must be personally pacifistic, only fighting when directed by the government and then not on his own behalf, but for those who are innocent victims of evil. The just war is designed to keep order and justice among societies. However, this perspective is often lost in the prevailing view of the Crusades. Crusading is frequently viewed through the lens of personal pilgrimage, with the crusader fighting on behalf of his own salvation, *pro remedia animae*, for the remedy of his soul. There has been too much attention paid to the spiritual benefits accruing to the crusaders and not enough recognition of the societal implications involved. The reason for the Crusades was the recovery of the Holy Land, not only for the crusading participants, nor even for the generations of pilgrims yet to come, but for all Christians everywhere. The just war emphasis on combat for the good of societal order and the protection of the innocents pertains to the act of crusading as well as serving as the underpinning of the entire enterprise. The unfettered access to the Holy Land for pilgrimage may not only have served as a significant ignition point for the Crusades but also continued to stand as a reason for crusading continuation, as the founding of the Knights Templar illustrates.

Further complicating the legacy of just war for crusading is the tendency of crusade chroniclers to emphasize individuals at the expense of groups. Christopher Tyerman has pointed out recently that when a king or magnate took the cross promising to go on crusade, his retinue followed suit.[37] The fervor that created the Crusades may have been based on individual attitude and choice but was realized by corporate action, a point often obscured by the emphasis on the frequent, and individualized, squabbling among the leaders of the Christian host. Chronicles also tend to feature the arrival of crusading forces as the singular arrival of a hero, much as in ancient Greek accounts of war. But these individual "heroes" were without fail accompanied by large groups of fighters. This elevation of "noble leaders" gives the further impression of the Crusades as individual efforts to remedy individual penitential needs. The group presence is obscured by the emphasis on singular leaders. Examples abound in the sources for the Baltic Crusades as well as in the sources for the better-known crusades to the Holy Land. Henry's *Livonian Chronicle* records under its entry for the year 1203 that Albert of Buxhövden brought back with him from his yearly recruitment journey "the noblemen Arnold of Meiendorf, Bernard of Seehausen, and his brother, Theodoric." Only as an afterthought was the phrase "with many respectable men and soldiers" added.[38] This became almost a type of literary *topos* as Henry later mentioned Gottschalk, the Count of Pyrmont, Albert of Anhalt, the Duke of Saxony, a Burgrave named Rudolf of Stotle, and "a certain young count" as making their appearances in turn to participate in the Baltic Crusades.[39] Each time it seems the leader is noted, but the size of the force accompanying them is not. But the armies assembled by Albert and his successors were large corporate efforts at missionary war, not individual sorties by warrior heroes. Viewed in this way, the just war theory has a legacy for the eventual emergence of crusading, perhaps even that variant that came to be known as missionary war.

Another seeming disconnect between the just war theory and medieval crusading lies in the apparently unfettered violence that informed the latter. A just warrior would, at least theoretically, be somewhat constrained in combat behavior regarding noncombatants, treaties, prisoners, and the like. Crusaders, especially those on campaign in the Baltic, seem to almost rejoice in bloody excess. However, the just war theory does not rest upon a presumption against violence, but rather on a presumption against injustice.[40] While the authorization of just war disappeared with the Roman state, the idea of a presumption against injustice, rather than one against violence, remained. One of Augustine's main quotes on the matter has been emphasized in part, rather than in the whole. The Bishop of Hippo opined in his tract *Contra Faustum* that some would die in order to provide peace for all and that the only "real evils in war" were love of violence, lust for power, and the like. What is not examined fully in this passage is Augustine's conclusion that good men "in obedience to God or some lawful authority" must make war.[41] The emphasis has been on Augustine's phrase requiring obedience to "some lawful authority" rather than the rest of his statement that included "obedience to God."

The lawful authority may have been missing but obedience to God surfaced in the post-Roman wars between the various tribal kingdoms of Western Europe. In the 530s, the Thuringian king Hermanfrid violated all the norms of hostage taking by executing, in the most horrific ways, young Frankish men and women in his custody. The Frankish king Theuderic, enraged by this, gave an emotional speech to his army to explain why these actions demanded a "just" military response. After citing all the gruesome particulars, Theuderic concluded with the rousing exclamation that "there is no doubt that we have right on our side. With God's help we must attack them!"[42] The translation leaves out the significant terminology that connects Theuderic's words to Augustine's "in obedience to God" phrase. What Gregory of Tours included in Theuderic's speech was the assertion that the Frankish army had a *verbum directum*, a direct word from God to authorize their just retribution.[43] This constitutes another bridge between the Christian Roman Empire's war permission and war permission in the post-Roman barbarian kingdoms. The legacy that certain wars were justified and even approved by God was passed on to succeeding kings and even churchmen.

The meso-prehistory phase was ushered in by the conversion of several barbarian kings such as Clovis in Gaul and Edwin in Northumbrian England. These kings were often led to Christianity by influential queens, but the trigger point in their journey to the faith was to be found on the battlefield. An important aspect of this model is that the royal would-be converts were drawn to the faith by the promise of victory, not as a consequence of their defeat in war. The association is a positive one: if the subject follows Christ, victory will ensue. This repeats the prototypical experience of Constantine, who experienced a vision while on campaign that included not only the Christian *labarum*, a symbol comprised of the first two Greek letters of "Christ," but the instruction to conquer in that sign. Military victory was intimately tied to coming to the faith.

A point must be made about the sources that convey these stories of the union of war and conversion. It is entirely possible that chroniclers, needing to validate Christian usage of war as a first step in conversion, inserted these types of accounts in order to establish the linkage. That is possible, but also beside the point. Their readership believed these battlefield pathways to conversion to be true and, as such, the received wisdom throughout the early Middle Ages was that victory in war was often a prerequisite to acceptance of the faith. The Frankish king Clovis, described by Gregory of Tours as impervious to conversion—"nothing could persuade him to accept Christianity"—was driven to the faith by the imminent prospect of his army being wiped out by an opposing barbarian tribe, the Alamanni. Gregory seems to insert a set piece featuring Clovis raising his eyes to heaven and bargaining with God: "If you will give me victory over my enemies . . . then I will believe in you and will be baptized in your name."[44] Clovis' battlefield fortunes turned immediately and the Alamanni were defeated soundly, with the denouement in Gregory's account being that the once recalcitrant king proceeded to the baptismal font.

King Edwin of Northumbria, about whom Bede had already prophesied that "as a sign that he would come to the faith and the heavenly kingdom, (he) . . . brought under his sway all the territories inhabited either by English or by Britons,"[45] found himself the central actor in one of the most tumultuous Easters in history. On that night, Edwin barely survived an assassination attempt and received the birth of his firstborn. In what might have been an understandable state of mental flux, the king "promised that if God would grant him life and victory over the king his enemy who had sent the assassin, he would renounce his idols and serve Christ."[46] As soon as he was sufficiently recovered from his wounds, Edwin marched to victory against the offending West Saxons and "either slew or forced to surrender all those who had plotted his murder."[47] After a full course of catechumenal instruction, the king was baptized.

Thus a union was created between monarch and religion that fit well with the preexisting barbarian view that the king stood before the gods for the entire people. If a barbarian king became Christian, it would be possible, so the church apparently thought, for that new Christian agent to conquer other peoples and thereby bring them into the Christian orbit as well. It was to this end that Bishop Avitus of Vienne, released from a tenuous existence under Arian rule in southern Gaul, would write to the newly baptized Clovis sometime after that king's decisive victory over the Visigoths in 507 AD, suggesting he use his new faith to "spread it to the peoples living beyond the Rhine."[48] That this was not a simple plea for missionary activity, but a precursor to a more violent form of mission, missionary war, is supported by the overall tenor of subsequent events. Clovis systematically removed rival Frankish warlord-kings in the north, often by the most devious means, and extended his control into Austrasia, or portions of the modern-day Rhineland.[49] However brutal and duplicitous, a newly converted barbarian king could be a powerful military agent in the spreading of the faith. Conquest and conversion seem to have become almost indistinguishable.

That this became an accepted viewpoint is echoed by the sharp criticism of kings who failed in this new mission. Gregory of Tours presents the finest example of this disapproval in his preface to the fifth book of his *Histories*. Expressing disgust at the penchant for civil war among the current Frankish kings, what he styled *bellorum civilium*, he lectures them on the proper use of war.

> If only you kings had occupied yourselves with wars like those in which your ancestors larded the ground with their sweat, then the other races of the earth, filled with awe at the peace which you imposed, might have been subjected to your power![50]

While Gregory does not explicitly link war and conquest with the spread of the faith, his view on Clovis' earlier victories suggests that this is implied: "Day in and day out God submitted the enemies of Clovis to his dominion and increased his power, for he walked before Him with an upright heart and did what was pleasing in His sight."[51] The apparent aggressively acquisitive nature of these statements places them at odds against the received principles of the just war, chief among which is the prohibition against offensive wars. Augustine had called *libido dominandi*, or "lust to dominate," a sin and made it a disqualifier for justness in war. Aggression and its concomitant product, conquest, were wrong. What then justified a missionary war that was directed at the conquest of pagan lands so as to effect the pagans' Christianization? Perhaps the move to conquest rather than defense was a corrupting move away from Christian just war toward a pagan view of war as a fully acceptable habit, aided by a type of loophole in the just war. Henrik Syse has noticed that "while the entire tradition" of just war requires armed force to be a reaction to wrongdoing, "there is no real opposition to *initiating* warfare for the sake of repelling injustice."[52] Augustine's codicil that just wars could be used to prevent greater evil, *ulciscuntur iniurias*, in practice could make a theoretically defensive campaign seem offensive.

When surveying the bevy of early medieval kings who used this union of war and religion to their benefit, there is a subject that must be addressed: the role of the influence of pagan approaches to war-making on the Christian world. The earlier paleo-prehistory phase consisted of the Christianization of an existing polity, the Roman Empire, from within. In the phase that followed, the

FIGURE 3 *Heavenfield battle site, near Newcastle, UK. Here in 635, the Christian king Oswald erected a cross (now symbolized by a modern wooden one) to dedicate his upcoming battle against the pagan forces of Cadwalla. His victory was yet another seal to the notion that warfare and Christianity could work in tandem; a significant step in the journey to missionary war. (Photo by the author)*

religion went outside the Roman population—first with the accommodation of invading peoples and then with religious forays into pagan lands. This process was to be ongoing from the period that saw the fall of Rome through Charlemagne's day to the period of the Baltic Crusades. The discussion of this matter usually takes the form of "the Germanization of the Church." James C. Russell believes Christianity, owing to its urban-centric orientation, did not address the fundamental concerns of the pagan Germans, which were largely military and agricultural. When these concerns were accommodated by Christian missionaries, "an unintended result . . . was the Germanization of early medieval Christianity."[53] As the just war theory, which permitted war under certain circumstances, was the creation of Christian bishops, notably Ambrose and Augustine, the move from the cautious, circumscribed approved war of that Christian creation to an enthusiastic embrace of war as an effective instrument of church policy must have been a corrupting by-product of contact with the pagan peoples beyond the Rhine.

This is an incomplete view. While the effects of Christian culture upon the Germans are obvious, as measured by their adoption of the faith and much of the social trappings that accompanied it, this position assumes rather less Christian Roman martial affinity than really existed. The Germans often sought to mimic Roman practice, which could include more than surnames, intermarriage, and the adoption of the large estate system. There was a congenial union of Roman and Germanic practice, and this extended to war.[54] J. M. Wallace-Hadrill offers his usual wise analysis: "Germanic pagan peoples had a clear sense that war was a religious undertaking. . . . Not surprisingly, Christian missionaries found this ineradicable, though not unadaptable to their own purposes."[55]

As the Germans became Christian, did Christians become Germanic in their view of war? Or was this "Germanization" more apparent than real—the product of a translation of Christian writings into a Germanic idiom for missionary purposes? An excellent example of this is *The Heliand*, the Saxon reworking of the Gospel. Written by an anonymous Saxon monk in about 830 AD, after Charlemagne's conquest and absorption of these people, it puts the story of Christ's ministry and passion in terms that resonated with the target audience.[56] The end product is redolent of martial terminology. Christ is the "chieftain of all mankind, born in David's hill-fort" and the disciples are called "thanes." The Last Supper is termed "the last mead-hall feast with the warrior-companions" and Peter's brandishing of the sword in the Garden of Gethsemane is not connected to a rebuke by Jesus to put away the weapon. Rather, the impetuous disciple is called "the mighty swordsman" who defended Christ "boldly."[57] The disciples were then made to form a defensive perimeter saying, "If it should be Your will that we be impaled here on their spear-points, wounded by their weapons, then nothing would be as good to us as to die here, pale from mortal wounds, for our Chieftain."[58] It appears that the military reimaging of the Gospel was more than just the use of a language medium to teach those new to the faith. The *Heliand* has been called "the meeting place of the Christian Gospel and Germanic culture" and its synthesis provided "an evangelical basis for the imaging of Christian discipleship in soldierly terms."[59] Even though this type of melding of Germanic culture with Christian tradition was not confined to Saxony, the Saxons' role as instigators of the Baltic Crusades makes the connection quite pertinent. That warfare became the essence of Saxon views of Christian government is attested by the coronation sermon delivered when Otto I was crowned in 936. Archbishop Hildebert of Mainz instructed the new king to "take this sword with which you shall defeat all the enemies of Christ, barbarians, and evil Christians."[60] It was at once a confirmation of the union of Germanic and Christian views as well as a chilling preview of the Saxons' role in the coming push to convert the peoples of the eastern frontier. The question remains, however, as to how the traditionally legitimate role of defensive war was subsumed under the barbarian notion of conquest.

Defense has long been a properly qualifying cause for war in the just war tradition. Pacifism, on the other hand, holds that the individual must waive the right of self-defense in the interest of opposing all forms of violence. But the just war theory also prohibits individual violence, a point that the noted American pacifist scholar John Howard Yoder employed to classify just war as one of his twenty-nine variations of pacifism in his book, *Nevertheless*.[61] The critical difference is that while both just warriors and pacifists may surrender their own right of self-defense, the just warrior cannot surrender those rights for others, particularly those that are innocent. If a war is in defense of innocent victims and is authorized by a properly constituted authority, the participants are seen to be just warriors.[62] As our available sources emphasize defense as the motive and note papal authorization for the military action, a case may be made for the Baltic Crusades as a just war, at least in the *ius ad bellum*, causative sense. Whether the wars were prosecuted in a proper, just fashion is a quite separate, and potentially disqualifying, issue. Apart from unjust battlefield behavior, the determination of innocence complicates the issue: Who are the innocent and who are the nocent? Theological questions of baptism and apostasy and their association with guilt and forgiveness would become controlling factors when that determination was made in the Baltic theater of operations.

All the above-mentioned factors point toward the union of warfare and religion with an additional complicating issue. It is not only the matter of just cause for war or even the just prosecution of the same that is at play here. Crusading was by definition a form of worship and worship is something that does not conform readily to limits. Believers, whatever the religious creed, have difficulty imagining what might be too much worship. A crusader, or even an earlier missionary warrior, viewing war as worship, may also have difficulty imagining what might be too much war. This could be a powerful impetus toward the adoption of violent pagan war practices and even the introduction of some new ones as well. The sacralization of combat in this missionary war format contains yet another temptation that caused the Baltic Crusades to veer into an aggressive, punitive mode of operation. When victory on the battlefield is anointed as God's plan, the differences between just and unjust causes blurs. The mechanics of victory override the original intent.

How does one go from defending the faith, or the faithful, to conquest for the faith? There must be some line of development that would move the sinful act of aggression as featured in offensive wars of conquest to a rationally acceptable activity for Christian just warriors. Here it seems there is an act of elision at play. Elision is usually defined as ignoring differences in order to make two things that are different the same. Often used in literary arguments, it can have an application here as well. Defensive war was acceptable in the just war scheme, but offensive war was not. Yet notions of defense are somewhat elastic, and thus suitable to cover even aggressive acts. At what point does the campaign cease being one to defend and become one to conquer? Tactically, repulsed and retreating armies may be pursued far beyond the boundaries of simple defensive protection. Miraculous, God-given victories in defense of coreligionists may be seen as a sanctification of war in general, even offensive ones.

It is a tempting shift from acceptable defensive war to protect new converts to an embrace of offensive war to make new converts. This often is done under the justifying rubric of God-granted victory: If God gives the crusaders an improbable win in a defensive campaign, perhaps He has sanctioned war as an instrument in an offensive nature as well. The elision from defensive to offensive war was already in place by the Baltic Crusade era, as Charlemagne's experience with the Saxons attests. But, as with religiously based violence in general, it needed a trigger. The repeated rebellions and attacks against the Christian presence by Slavic, and later Baltic, peoples meant that there would be no shortage of triggers to activate this shift. The received wisdom of the mid-twelfth century along the Baltic was, in Helmold of Bosau's words, that "of all the peoples of the northern nations, the country of the Slavs alone has remained more obdurate and slower of belief than the rest."[63] Noting Slavic rebellions in 983, 1018, and again in 1066, Bysted even credits this repeated recalcitrance as the reason the Wends, rather than the Danes, suffered the full force of a crusade. While the Danes, once converted, remained relatively stable in their Christianity, the Wends did not: "Every fresh attempt to re-establish organized Christian life was forestalled by a new pagan revolt."[64] The Baltic crusaders would not feel a twinge of apprehension as they moved from defending new converts to conquering previously unreached peoples.

But there is also the seductive elision of war practice at play here. As combat is enjoined, whether for defensive or offensive purposes, the tendency to adopt the "coinage of the realm" on the battlefield is almost irresistible. An army can hold itself to higher standards of war practice, at least in theory, but the tendency for a type of martial sympathetic magic with "like begetting like" can take over. Therefore supposedly upright Christian soldiers can find themselves drawn into the vortex of violent behavior bordering on atrocity. The "preaching" could most definitely take place with "a tongue of iron." William Urban has taken the position that the primary goal of the Baltic Crusade was "to protect missionaries and merchants" while the second was "to protect the converts."[65] One might quibble with this order of importance as the vague line drawn in the late medieval period between the status of merchant, crusader, and even missionary makes for difficulty in classification. The sources do seem, however, rather insistent on the need to protect new converts, placing the enterprise in the category of a justifiable war. We must, as Urban wisely cautions, refrain from the "extremes of defending every action of the crusaders" since a just cause can often result in an unjust effect.[66] Yet the need to protect fellow Christians even worked its way into the template for English coronation oaths by the tenth century. Apparently the solemn pledge made by King Edgar in 973 included the pious wish that the king "by his power both terrify infidels and bring joyful peace to those that fight for thee (God)."[67] The bright line between conquest for the faith and military action only to protect fellow Christians was dimming.

If we are to credit the Baltic Crusade sources' assertion that crusading military force was used in defense of newly converted Christian enclaves, it opens up an issue that still bedevils international relations: the justness and acceptable extent of intervention. Modern students of the matter note that once military intervention is permitted as an exceptional case, the practice tends to become more and more unexceptional.[68] It is, indeed, a "slippery slope" that almost irresistibly leads to expanded action. This may well be at play in the Baltic, as it was in earlier centuries also. As a type of medieval "mission creep" Christian forces sent to protect soon remained to conquer. By 1245, Pope Innocent IV (r. 1243–54 AD) issued an opinion, in the *Decretum*, on the issue, holding that "warfare opening the way for Christian preachers is lawful."[69] Benjamin Kedar believes this reconciled "the fundamental principle of free choice (regarding baptism) with the popularly evolved notion of Christianization as one of the goals of crusading."[70] This further produces a rolling wave of intervention that courses eastward to eventually touch the shore of Christian Russia.

The papacy was not slow to participate in this authorization of force as a legitimate protection of the church. Arguably the greatest of medieval pontiffs, Gregory I (r. 590–604 AD) lived and worked, in his colorful phrase, "among swords."[71] The swords were wielded by the predatory Lombards, who had conquered large portions of the Italian Peninsula and threatened to take Rome as well. This gave Gregory no choice but to enter "the sphere of military and political affairs,"[72] and the pontiff deployed troops, consulted with commanders of imperial forces, and generally authorized the church to use warfare as an instrument of defense. Later popes, when pressed by circumstances, elaborated on this position. Leo IV (r. 847–55 AD), preparing for an imminent invasion by Muslim forces, ruled that "the kingdom of heaven will be given as a reward to those who shall be killed" in defense of the church,[73] while Nicholas I (r. 858–67) seemed to extend approval for those who fought in defense of the church but survived the conflict. John VIII (r. 872–82) held that those who fought in battle "against pagans and infidels" (*contra paganos atque infideles*) would receive an *indulgentia*.[74] What this indulgence meant has been a matter of discussion, but the merit of fighting for defense of the church was strengthened. Once this position was established, it percolated throughout the Western church.

Janet Nelson has examined the increasing ninth-century tendency of the church to incorporate detachments of soldiers under the normal purview of high-ranking ecclesiastical positions. Using

Hincmar of Rheims' *De Ecclesiis et Capellis*, written c. 857/58 AD, Nelson notes that in Frankish lands clerics were apportioned funds in several parts: one each for their own upkeep, one for church maintenance such as lighting, one for poor relief, and one for the bishop. Most significantly for our purpose, there was also a share for "the fighting-men who are listed under the name of 'housed ones' (*casati*)."[75] Styled the *militia ecclesiae*, these troops became the "key element in the ninth-century system . . . composed of bodies of virtually full-time soldiers, maintained out of churches' moveable resources and available for service alongside the king's and his counts' and magnates' own household troops."[76]

That this was not confined to the growing Frankish Empire is attested by the *Anglo-Saxon Chronicle* which includes multiple mentions of bishops leading contingents of soldiers into battle.[77] In Ireland, beginning in the middle of the eighth century, monasteries fielded actual armies to defend, and sometimes expand, their holdings. A cursory glance at the contemporary Irish annals will reveal multiple "wars" fought between monastic settlements from at least 759 right on up to the 820s, notably before the supposedly polluting Viking Age.[78] That these armies were not just for show is made plain by the terminology. The battle between the monastic houses of Ferns and Taghamon in 817 killed some four hundred and was listed as a *bellum*, or war, in the sources while the dynastic struggle between Brega and the Cianachta of Louth was merely called a *belliolum*, or "little war."[79] While most of the scholarly examination of these Irish monastic armies has revolved around the question of whether monks were the actual combatants—consensus now is that the warriors were *manaich*, or lay clients of the monastic towns—the unmistakable conclusion is that churchmen, even those of the monastic calling, were fully invested in war for defensive as well as occasionally offensive purposes.[80] While it seems that churchmen supported and directed war, they were still not permitted to actually fight. Odo, Abbot of Corbie, fought against the Vikings in 859 and was chastised by Lupus of Ferrieres for his personal participation.

> I advise you, out of well-wishing affection, be content with only putting your troops in position—for that's as much as is suitable to your (monastic) vow—and leave it to the fighting men (*armati*) to carry out their "profession" with instruments of war.[81]

It is one thing for the church to take the initiative to lead troops into battle for defensive purposes, quite another for them to engage in missionary war.

If the paleo-phase of the prehistory of missionary war consisted in the Constantinian revolution and the just war theory that it provoked, the meso-prehistory phase, while it began with the equation of conversion with military victory that barbarian kings from Clovis to Edwin experienced, flowered in Charlemagne's enthusiastic embrace of the just war concept in his struggle with the Saxons. This implies, however, that what Charlemagne did was novel. Yet even such a gaudy use of missionary war by the first Holy Roman emperor had its precedents. The emperor's grandfather, also named Charles and nicknamed "Martel" or "the Hammer," was far more than just the victorious commander at the Battle of Poitiers in October 733. This Charles was not the actual king of the Franks, but as *major palatii*, or "mayor of the palace," the Frankish host was at his command. Overshadowed by his dramatic defeat of Muslim forces was his steadfast military support for missionary activity among his pagan German neighbors. By supporting these conversion efforts with arms, Charles Martel moved the concept of missionary war ever closer.

This is shown by the principal, but not the only, missionary to the pagan northern reaches of Frankish influence, the English churchman Boniface (c.685–754 AD). Born Wynfryth at Crediton in Wessex, he took the name Boniface and played a pivotal role in missionary activity among the Frisians and Germans until his martyrdom on June 5, 754. Boniface's letters, an important source in this lightly illuminated age, testify to his dependence on Charles Martel's military backing for success in his mission. Early on in his mission, in 723, Boniface apparently appealed to Charles Martel for protection from his enemies. These enemies included ecclesiastical rivals, but also threatening pagans. Charles answered his request with "pleasure" affirming that "he shall with our love and protection remain unmolested and undisturbed."[82]

This governmental protection was even more sharply focused some eighteen years later when Boniface sought to reaffirm his status with Grifo, the son of the recently deceased Charles Martel and now the *major palatii*. Boniface asked "that you will protect the Christians from the hostility of the heathens so that they may not be destroyed by them" and reminded Grifo that "this your father desired during his lifetime."⁸³ When Boniface was martyred by a band of pagans, the local Christian population raised "a large avenging force" and killed pagans "in great numbers." In a chilling adumbration of the Baltic Crusades, the winning army took as spoil "the wives and children" of the losing side with the result that the pagans "struck with terror at the visitation of God's vengeance . . . embraced after Boniface's death the teaching they had rejected while he still lived."⁸⁴ The reaction to the martyrdom of the missionary was a type of missionary war. This background to the age of Charlemagne highlights the central point: Charles Martel's military was employed in defense of Christian missionary efforts. The sad tale of St. Patrick, watching his new and defenseless flock slaughtered at the hands of a hostile force, would not occur in the land of the Franks.

This protective assignment only increased under Charlemagne. The *Life of St. Lebuin*, probably penned about 850 AD, after Charlemagne's conquest of Saxony, and therefore an example of the received wisdom of an earlier age, the 770s, featured the saint

FIGURE 4 *Charlemagne's chapel at Aachen, Germany. With Charlemagne's rule (768–814) the idea of a reconstituted Christian empire emerged. He was not merely a Christian king seeking to be protected from his pagan enemies, but an emperor who aggressively sought to expand his empire for God, using missionary war. (Photo by the author)*

warning the Saxon assembly of the dangers of repeated attacks on Christian enclaves: "If you are unwilling to accept God's commands, a king has been prepared nearby who will invade your lands ... slay you with the sword, and hand over your possessions to whom he has in mind."[85] This is a clear-eyed retrospective on Charlemagne's actions as well as an accurate prediction of what was to come along the Baltic coastline.

The vaunted Carolingian army that eventually conquered the Saxons after some thirty-three consecutive years of campaigning included churchmen and their forces, further illustrating the union of Christianity and war. The capitulary that is often cited as an example of the standard summons for Charlemagne's army was addressed to the abbot Fulrad of the monastery of St. Denis in Paris, sometime after 804. Charlemagne was holding his general assembly in newly conquered Saxon territory and called the famed Abbot to the colors. The language is revealing.

> Therefore we have commanded you to come to the aforesaid place, with all your men well armed and prepared. . . . Come, accordingly, so equipped with your men ... with arms and gear also, and other equipment for war in food and clothing. So that each horseman shall have a shield, lance, sword, dagger, bow and quivers with arrows.[86]

The widespread existence of the *militia ecclesiae*—Nelson has found evidence of its presence in Italy and England as well as in the kingdom of the Franks—was a fertile seedbed for the next phase of the prehistory of missionary war: the use of armed contingents to enforce church decrees and/or defeat foes of papal policies. Once again Janet Nelson has closed the circle concerning the *militia ecclesiae*:

> Can we believe that any wide gulf separates these *milites* from, on the one hand, those warriors of Carolingian bishops and abbots and abbesses who went to war behind their banners and kept their mail-shirts in holy places, as on the other, the *militia sancti Petri* and the soldiers of Christ?[87]

It is to the line of development that led to this neo-prehistory phase of missionary war, and the *militia sancti Petri* it produced, that we must now turn.

The existence of military retinues associated with the church, whether monastic armies or *casati*, and used by the government to accomplish defensive and protective purposes, still allows for some daylight between church and state. What would finish the structure of the prehistory of missionary war would be the use of such forces to accomplish the church's purposes whether expansionist or punitive. It is one thing to contribute to the general defense of the faith in conjunction with the governing secular authorities, quite another to establish a body designed to make war for the faith. Ironically, one gateway to this was via the pursuit of peace.

The rampant violence of the late tenth and early eleventh century provoked a justifiable reaction from the Christian authorities: How might the destruction be mitigated? Springing up in France, but not confined there, reform movements dedicated to limiting violence sought compliance with their developing strictures. Commonly called "the Peace of God" and "the Truce of God," these concepts placed certain classes of people off limits for war as well as attempted to establish times that warfare was prohibited, whether holy days or a long weekend.[88] Potentially violent feudal lords were brought together to swear on holy relics that they would obey these restrictions on their behavior. But pledges were seen to be insufficient in dealing with recalcitrant offenders. To enforce the commitments that wayward lords had sworn to honor, the church turned to the use of force to battle force. Unacceptable war, such as attacks on churchmen or unarmed peasants, was bolstered by the creation of a category of an acceptable, church-originated militia. At one of the foundational meetings that brought about this development, the presiding cleric, Archbishop Aimon of Bourges, put forth the entry oath for this peace movement. It included a vow that they "would go after those who repudiated the oath with arms."[89] The church has moved from supplying troops to creating an early version of a church army, to be used to enforce compliance with ecclesiastical rulings. Christopher Tyerman has called it a turning point in the prehistory of crusading in general, saying it provided "a pattern for the clergy that directly influenced the inception of the First Crusade," noting that "the role of the knight was couched in positive language, as protector of Christian peace, specifically of the Church and its interests."[90]

By the 1070s, this idea was taken over by Pope Gregory VII (r. 1073–85), as part of his reform papacy. Since reform placed the church in opposition to kings and emperors who had large military assets, it might need more than the unreliable sword arms of secular allies. Gregory envisioned, and then brought to life, a *militia sancti Petri* or "army of St. Peter." Earlier the *militia Christi* had been understood as those clergy who fought for Christ with the weapons of prayerful peace; now it was reified in war. This *ordo pugnatorum*, or "order of warriors," was publicized by key thinkers in the church, notably Anselm II of Lucca and Bonizio of Sutri. Bonizio, writing in the early 1090s, created a catalog of duties of the Christian knight, giving them their own professional and religious standing.[91] This new class was based on the notion of *fidelitas*, faithful service like feudal vassals. Thomas Asbridge believes this choice of words was pivotal in that it emphasized the "implication of service and vassalage to suggest that all Latin Christians were, in fact 'vassals of St. Peter' and so by implication vassals of the pope."[92] A ready-made mechanism for attaining protection, correction, and even conversion for the church is available. Hans Eberhard Mayer believes that "a crusade was possible only after the church had prepared the ground for it by working out a theory of holy war and by creating a class of Christian knights. This was what Bernard of Clairvaux did at the Council of Troyes in 1129, with his work *De laude novae militiae*, 'In Praise of the New Knighthood,' authorizing the emergent Knights Templar order."[93] This "new knighthood" was provoked into being by the need to protect Christians from predatory nonbelievers, as Bernard made clear: "I do not mean to say that the pagans are to be slaughtered when there is any other way to prevent them from harassing and persecuting the faithful."[94] By this juncture the prehistory of missionary war had reached the point where it could become the actual history of missionary war in the Baltic. All that would be needed would be a triggering event, such as that which transpired at Frankfurt in March 1147.

Once missionary war was realized in the Baltic Crusades, it opened up a "Pandora's Box" of associated questions and practices: how to solidify the Christian status of conquered pagans; how to fit this form of military campaigning into the rubric of crusading, especially as it concerned pilgrimage; what, if any, battlefield behaviors may be permissible; and perhaps the most vexing question of all, who among the various Christian entities participating in these conflicts will have political and ecclesiastical control over the newly expanded frontier of Christendom? Missionary war thus became a type of enabling legislation that opened up unintended consequences, many of which comprise the most distasteful aspects of the Baltic Crusades for modern scholars. We shall look at some of these in turn.

Questions for discussion

How can Christianity and war be reconciled? What triggered the first efforts to do this?

Were early Christians pacifistic? Was there a presumption against violence, or injustice?

What is "missionary war"? Is the name an accurate one?

How does missionary war intersect with the just war theory?

How can missionary war be linked to crusade?

Why is it easy to slide from defense of the faith to the use of offensive war to spread the faith?

How might missionaries and their newly converted flock be protected from attack if not by war? Should they be protected from attack?

How are the Baltic Crusades and missionary war different from the Muslim concept of *fath*?

6

Baptism by treaty

Once the concept of missionary war, whether it meant the use of armed force as a defensive measure to protect Christian enclaves or meant the use of armed force as a means of conversion, had been adopted, the question arose as to how exactly conversion might be accomplished. Would it be enough to conquer a pagan kingdom to allow Christianity to percolate slowly through the nation, or would the immediate enforcement of the Christian faith be required? The first option allows for individual choice—a person could convert via the long process of instruction in the faith or through the slow realization that "going along to get along" might be the best path for those living under the new rule of the conquerors. But this approach would likely be glacially slow and given the ebb and flow of military power and the possible reversal of conquests, the process might never produce full results. The second option promised a rather full compliance with the faith, even if the depth of that new faith was, owing to little or no instruction, quite shallow. In this case, the target population would be forced to accept the new religion, whether understood or not.

The answer to this question of how to produce instant Christians appeared to be the rite of baptism. But to baptize without full instruction via the process of the catechumenate was opposite to church tradition. By the sixth century the status of the catechumen had been subdivided into three stages: the *audiente*, or "hearer," who was taught the basics of the faith, the *competente*, or "prepared, competent one," who was now ready for baptism, and the *candidatus*, or "candidate," so called because he or she was to be baptized and receive the white robe, or *candida*, of the new Christian. This multilayered progress would often take a year with baptism done at Easter.[1] To circumvent this slow growth in understanding would violate the whole nature of the faith. Even the scriptural instance of a quick baptism, that of the "Ethiopian" eunuch in Acts 8:26-40, was not nearly as quick as it seemed. This educated man, the chief advisor to the royal family in the Kushite kingdom of Nubia, was apparently conversant with the Scriptures, and was instructed, albeit "on the fly," by the Apostle Philip.[2] The pagan peoples targeted by missionary war would not likely rise to the same level of understanding as this Ethiopian. Further, most of the instruction for the catechumen was based on dealing with late Roman converts, who could be expected to be aware of at least some of the contours of Christianity and shared in a common culture with their religious mentors.[3] In spite of its apparent dangers and objections from many quarters, the use of baptism en masse to finalize victory in a missionary war appeared to be a choice too promising to resist.

This choice to use the second option and its reliance on mass baptism produced some of the most peculiar scenes in the Baltic Crusades, an enterprise that had no shortage of peculiar vignettes. Thus it was that sometime in 1187, the newly conquered, converted, and baptized Livonians living in Holm reneged on their agreement to be Christian if provided with stone forts by the freshly minted Bishop Meinhard of Uexküll. To show their rejection of the agreement, they plunged as a group into the Daugava River. "They thought," in the judgment of Henry's *Livonian Chronicle*, "that since they had been baptized with water, they could remove their baptism by washing themselves in the Daugava and thus send it back to Germany."[4] This was the beginning of a pattern of behavior. Eleven years later the second bishop to the Livonians, Berthold, encountered a similar reaction. After his forces had won a battle near Riga, baptized the defeated survivors, and sailed away fully confident that the faith had been planted anew, the Livonians "poured water from the Daugava River over themselves saying, 'We now remove the water of baptism and Christianity itself with the water of the river. Scrubbing off the faith we have received, we send it back after the withdrawing Saxons.'"[5]

So common was this practice of washing away a baptism that it became almost a literary *topos* in Henry's *Livonian Chronicle* and apparently became a part of the received wisdom of the Livonians, as "they often said they had removed it (baptism) by bathing in the Daugava."[6] The belief that baptismal water was magically essential was even a part of the great pagan resurgence in Esthonia in 1223: "They washed themselves, their houses, and their forts with brooms and water, trying thus to erase the sacrament of baptism in their territory."[7] Recent scholarship has determined that this washing off of baptism was, in fact, an acknowledgment of its power—only the power was seen as evil. It was not "a symbolic act freeing oneself from something in which one does not believe."[8] The Livs validated the rite as they rejected it.

Apart from the obvious ignorance on the part of the Livonians, Esthonians, and other Baltic region tribes that baptism is a spiritual condition and cannot be simply washed away, what are we to make of this strange practice? In defense of the pagans, it must be said that they were coming from a position of sympathetic magic. The belief that "like begats like" was deeply engrained in their culture as evidenced by the brutal treatment of a Christian magistrate named Hebbus at the hands of the rampaging Saccalians. Having "plucked out Hebbus' heart from his bosom while he was still alive," the pagans cooked and ate it. Their motivation for this barbaric act was "that they would be made strong against the Christians."[9] This type of ritual cannibalism was based on the notion that consuming the enemy would grant the eater the strength of the victim. Thus if water applied can make one a Christian, then washing that application off with the waters of your home river should nullify the condition. They had no way, absent teaching in the faith, to know that the water of baptism was an external sign of an inward condition.

If the pagan tribes did not understand the theological nuances involved in baptism, they seemed all too aware of the political and military significances of this particular version of the rite. These riverine reversals of baptism seem to be tied tightly to victory or defeat in battle. In our context, this places it firmly in the realm of missionary war. One does not have to look far for evidence of this union of victory in war and baptism of the defeated. Early in 1208, the Swordbrothers advised their Selone opponents at Selburg thus:

> If you wish true peace, renounce idolatry and receive the true Peacemaker, Who is Christ, into your camp, be baptized and, moreover, remove the enemies of Christ's name, the Lithuanians, from your fort.[10]

Much like the terms of a treaty, it was not enough for the Selones to be baptized, they had also to renounce any alliance with the Lithuanians as well. This type of treaty-based baptism was not just something that happened after a military loss but was understood in advance of hostilities. After a brutal war in which a coalition of Letts, Germans, and converted Livonians defeated the Ungannian Esthonians in 1215, the vanquished "asked to be baptized, so that they could get a true peace and perpetual brotherly friendship with the Germans and Letts."[11] Hearing of the outcome, a nearby people, the Saccalians, then sent emissaries to the winning Christian side requesting baptism as a type of protective treaty so that "they might become friends of the Christians."[12] That baptism had become an essential part of treaty making it attested by the ultimatum that the newly converted Letts gave their Esthonian opponents: "Neither can there be one heart and soul nor a firm treaty of peace between Christians and pagans unless you accept with us the same yoke of Christianity and . . . serve the one God."[13] The Letts were simply passing on what had been done to them in the preceding decade of crusading. In this, they were also echoing a centuries-old belief. As Widukind of Corvey wrote of the Saxons some 250 years earlier, Charlemagne's brutal conquest cum Christianity had produced a full blending of the formerly bitter enemies: "As we see today, it was as if they had been transformed into one people through their Christian faith."[14] No *pacis firma*, or lasting peace, much less a union of heart and soul, could exist until the religious nature of the treaty via baptism had been satisfied.

Baptism had thus become a by-product of military and diplomatic relations. It seemed a surer way to finalize a conquest and conversion. Charlemagne had negotiated some fifteen treaties in only thirteen years with the Saxons, all were broken prompting him to his ultimate military victory.[15] Of course, reducing the sacrament of baptism to a treaty provision carries with it the risk that, like a treaty, baptism can be renounced, or negotiated. Rasa Mazeika has shown that Lithuanian kings in the thirteenth and fourteenth centuries used baptism as a bargaining chip in treaty deliberations, indicating that a timeless spiritual condition had been transferred to the kaleidoscopic reconfigurations of the political landscape.[16] Much later in the Baltic Crusades there would be a retreat from the practice, particularly among the Teutonic Knights, who were upset that their Lithuanian opponents had joined in the faith with Poland

and thus could no longer be classified as pagans worthy of attack. But the precedent, as well as much of the damage, had been done. It is as if baptism had become, like Clausewitz's famous dictum on war, "a mere continuation of policy by another means."[17]

This phenomenon has been called "baptism by treaty"[18] and it creates many appealing lines of investigation. The objective of baptism by treaty appears not to be the actual Christianization of the pagan tribe, but the pacification of an enemy polity. The assumption was that should the Livonians, Ungannians, Saccalians, or any of the sequential roster of predators on the infant Christian community, be baptized, they would, as coreligionists, be in peaceful relations with their Christian neighbors. Baptism by treaty seemed a cure for the constant attacks on the church and a recipe for peace.

For our purposes of prehistory, the chief question is where this linkage between victory in war and baptism originated and how it made its way to the bloody battlefields of the Baltic Crusades. Generally, exploration of this question takes one of two tracks: a theological one that concentrates on the relative efficacy of the administration of the sacrament to those ignorant of Christian doctrine, and an ethno-political one that examines the interplay between Christianization, conquest, and tribal identity. Both these approaches have a long and productive history. Often, however, the theological track does not move forward chronologically from the catechumenal instructions of Augustine and the implementation of these ordinances for barbarians as detailed by Martin of Braga, and later Alcuin. The need for Christian instruction is critical and obvious, but not particularly relevant to the actual practices in the Baltic that featured baptism first, then instruction later. As Henry's *Livonian Chronicle* bluntly admitted, theological teachings were to follow, not precede, conquest.[19]

Conversely, the ethno-political track stops short of reaching back to the true point of origin for the practice—its prehistory. Generally, it begins with the Carolingian policies made infamous by Charlemagne. But baptism by treaty did not suddenly appear *ex nihilo* among the Baltic lands, nor even in Charlemagne's epic struggles with the Saxons some four centuries earlier. The prehistory of the baptism by treaty model may extend back to the earliest stages of the expansion of late Roman Christianity. It is quite literally a journey of a millennium.

Before tracing this journey, it may be productive to deal with the issue of forced baptism. Typically when baptism by treaty is mentioned, it is conflated with the idea of forcing an unwilling pagan, heretic, or Jew to the baptismal font.[20] While baptism by treaty is indeed the by-product of force—waging a war and conquering territory is a bloody and violent use of force indeed—it is categorically different than the individual compulsion involved in dunking an unwilling soul in the baptismal waters. It may better be described as "consequential baptism." In both forced baptism and consequential baptism, no true assent is given, yet in consequential baptism a situational assent, after a loss in battle, is granted. Force is indeed a part of the equation that brings pagans to the font en masse, but it is force applied in advance and not in the actual performance of the rite. As such, it is a type of judgment, akin to trial by combat. This baptism is the end result of the victory of one god over another, making baptism an epiphenomenon of battlefield triumph. This was made plain in the account of the siege of Fellin in March 1211. After six days of intense fighting, the Christian coalition of Germans converted Letts and Livonians and gave the Esthonians an ultimatum: "Do you still resist and refuse to acknowledge our Creator?" Recognizing their impending defeat, the pagan Esthonians replied:

> We acknowledge your God to be greater than our gods. By overcoming us, He has inclined our hearts to worship Him. We beg, therefore, that you spare us and mercifully impose the yoke of Christianity upon us as you have upon the Livonians and Letts.[21]

The promise of baptism was not fulfilled as the Christian forces left before completing the rites. The Esthonians, seeing their enemies depart, promptly renewed hostilities.[22] This episode points up a major flaw in the concept: since baptism is situational, it is revocable, subject to repudiation as the situation changes. This is more than a distinction without a difference in that mass, treaty-based baptism can and did produce mass apostasy; a transgression that was used by crusaders as justification in further punitive campaigns.

As it is tempting to see baptism by treaty as merely another example of forced baptism, it is equally tempting to see it as a copy of Muslim *fath*. Meaning "opening," *fath* was the conquest of a territory in order to make it available to Islam. During the period from the prophet Muhammad's death in 632 to the mid-eighth century, Muslim forces swept across the Near East, North Africa, most of Spain and into southern France. This great age of *futuh*, the plural of *fath*, is celebrated in many sources as the point at which the Muslim world of *Dar-al-Islam* established its greatest gains.[23] On the surface it sounds like missionary war, but there was a critical difference. While it has been said that the most certain way to incorporate alien, conquered peoples into the conquering society is to make entry into that society religious rather than ethnic,[24] Muslim conquerors did not demand that the conquered become Muslim. In fact, they were among the most religiously tolerant societies in the seventh century as witnessed by the famous *Pact of Omar*, creating a status, *dhimmi*, for those not Muslim. While the *dhimmi* had serious limitations on his or her freedom to worship and participate in public life, for the seventh century *dhimmitude* was a relatively lenient condition. It appears that the Muslim forces did not expect immediate conversion to Islam, feeling instead that Allah had given them the territories and peoples as booty, not as coreligionists. Robert Hoyland has likened it to "an immigrant society" with the exception that they were "not migrating from one country to another . . . but from the ranks of the conquered to the society of the conquerors."[25] Migration was necessarily a slow and piecemeal process, not a sudden, imposed transformation. As a result, those who did wish to become Muslim were required to have a sponsor, or *mawla*, an already practicing Muslim, in order to enter the faith.[26] The use of this client sponsor was not, incidentally, confined to individuals but could be applied to "entire tribal groups," much like the baptism by treaty model.[27]

Despite the superficial similarities, Christian missionary war had no such institution for newly baptized defeated foes. Without a client instructor to shepherd them through the intricacies of Christianity, the battlefield converts were expected to adhere to a rather full set of Christian behaviors that seemed mysterious given that they were not taught. The lack of a catechumen status meant that the situation was ripe for the renunciation of baptism. It is true that like Muslim *fath*, missionary war had the same aim: to expand the territory under the faith, but the means of accomplishing this were significantly different. Baptism represented full, and immediate, membership in the Christian religion, even if the new member had no real idea as to what that meant.

As an agent of so much generational change and strife it is necessary to seek the origins of this practice. The church has always opposed forced baptism, even our nuanced, "consequential" version, but the paleo-prehistory stage of the development of baptism by treaty begins with a controversy that played out on the far away shores of the North African coast some seven centuries before our Baltic application. Here the question was not forced baptism but whether or not the rite, once applied, was valid. If a baptism is effective, no matter how applied, then the use of baptism by treaty seen in many circles as wholly inappropriate use of the rite, can exist.

In the last years of the Roman Empire the great persecution of Christians under the Emperor Diocletian (r. 284–305 AD) created a dilemma. Some of the Christian priests—the number is forever beyond our reach—renounced their religion in order to preserve their lives. When the persecutions ended, with the miraculous victory of the self-identified Christian emperor Constantine, many of these churchmen rejoined the ranks of the faithful. Called *traditors* after the provision in the Persecution Edict that demanded the surrender of all Christian writings, a type of *traditio*, or handing over, the sacramental applications of these formerly traitorous churchmen were viewed with suspicion, if not outright hostility by those who had maintained their theological purity. This brought the question of the validity of baptisms performed by these onetime apostates to the fore. A section of the Christian church in North Africa, nicknamed the Donatists after their leader, held that any baptisms done by such priests were of no effect.[28] The Donatists believed that those churchmen who had renounced their allegiance to Christianity during the great persecution of the early fourth century were unfit. Any baptisms they administered were therefore invalid. The division between those who believed that these baptisms were legitimate and those who did not was splitting the church in North Africa.

Eventually the ecclesiastical authorities established, at the behest of Augustine (354–430 AD), the influential bishop of Hippo Regius in modern-day Tunisia, that baptism, even if applied by an improper agent, was still valid. This has been seen as a reaction to Augustine's Donatist opponents, who believed the inner, spiritual purity of the administering cleric determined the efficacy of the sacrament for the baptized. But it is more than the question of baptisms done by worthy churchmen. Augustine's stance tended to advocate for the interpretation that baptism was not the completion of entrance into Christian life but the beginning of a process. Garry Wills believes Augustine's view was "legalistic, almost mechanical, with further steps often needed to reach the full Christian life." He has noted that the Donatists had, therefore, a "maximalist" view of baptism while Augustine's emphasis on the rite itself over the purity of the officiant was a "minimalist" position.[29] The focus was redirected from the inner spiritual condition of the participants, both churchman and baptismal candidate, to the external application of the rite. The mechanics and the intent of the recipient, rather than the worth of the applicant, were what mattered. Baptism had become a starting point rather than a destination. It is important to note that the baptisms in question were not forced, however, but administered by schismatic Donatists to willing catechumens. Since Augustine's position that a baptism once given remains valid became normative, these Donatist baptisms need not be redone in order to be effective.[30] Baptism became once and for all the external application that granted entry into Christianity, a matter that had the side effect of encouraging infant baptism as well.[31] If uninstructed babies could be entered into the church, then so too could entire tribes, equally uninstructed. The sacrament is efficacious regardless of the level of awareness of the recipient. The Augustinian emphasis on the rite of baptism being of paramount importance opens the door for baptism by treaty; the baptism does the trick, not the internal understanding and surrender. This "imputation of righteousness and infusion of grace," in Bryan Spinks' terms, acted "as an insurance policy or protection against eternal punishment" and tended to dominate popular understanding of the sacrament.[32]

Much of the attention to this dispute has focused on the question of the worthiness of the baptizing minister, but a coequal issue was that of rebaptism. Should the Donatist believers, already baptized under their rite, be rebaptized when entering the Catholic fold? And what was to be done with Donatist converts from Catholicism who had been baptized twice, once by an apostate *traditor* and secondly by a "pure" Donatist priest? Should they be baptized again upon re-entry to the Catholic fellowship? Augustine thought not. Once again, a baptism however applied was final.[33] The controversy produced as a side effect the argument that one who had been baptized twice was not in error because, as W. H. C. Frend pointed out, "it was not that individuals were baptized twice but that the sacrament given by a *traditor* or persecutor was not baptism at all."[34] While this is a precursor of the position of the sixteenth-century Anabaptists, who held that traditional Catholic infant baptism was not a true baptism, at this point it played into Augustine's idea that one valid baptism was all that mattered.[35]

What did a sacramental controversy in fourth- and fifth-century North Africa have to do with behavior in the Baltic region more than seven centuries later? It marked the first step toward making baptism by treaty feasible. If baptism represented the culmination of training and the attainment of Christian life, such as the "maximalist" view held, then the baptism by treaty of masses of pagans who know little or nothing about Christianity makes no sense. But if baptism is seen as an initial step in the process of Christianization, then baptism by treaty may be an option. The theology will follow after the baptism in order for the subject to become fully Christianized, as Henry's *Livonian Chronicle* frankly stated. Further, as a paleo-prehistory of baptism by treaty, this stage of development creates the notion that baptism is permanent, even if applied incorrectly. However, this new situation of irreversibility, as León Arsenal has termed it,[36] created a new problem, particularly for areas of the post-Roman West that featured serious religious diversity. Spain was such an area.

The Fourth Council of Toledo, meeting in the Visigothic Spanish capital in December 633, took matters a step further.[37] Under the presidency of the renowned early medieval polymath, Isidore of Seville, the Council was convened to address a number of church matters, including the question of how to incorporate the Arian Christians into the newly unified Catholic Church. The Council inevitably had to rule on the issue of proper baptism. The Arians had required any Catholic who chose to enter their ranks to be rebaptized, and when Arians sought to reconcile with the Catholic communion, they believed that a rebaptism into the Catholic worship was also necessary. But the church had long held that rebaptism was an affront to the faith and subject to punishment. Taking this into account, as the Council considered the issue of rebaptism, as had Augustine earlier with the Donatists, they ruled that the sacrament once done was a final and permanent event.

As there could be no rebaptism, there could be no "unbaptism." Considering the plight of Jews who had been forced to the baptismal font by Christians, they disapproved of the force, agreeing with Isidore's previously stated position that those who should have been persuaded by a rational presentation of the faith should not have been constrained by force.[38] Indeed, Isidore had condemned an earlier Visigothic king, Sisebut (r. 612–21 AD), who had, "acting with zeal, but not according to knowledge," compelled "by force those who should have been called to the faith through reason."[39] But, ominously, the Council affirmed that once applied, even in this way, baptism was still valid. Thus the door was open for a variant of "if the deed accuses, the result excuses" rationale. Baptism forcefully administered is wrong and to be avoided, but once done legitimate and permanent. This was the thin edge of what would become a very large wedge as the occasional Jew made to receive laving in the font could serve as a model for whole tribes and peoples being coerced by military defeat into baptism. The mechanism permitting this was in place by the seventh century, and Isidore's warning in protest that "in those on whom it is forced by violence it is not permanent" would have a long and tragic future even into the Baltic Crusades of the later Middle Ages.[40]

This leads us to the middle, or meso-prehistory, level of development for baptism by treaty: the compulsory baptism of Saxons by the forces of Charlemagne during his long missionary wars against these pagan people. This has been a typical default setting for anyone looking at baptism by treaty. For Charlemagne seems a role model, perhaps even a prototype, of what would become normative on the Baltic frontier. His actions, called "a massive change in policy,"[41] seem so novel as to be a radical departure for the Christian West: the creation of a new paradigm. Marcia L. Colish has called these measures a "substitution of coercion for the prescriptions of canon law" and believes it "placed Christian missionary activity on a new and violent path."[42] But was Charlemagne's approach all that new? Or was it a logical step in a progression already well underway?

The first Holy Roman Emperor and King of the Franks sought unity among the various regional magnates and tribal cultures that he either inherited or conquered. Could it be any different with newly incorporated pagans such as the Saxons? Christian liturgy and sacramental practice was a means to establish uniformity in the *regnum* and thereby ensure governmental control. Baptism, the admission ritual to Christendom, played a pivotal role in the use of Christianity to consolidate Charlemagne's reign.[43] This consolidation was at least as much cultural as political. S. A. Keefe has noted that baptism "put its stamp on every individual not only as part of the church, but as a member of society" and this "was often the only thing that distinguished the peoples of the newly conquered borders of the Carolingian empire from the pagan tribes."[44] As J. M. Wallace-Hadrill wisely observed, "Thus military occupation and forced conversion went hand in hand."[45]

Therefore the great emperor issued an extremely draconian capitulary, or ruling, sometime during his wars against the Saxons, the date varies from 785 to 795 depending on the historian asked, that mandated baptism for all the conquered peoples in Saxony. The question remains, however, as to where Charlemagne got this new idea. A recent effort, Yitzhak Hen's provocative article titled, also provocatively, "Charlemagne's Jihad,"[46] locates the great emperor's inspiration in the thinking of a refugee to his court at Aachen, Theodulf of Orléans. Despite his name, Theodulf came from newly conquered Saragossa in now-Muslim Spain and Hen believes he brought the Islamic idea of religious war north with him. The type of treaty by baptism as enforced by Charlemagne against the Saxons is thus a direct derivative from Muslim practice. Hen says, "I would like to suggest that it was indeed the notion of *jihad* ... that stood behind the formation of the *Capitulatio*'s forced conversion policy."[47]

Yitzhak Hen is one of the finest scholars working today on the issue of the intersection of crusading and conversion,[48] and no doubt is right to speculate on the origins of missionary war as practiced by Charlemagne, whether finding its impulse in Theodulf or not. But it is one thing to note the similarities between Charlemagne's policy of missionary war and Muslim *fath,* and quite another to miss the differences. Conquest purpose-built to allow the faith to work its way through society, as in the Muslim model, should not be conflated with conquest designed to immediately incorporate the target peoples into the faith. Aside from making Charlemagne's approach a mere copy, a mimesis, of Muslim practice,[49] this view misses the provisions of the *Capitulatio de partibus Saxoniae* that not only require baptism for the Saxons to become full members of the Christian community but also mandate adherence to a rather complete set of Christian religious behaviors. The capitulary details at length the exact practices required and the precise penalties incurred for violating these stipulations. Apart from the obvious, albeit exceedingly harsh, requirement that failure to be baptized earned the death penalty, a pagan could also be executed for the insufficient practice of Christian life such as failing to observe the Lenten fast.[50]

While Charlemagne often allowed subject peoples who readily accepted his rule to remain pagan, and convert slowly via missionary activity,[51] he apparently did not confine his baptism by treaty efforts to the recalcitrant Saxons, even though their stubborn refusal to adhere to the settlement occupied thirty-three years of the emperor's reign. The Avars, a central Asiatic people who had developed an empire in central Europe, were conquered by Charlemagne in the 790s. After a decisive defeat, the Avar leader, or *tudun*, "wished, with his land and his people, to submit to the king and on his instruction accept the Christian faith."[52] Later in the year the *tudun* made good on his promise when "he and his people were baptized." But the *tudun* predictably "was not willing to keep long the fealty he had pledged"[53] and renounced his Christianity; a foretaste of the repeated pattern that would occupy much of the Baltic Crusades.

By concentrating on the similarities, real or perceived, between Carolingian missionary war and Muslim *fath*, the further investigation of Christian origins of baptism by treaty is foreclosed. The line of prehistory stops with Charlemagne's adoption and slight modification of Islamic practices. But Charlemagne's Saxon Wars seem to only represent the middle stage in the development of baptism by treaty. Even the baptism of the Danish royal pretender, Harald Klak, at the hands of his new godfather and Charlemagne's son Louis the Pious in 826, proved somewhat fruitless in that Harald was unable to take the throne, and therefore require the Danes to be baptized as well. He settled for control of the Frisian county of Rüstringen as a forward base for future futile attempts at kingship.[54] Even with that benefice Harald apostasized upon failing to gain the Danish throne. The Danish historian Saxo Grammaticus records the moral of the story: "As he had been the leading pattern for the new belief he was the first to display its neglect; from being a glorious promoter of this faith he emerged a notorious apostate."[55] That the baptism by treaty procedure permeated the political give-and-take in the century after

Charlemagne is attested by the post-battle treaty between Alfred the Great of Wessex and his Viking opponent, Guthrum. After Alfred's victory at Edington in 878, the *Anglo-Saxon Chronicle* records that the beaten Vikings agreed to leave his kingdom and "promised him in addition that their king (Guthrum) would receive baptism."[56] Three weeks later the rite was solemnized and Guthrum, along with thirty of his best men, was baptized with Alfred standing as "sponsor" to his former enemy.[57] It seems the use of baptism to finalize relations between Christian and pagan forces, regardless of which side initiated hostilities, became a fairly common policy along the fault lines between these dueling religions. When the powerful Saxon king Henry "the Fowler" retaliated against the Danes because they had "launched naval raids against the Frisians" in 934 AD, he forced the Danes to pay tribute and "had their king, named Knuba, receive baptism."[58] The fact that this "king" was apparently only the local lord of the trading center of Hedeby merely means that the baptism by treaty mechanism was applicable in multiple contexts. The prehistory of the practice might reach much farther back into the roots of the Christian West than Charlemagne's push against the recalcitrant Saxons, or the occasional baptism of an ambitious prince, or a predatory Viking.

If these roots are not to be found in Charlemagne's policies, then where and when do they appear? We have already seen that the sacrament of baptism had been analyzed to the point of permitting, even without official sanction, a baptism that was forcibly applied. But how does the forced baptism of the individual, a type of micro issue, balloon into forced, or even "consequential" baptism of the masses, a decidedly macro event? It is tempting to follow the incremental development of Christian approval of warfare, the origins of missionary war, as the true beginnings of baptism by treaty. But a Christian force can practice missionary war without requiring their defeated opponents to straightaway become full members of the church. Where was the origin of the linkage between a Christian army defeating a pagan one and then demanding baptism en masse?

It is true that the political entente that existed between the first Christian emperor, Constantine, and his rival coruler, Licinius, featured the latter accepting the Christian God at Milan in 313, and his subsequent utilization of the prayer to this new God written by Constantine himself, only to later renounce that faith and institute his own persecution of Christians. Although neither he nor Constantine were baptized at that point, Constantine waiting until his deathbed some twenty-four years later, Licinius' dalliance with Christianity represents an early example of the union of faith and politics, setting in motion a developmental trend that would eventually reach fruition in baptism by treaty.[59] An imperial model had been established that automatically included adherence to Christianity as an essential part of membership in the Empire. This would be useful as the empire of the faith that replaced, and in some important ways replicated, the Roman one would expand ever deeper into the pagan lands beyond.

Yet, earlier, pre-Carolingian wars sanctioned by the church were not ones that featured a Christian force invading a pagan land with the express purpose of converting them by the sword to the faith. Constantine's wars as well as those of the Emperor Theodosius I (r. 379–95) were civil wars, albeit of cosmic Christian versus pagan scope. The pagan foes of the first Christian emperors were as Roman as they giving a certain internecine flavor to the conflicts. The battles sanctioned as holy defense during the barbarian invasions of Rome were not missionary wars, but wars of desperate self-defense. That is why Augustine felt compelled to write to Count Boniface, the chief military commander against the Vandal invaders of North Africa, to assure him that fighting for the preservation of the faith and civilization was acceptable.[60] Even later struggles, such as the one involving the newly baptized king of the Franks, Clovis, who was depicted as "holding it hard to go on seeing these Arians occupy a part of Gaul," in Gregory of Tours' florid prose,[61] do not rise to the standard of a Christian polity invading an alien, pagan land and people in a missionary war. The Visigothic Arians that Clovis targeted successfully at the great Battle of Vouillé in the spring of 507, were after all a heretical branch of Christianity. Where, in Carl Erdmann's terms, is "the origin of the idea" of baptism by treaty?

The paleo-prehistory of baptism by treaty may not lie on the military side of things, but rather in the religious and political portions of the concept. Perhaps its beginning is not to be found on the battlefield but in the missionary strategies for expanding the faith that emerged in the late antique church. The path to conversion for a pagan nation had the potential to morph into a violent union of sacrament and slaughter.

It may have all started innocently enough with the church seeking to encounter pagan peoples on their own terms. Scholars have noted a common social and cultural essence to tribal societies, often called "syntality," or a group personality.[62] One feature of this syntality was that the tribes of early medieval Europe generally subscribed to a version of what the Germans called *blot*, a belief that their king stood before the gods for the whole people. The Latins described this as *rex et sacerdos*, "king and priest," indicating that the barbarian leaders had a dual function as military and religious standard bearer for their tribe. J. M. Wallace-Hadrill has summed it up, "kings without being priests could link the gods with those they ruled; they could appease and placate the gods and be deposed in sacrificial propitiation when things went wrong."[63]

There were priests to be sure, one thinks of Bede's account of the pagan priest Coifi and his dramatic approval of King Edwin's move to Christianity in Northumbrian England.[64] Provocatively, Coifi, a priest who had been forbidden to bear arms by pagan custom, requested a sword to use in his profanation of the pagan altars. "Girded with a sword and with a spear in his hand, he mounted the king's stallion" and destroyed the pagan shrines, "full of joy at his knowledge of the worship of the true God."[65] This vignette seems a foretaste of the warlike posture of the Christian priests that would emerge in coming years. But while there were specialist priests, armed or not, the king was the guarantor of the people's weal and his religious standing was critical to the people's religious standing as well. This is a hard concept to verify as the "lack of a more profound knowledge of primitive" Slavic and Baltic civilization in their preliterate state leaves only archaeology and folklore to explain similarities between the early kingship characteristics of northern Europe.[66] Marija Gimbutas even went so far as to assert that the power of Baltic priests was a recent development, spurred by the attacks of the crusaders on native culture, "the emergence of priestly power in the fourteenth century may have resulted from the old religion being endangered at this particular period by the invasion of Christian enemies."[67]

Despite the seeming similarities "a nervous caution nips persistently at the heels of those seeking to address" this issue.[68] Opinions vary from the certainty of Dvornik, "the basis of the social organization of the primitive Slavs *was the same* as that of the other Indo-European peoples,"[69] to the uncertainty of Gimbutas, "The social organization of the primitive Slavs was *probably* very much like that of the Germanic peoples before the migration."[70] While we may never dispel doubt about the parallel views of kingship among the Germanic, Slavic, and Baltic peoples, the possible similarity of structure offers an enticing model for understanding the origins of baptism by treaty.

The church sought to use this concept to its advantage for mass conversion, so much so that it rose to the level of a standard practice. Torben K. Nielsen has expressed this conclusion well:

> The common assumption that, were the mission to succeed, it would be necessary first to convert the pagan leaders. In the history of the Christian mission it is a commonplace that conversion—if successful—should be aimed primarily at the leading strata of pagan society, the assumption being that if the leaders are converted, the people will follow.[71]

German scholars have labeled this approach *adelskirche*, or "church of the nobility," and it encompassed more than kings. Early medieval sources are rather full of accounts of church growth, whether monastic or political—if one can separate the two in this era—resulting from the wooing of nobles and kings into the Christian fold. The celebrated successes of the Irish wandering monastic founder, Columbanus, are dependent upon his gaining of royal patronage and his almost magnetic appeal to the nobility in the lands he affected.[72] It is, however, one thing for a ranking noble to change religion and quite another for a king, who stands before the gods in behalf of his people, to change his beliefs. Should the king be persuaded to forsake paganism in favor of Christianity, one of two things might happen: either the people would rebel and oust the king who had the audacity to endanger their religious status, a very real possibility in a custom-oriented tribal world, or the conversion of the king would lead to the conversion of the whole tribe as the people continued in the same religion as their leader.

Despite its inherent dangers, this "get the king, get the people" strategy was much in vogue in the post-Roman expansion of Christianity during the sixth and seventh centuries. Sometime around 500 AD, Clovis, convinced by St. Remigius to change his religion and become Christian, worried that his willingness to accept the new faith would be rejected by his Frankish followers saying,

"There remains one obstacle. The people under my command will not agree to forsake their gods. I will go and put to them what you have just said to me."[73] Nearly a century later a similar scene unfolded when Aethelbehrt, king of Kent in southeastern England, told the Roman missionaries that while their words were "fair ineed" he could not "accept them and abandon the age-old beliefs that I have held together with the whole English nation."[74] The Visigothic king Reccared (r. 586–601), convinced in the first year of his reign to leave Arianism and adopt the Trinitarian view, timidly built a Catholic church just outside the walls of Toledo dedicated to St. Leocadia, to see if his people would revolt at his changed religion. When they did not, he confirmed the switch at the famous Third Council of Toledo in 589.[75] The Council enthusiastically affirmed his decision, saying of Reccared, "He is the conqueror of new peoples for the Catholic Church!" and labeling him an "apostle."[76]

In these cases, the missionary strategy to convert the king in order to reach the people worked quite well. Clovis

> arranged a meeting with his people, but God in his power had preceded him, and before he could say a word all those present shouted in unison: "We will give up worshipping our mortal gods, pious King, and we are prepared to follow the immortal God about whom Remigius preaches."[77]

Of course we must be a bit suspicious of the rather overly dramatic depiction by Gregory of Tours, written about eighty years later. But we can know that Clovis did change religion and his Frankish followers did not remove him from the throne. Aethelbehrt also was baptized in the little, pre-invasion period Church of St. Martin at Canterbury and his people dutifully followed him into a new religion.[78]

But there were other, less successful, attempts. Gregory of Tours tells us of the failed mission of Bishop Avitus of Vienne to Gundobad, king of the Burgundians (r. 474–516). When the king demurred on changing to Catholicism from Arianism, the fearless bishop lectured him.

> You are afraid of your people. Do you not realize that it is better that the people should accept your belief, rather than that you, a king, should pander to their every whim? You are the leader of your people; your people is not there to lord it over you.[79]

Gundobad was not moved by this chastisement and "persisted in his obstinacy" until his death (*usque ad exitum vitae sude in hac insania perduravit*).[80] This sixth-century scenario is almost perfectly mirrored in the twelfth-century Baltic. When the pagan cult center of Arkona on the island of Rügen was taken by the Danish crusader king Valdemar "the Great," the Rugian princes, Jarimar and Tetislav, were lectured by an accompanying bishop that

> the people were supposed to obey their masters, not the masters their people, and that it was not right that magnates should bend to follow the whims of lesser people. Was it not the greatest victory one could wish for, to force pagan people not only to pay taxes, but also to become subjects of the Christian church?[81]

The Rugian princes were baptized, as were their people.

The targeting of the king to get the whole people was not only occasionally unsuccessful, but could be reversible, as Aethelbehrt's son, Eadbald, led a pagan reaction in Kent upon his father's death in 616. It took one of the missionaries, Laurence, appearing before the king to show him supernaturally inflicted wounds to convince Eadbald that he should follow in his father's Christian footsteps.[82]

Yet the position of the king as the key to reaching the people might be the effective gateway to the shift from peaceful missionary preaching to missionary war and its resultant baptism by treaty. If the church could convert the king to get the people, could not the church conquer a recalcitrant king with the same result? This might be especially appealing when the church came to view the converted king as consecrated, thereby uniting faith with polity. Since the barbarian target populations already saw religion and government as a unity, the stage was set for both the invader and the invaded to subscribe to a similar worldview: religion and *natio* are one. The gentle blandishments of missionary preaching could easily elide into a policy that would earn the chilling sobriquet "preaching with a tongue of iron." Add to this confluence of ideas the conversion stories of kings, from Clovis in Gaul right through to Edwin in Northumbria, that often featured victory in war as the trigger event,[83] and the union of king, people and war could be planted in the consciousness of the church as well as the monarchs of Christendom. With this background the missionary war efforts of Charlemagne lose some of their startling novelty, seeming more like a logical progression than a radical departure. This would also explain, as Friedrich Lotter has done, the seemingly barbaric statement of St. Bernard of Clairvaux, who wrote shortly after the initiation of the opening campaign of what would become the Baltic Crusades, the Wendish Crusade of 1147, that the goal was: *Donec auxiliante Deo aut ritus ipse aut natio deleatur* (with the help of God either the rite/customs or the people should be destroyed).[84]

When viewed through the prism of baptism by treaty this statement loses some of its genocidal quality and becomes an issue of enforcing previously agreed treaty obligations, although the exact way to enforce those obligations remained problematic. The Wends of 1147, as those tribes encountered in the next quarter millennium, should either be made to obey their baptismal vows or punished as apostates. The pagan rites should be extinguished, as Henry noted after two consecutive weeks of marathon baptizing of the inhabitants of Wierland in 1220, "when the baptism was finished, even in these parts they had wiped out the pagan rites."[85] It was to prove a much more complex undertaking than that, and not simply for the difficulties involved in baptizing large numbers in a short time. The priests tasked with this daunting undertaking often were forced to use a simplified version of the rite called *aspersio*, rather than the full, time-consuming ritual called *immersio*.[86]

The examples of baptism by treaty that immediately preceded the Baltic Crusades, the neo-prehistory phase, followed the pattern established by the union of "get the king, get the people" backed by the threat of military or political force. The generations before the onset of the crusades in the Baltic saw the advancing line of Christian conversion move north to Scandinavia and eastward into what would become Russia.

The legendary trappings around the conversion of Harald Bluetooth in the late tenth century, as recorded 300 years later by the Icelandic writer Snorri Sturluson, hold that Harald was forced into baptism after losing a battle with the Emperor Otto. However, we do not know if it is Otto I or Otto II who won the day, making the approximate date for the event either the 960s or 980s. The mythical imprecision should not obscure the fact that in Snorri's day, contemporaneous with the Baltic Crusades, the received wisdom was that a loss in battle created a treaty that included baptism as the seal. Further, the legend relates that Harald "let himself be baptized, together with the whole Danish army" and then forced one of his principal, and often recalcitrant, nobles, Earl Hakon, to be baptized with "all the men who had accompanied him."[87] As a preview of affairs on the Baltic, Earl Hakon promptly sacrificed to Odin in his next campaign, confirming the shape-shifting nature of his baptism.

The Norwegians followed suit in 994, when Olaf Tryggvason received 16,000 pounds of tribute from King Aethelred of England, his baptizing godfather, and used that to finance his takeover of Norway.[88] The new king vowed that "he would succeed in christening all of Norway or else die."[89] That he meant business is confirmed by Snorri's terse evaluation: "In the end the king offered them two alternatives: either to accept Christianity and be baptized, or else to fight it out with him."[90] So threatening was Olaf's baptismal campaign that the inhabitants of Iceland voted in 999 as to accept or reject the baptism offered by Olaf's missionary Thangbrand. The pagan "lawspeaker" considered it better to change religion than to battle Olaf, saying, "all men should have one law and one faith" and that "if we break the law in pieces then we break the peace in pieces too."[91] All the people were promptly baptized. After Olaf Tryggvason died in battle in 1000 AD, the torch was carried by Olaf Haraldson, who was baptized at the Norman capital of Rouen in the winter of 1013/14, once again as an ally of Aethelred of England. This Olaf, later to be memorialized as St. Olaf, gained the Norwegian throne in 1015 and promptly campaigned throughout the land enforcing baptism as a mechanism of royal unification. The king

> laid such stress on (the right faith) that if he found anyone who did not want to abandon heathendom, he drove him out of the land. Some he had maimed, having their hands and feet lopped off or their eyes gouged out, others he had hanged or beheaded, but left no one unchastised who refused to serve God.[92]

Noting that Christianity had the cachet of Imperial Rome attached to it, Anders Winroth believes that these monarchs brought the faith to Scandinavia "to gain a share in that prestige for themselves—in other words, for the same reason that they brought trade goods."[93] He sees it as a commodity that could buy allegiance, and thus political power, much like the early Germanic *goldwine*, or "gold friend" war leader. It was not an outside force conquering Scandinavia for Christianity, but major actors in their own political play who used Christianity as a weapon to gain power: "Silver, swords, baptism: they all served as gifts in the gift exchange system of early medieval Scandinavia, and that exchange of gifts greased the wheels of Scandinavian politics."[94] Whether used as a pretext for conquest via missionary war, or as a wedge to drive home a quest for royal power, the political and the religious were laminated in a baptism by treaty construct.

A similar scenario played out far to the east in the riverine strongholds that would coalesce into Russia. The Russians had been Christianized by a treaty negotiation when Vladimir of Kiev supported the winning side in a Byzantine civil war and was rewarded with an imperial bride in the year 988. The clincher for the deal was that Vladimir would be baptized. The Russian prince complied and forced his people to be baptized in the Dnieper River as well, compelling them with the threat that their noncompliance would make them "enemies of the king."[95] He then used his Christian status and baptism to consolidate his hold over the emerging Russian state. This emergence would play a major role in the Baltic Crusades. Therefore, when the Danish crusader king Valdemar "the Great" conquered the Rugians and burned their pagan idol in 1168, it was almost given that the prince of Rügen "was eager to be baptized and commanded all his people to convert."[96]

The use of baptism by treaty, whether spurred by a desire to secure protection for fledgling Christian communities, or to convert forcibly the adjacent tribes, can be shown to be a practice that did not suddenly arise out of a renaissance of Carolingian policies but rather grew organically out of the missionary strategy of the early Middle Ages. It reached fruition in Charlemagne's Saxon Wars, and then continued as an effective tool for both the church and the Christianized state in successive bursts of expansion throughout the still pagan north of Europe. It also persisted throughout the Baltic Crusades. The anonymous author of the *Livonian Rhymed Chronicle*, writing sometime after 1290, summed up the intended scope of his work in this way:

> (to describe) . . . how God's grace sent Christianity into many lands where no apostle had gone. Even after God had taken them into heaven, many rulers who lived in later times, were converted by their teachings, received baptism and led others to do likewise.[97]

The remaining issues relating to the success of this enduring practice involve the question of how all this fits into the mechanism of crusade. Can a crusading army engage in native war practices and still remain signed with the cross? Further, a critical point to the participants was the status of the Christian warriors as "pilgrims." Without clear decisions on these issues, the Baltic Crusades would slide out of the category of crusade and become, as some critics still maintain, merely shabby border land grabs dressed up in the cosmetic finery of theology. Our next two chapters will address these questions.

Questions for discussion

How did "baptism by treaty" work? What are its benefits and what are its drawbacks?

What role did Christian instruction play in baptism?

What did Augustine have to do with creating the possibility of baptism by treaty?

Where did baptism by treaty originate and why?

How did sympathetic magic figure into the pagan view on baptism by treaty?

Was baptism by treaty a "normal" procedure in the spread of Christianity in Europe? Or was it merely a Baltic phenomenon?

7

The ministry of shields and swords

After the notion of missionary war had been accepted and baptism by treaty made a part of the package, the further question was: How does one actually do this combination of military and religious war? That the crusaders saw their martial efforts as religious is starkly revealed by an offhanded comment by Henry in his *Livonian Chronicle*. He was both a priest and a crusader, often betraying that fact by using the pronouns "we" and "us" when describing the flow of action. In 1219, the pagan Ungannians devastated a neighboring province called Pudiviru. The suffering people appealed to the Swordbrothers to intervene on their behalf and were given the typical terms that their conversion and baptism must precede any military help. As they complied, and the baptisms were underway, the process was stopped suddenly when, in Henry's words, "a great clamor arose (with) a rushing of our army through all the streets and everyone ran to arms, crying that a great host of pagans was coming against us. We immediately put down the holy chrism and the other holy articles, therefore, and hurried to the ministry of shields and swords."[1]

The alarm of an approaching pagan force proved to be false, but the sentiment expressed was not. While it is certainly possible to read too much into Henry's catchy phrase, one wonders if the word order has significance. He mentioned a primarily defensive instrument, the shield, first over the offensive weapon of the sword. Since the Baltic Crusades were predicated on the notion that the warfare was conducted as a defensive measure to protect vulnerable Christian communities, the word order might be a self-conscious attempt to make that point yet again.

Whatever the case with the term, it remains true that the Baltic Crusades were seen as a "ministry of shields and swords." But that raised far more questions than it answered. For how was this "ministry" to be done? And, what might be the justification for it? The latter question was, by virtue of the mechanism of mass baptism and the association of that rite with military treaty obligations, easier to answer: the targets of the ministry of shields and swords were apostates and thus fully deserving of the correction of military punishment.

The terms apostate and apostasy are sprinkled throughout the chronicles of the Baltic Crusades. The crusaders are to seek *victoriam de gentibus apostatantibus*, or "victory over apostate peoples" while the most often used justification of invasion and/or battle is that it is *contra apostatas*, "against apostates."[2] This was apparent early in the efforts to conquer and convert the Livonians in the last years of the twelfth century. The new bishop, Berthold brought an army to punish the Livonians. When they inquired as to why he had brought forces against them, he quoted the line from Proverbs 26:11, and II Peter 2:22, that "as dogs return to their vomit, so they had returned too often from the faith to paganism."[3] Even though the Livonians earnestly promised to "do away with this reason" for bringing an army against them, negotiations fell apart and war ensued.

The concept of apostasy is an old one, based on the Greek words for "stepping away,"[4] and it offers the threat of reversing any gains made in the conversion of the populace of a given region. The dynamic is one that was described by the great Dutch historian, Johan Huizinga, who noted that the outlaw was often regarded as less of a threat than the apostate in that the former validated the very rules he broke, while the latter dismissed the whole structure of the rules.[5] The outlaw could be corrected and brought back to the fold, but the apostate, mocking the faith and the system it represented, deserved extinction. Further, the apostate cannot be allowed simple coexistence with the faithful as their oppositional message, and indeed their very existence within the communion, undermines the work of the church. Phillip W. Gray sums it up this way: "By allowing schismatics to coexist peaceably ... with the true representatives of God, there is no peace conducive to the Heavenly City, and the church is stymied."[6] Whether an individual or a group apostasy, the abandoning of the Christian faith challenged the whole system. The church responded to a contrite apostate with a graded system of penance, designed to reintegrate the offender into the Christian communion.[7] But for a recalcitrant apostate, unwilling to admit wrong, the punishment was exclusion from the Christian community. In a situation where the offenders were entire tribes, who had been brought to the faith by "the ministry of shields and swords," the punishment, or even the remedy, was not exclusion but attack.

The earliest manifestation of this approach might be found in the months just after Constantine's "conversion" and victory in the civil war of the Western Roman Empire in 313. Moving to Milan, the then Western capital, he allied with Licinius, the leading contender for Eastern hegemony, by marrying his half-sister, Constantia, to him and requiring Licinius to convert. Licinius dutifully used the "prayer prescribed by Constantine" for his troops in their victorious campaign against his Eastern rival, Maximin, only to later apostasize and begin a persecution of Christians. This provoked Constantine to attack, "led by the *Labarum*, the imperial banner with the (Christian) *chi-rho* monogram on its stave," and conquer the rest of the previously divided empire.[8] By the era of the Baltic Crusades, punitive military intervention was a customary punishment for apostate peoples.

Most modern studies, however, emphasize the individual rejection of the faith, while the Baltic context appears to be much more group or tribally situated. Recent studies do stress that the formulation of the concept of apostasy derives from the existing social structure of both the apostate and the church,[9] and the social context seems to be paramount in the Baltic Crusades. In most modern studies, however, the assumption that both the apostate and the church share in the same social structure is paramount. While this may work well for the early Christian, late Roman world, with at least the pretense of a commonly held culture, it is ill suited for the Baltic and its hallmark clash of cultures.

Further, as apostates must by definition be Christian, it becomes difficult to differentiate between heresy, the belief and teaching of incorrect doctrine, and the act of apostasy. There are gradations of distance between the two that often make it hard to pinpoint the exact change in degree that becomes a change in kind. Could one "step away" from a particular theological point without stepping away from Christianity as a whole? The matter is further complicated by the canon law tendency to classify the punishments for heretics and apostates as similar, if not identical. But for our purposes, the Baltic context does not prove as slippery. The apostate tribes in conflict with the crusaders were involved in a rather full-throated rejection of Christianity, not simply a different interpretation of a theological doctrine. The sure proof of their "stepping away" was the wholesale return to pagan practices. While scholars agree that the use of lethal force against heretics has long been acceptable, it has never been approved for the conversion of pagans.[10] Yet, should the pagans be classified as apostates, the prohibition against violence and thus crusading would no longer be in force.

Henry's *Livonian Chronicle* gives us a good picture of how this transgression of apostasy played out in the Baltic context. When the once-baptized Livonians washed off, yet again, their baptism in 1212, and revolted against the Christian forces of Bishop Albert and the Swordbrothers with the battle cry, "Take heart and fight, Livonians, lest you be slaves to the Germans,"[11] their stronghold at Dobrel was eventually reduced to surrender. Appealing to the bishop, they were lectured on their sin of apostasy by the venerable prelate who predictably cited their rejection of the faith and their warmaking. In a peculiarly Baltic twist, Albert chided them for throwing "goats and other animals which you had immolated to the pagan gods in our face and in the face of the whole army." The remedy was simple: "We therefore demand a moderate sum of silver from your entire province."[12] Far from the textbook theological definition of apostasy is one that accounts for sacrificial meat serving as an insult and the payment of silver as a means of reconciliation. Yet this was the practical, everyday reality in the Baltic of the crusading era.

The practice of baptism by treaty therefore became a self-reinforcing agent for the Baltic Crusade. Those washing off their baptism because of the perceived change in military hegemony were by definition apostates deserving of further military attack. The notion that creating coreligionists would promote peace, perhaps the driving force behind mass baptisms in the first place, was an obviously dubious proposition given the dismal historical record of wars among adherents of the same faith. The belief that there could be "one heart and soul" and a firm treaty of peace between Christians and pagans was shown to be mere wishful thinking. Baptism by treaty often was productive of more, not less, warfare as newly laved apostates required the discipline of reconquest, yet another use of the ministry of shields and swords.

When imagining this warfare, one should not envisage a scene where well-armored Christian knights battle against poorly equipped pagan forces who trust only in leather, fur, and fire-hardened wooden spears. The sources are peppered with descriptions of the pagan armies glittering in polished armor and brandishing state of the art swords and spears. They may have been lacking in fortification and siege skills and equipment, as the story of Bishop Meinhard's promise of stone forts indicates, but they learned, adopted, and adapted to new weapons systems and strategy with speed and effectiveness. The cover illustration for this book, showing armored crusaders battling equally armed opponents, while depicting the fighting between Teutonic Knights and Polish-Lithuanian forces in 1410, is nevertheless eerily accurate as a mention in the *Livonian Rhymed Chronicle* from 1288 shows: "The Brother (a Teutonic Knight warrior) who carried the banner in his one hand used the other to strike down and kill whomever was in his way."[13]

But the prosecution of this kind of missionary war, regardless of arms and armament, almost inevitably brought a sense of anomie, or the breakdown of customary social norms, to the pagans as their very worldview was either transformed or modified in blood. This could not but affect the crusaders as well. The appearance of monotheistic warriors on the borders of the pagan world predictably created a sense of disorientation among these tribal peoples, especially when defeated. Yet it should not surprise us that a certain amount of anomie would arise in the Christian invaders, producing in its wake a syncretistic synthesis. The old aphorism "the bee fertilizes the flower that it robs" may well apply in this violent cultural interaction known as the Baltic Crusades. Richard Fletcher describes this tendency to syncretism as "the convert carrying a certain amount of traditional cultural equipment, as it were a duty-free cultural allowance, over the threshold of Christianity."[14] This is an excellent description of the tendency to syncretism, but it must be noted that syncretism is a two-way street. It is not just that the new religion, in this case Christianity, is altered by the inclusion of an alien people, but that the adherents of the new religion might choose to alter their religion accordingly. In the exchange between cultures and religions via missionary war pagans may become only partly Christian, yet Christians may just as easily become partly pagan. While the pagans were adopting Christian ways, the Christians were, sometimes unwittingly, sometimes wholeheartedly, adopting the practices of the pagan world, creating a strange hybrid of religious war. Hamilton Gibb has pointed out that "it is rarely, if ever, that any element from a foreign culture is introduced or taken over as an entirely new constituent in the receiving culture."[15]

Calling it his "first law," Gibb believes that "genuinely assimilated elements" are preceded by something similar in the receiving culture, and "that it is this existing activity which creates the factor of attraction without which no creative assimilation can take place."[16] That which is completely alien, or repulsive, to the receiving culture is not likely to be adopted. This seems a type of "prevenient acculturation," a cultural attraction that goes before, wherein the receiving culture adopts that which already resembles their practice. If so, the Baltic Crusades might qualify. The question is: How much traditional cultural equipment of the pagan peoples did the crusaders appropriate?

These crusaders, steeped in a world of violent war behavior, if given permission to use war in service to the faith, would find no bar to adopting an even more extreme standard of violence. This point has escaped many who analyze the Crusades from a moral perspective. Edward LeRoy Long, Jr. provides a good example of what has become an all too standard interpretation of the act of crusading, whether in the Baltic or any other theater of operations: "Many of the most flagrant excesses in war—brutalities in method, barbarism in action, and a lust for total revenge—have stemmed from campaigns undertaken with the self-righteous motivations of the religious crusader."[17]

This has the benefit of providing an easy condemnation of violence in the name of faith without the troublesome contextual nuances that might reorient that judgment. While few, if any, would praise the barbarities of medieval warfare, whether crusading or not, a blanket evaluation such as this misses an important point: it presupposes that the crusaders were *more barbaric* than their opponents when the problem might be that "Christian" crusaders became as *barbaric* as their pagan counterparts. There is a tinge of noble savage reasoning here, implying that the targets of crusading were peaceable and pure until defiled by the violent excesses of crusading practice. But the real issue is that these targeted peoples, already living and functioning from immemorial times in an intensely violent milieu, were not transformed into a gentler folk by the forcible advent of Christianity, rather that they escorted the crusaders, already violent as well, into an even more brutal system of practice. It was an act of mimicry in which the putatively higher Christian standard was accommodated to the lower one. In short, as the crusaders won the pagan lands for Christ, the pagan lands won their habits of the heart.

This was decidedly not a new phenomenon. When Otto I (r. 936–73 AD), a monarch and emperor so impressive as to become the eponymous founder of a "renaissance" in Europe, defeated a rebellious Slavic leader named Stoinef, he was presented his opponent's head as a trophy. Otto was greatly moved by this gesture: "The reward for this famous deed was an imperial grant with an income equivalent to twenty farms."[18] That this cannot be dismissed as the action of an embarrassed leader wishing to avoid insulting an over-eager supporter is demonstrated by the aftermath: "The next morning the head . . . was placed in a field. Around it, seven hundred prisoners were beheaded. The eyes of his adviser were torn out, as was his tongue. He was then left helpless in the midst of the corpses."[19] The chronicler Widukind of Corvey summed up this episode with the observation that Otto had "awakened both fear and support among many kings and peoples" and that "the hope of all Christians everywhere rested on him."[20]

Correspondingly, the crusaders seemed comfortable with a close proximity of pagan and Christian practices in their everyday dealings with the Baltic peoples. In 1207, the missionary priest, Alabrand, when successfully persuading the Letts living by the Sedde River to receive baptism, was forced to wait while they cast lots to determine if they should be baptized in the Latin or Eastern Orthodox rite. Apparently the Russians had already baptized some of the Letts as tributary people, creating a conflict of allegiance between the eastern and western halves of Christendom. The chronicler Henry was pleased to conclude his description by announcing that "The lot fell to the Latins, however, and they were counted with the Rigans as members of the Livonian church."[21] Later, in 1263, the Teutonic Knights used this same pagan approach when contemplating a campaign into Kurland. The *Livonian Rhymed Chronicle* stated rather matter-of-factly that, "Their oracle sticks fell propitiously," causing them to conclude "that everything would go well for them."[22] This use of chance as a predictor of right action calls to mind the early Christian practice of the *sortes Biblicae*, or letting the Bible fall open to whatever random passage as a way of discerning God's will. It is worth noting that the church had frowned upon this as being too much like pagan behavior. On the Baltic seacoast, such behavior could coexist and be incorporated into the process of conversion.

One dangerous by-product of missionary war and its concomitant baptism by treaty structure is found in the temptation to import other local warmaking traditions into the mix. If warfare is accepted as a legitimate instrument for expanding the faith, then what, if any, of the practices of warfare are off limits? James Brundage has noted that the Baltic crusaders routinely used "local rulers and their forces" to assist in the campaigns and that the crusaders as well as the regional chieftains used the disruption of war to further their own causes. As we have already noted, native leaders often "seized the opportunities that the invasions afforded to attack traditional enemies with whom they had often struggled before the German armies arrived."[23] This had the effect of injecting religion into local disputes that had existed immemorially, thus opening the door for behaviors associated with these traditional conflicts to come into the crusading practice.

The appearance of pagan practices in the Christian ranks is not due to the tradition of keeping some familiar aspects of old worship in order to ease the abrupt transition to the new faith. First, it must be said that it was not merely the newly converted Baltic contingents among the Christian armies who continued pagan war tactics such as women-stealing. The German crusaders willingly participated. Secondly, the tradition of accommodation, as famously ruled by Pope Gregory the Great, six centuries earlier, allowed only consecrated, and thus cleansed, pagan trappings to remain, such as feasts, now dedicated to God or the saints rather than to pagan deities. The intent was that pagans would still feel comfortable in their new religious setting. It was a type of repurposing of familiar ritual. As Gregory phrased it:

> If the people are allowed some worldly pleasures in this way, they will more readily come to desire the joys of the spirit. For it is certainly impossible to eradicate all errors from obstinate minds at one stroke, and whoever wishes to climb to a mountain top climbs gradually step by step, and not in one leap.[24]

Culturally generous as this is, it is far from the wholesale adoption of pagan practices diametrically opposed to Christian principles.

The traditional just war theory had come into existence to limit the impact of conflict by declaring some war behaviors as impermissible: the breaking of treaties and truces, maltreatment of prisoners and civilians, and the like. But in the heat of a violent campaign, with the opponent already classified as an apostate deserving of punishment, customary techniques of war could and did pass muster as legitimate. Added to this was the reality that a union of religion and polity existed among the target people, leading the crusading forces to do whatever had traditionally worked in breaking the opponent's resistance. In the crusading context along the Baltic, what might that be? Devastating the pastures and farmlands of the opposing pagan tribes would be, as was pointed out at the outset of the Wendish Crusade of 1147, destroying what soon would be the crusaders' own property. Conquering a destroyed land, even one full of newly minted converts, would be quite counter-productive.

It is tempting to assume that the extremely violent nature of missionary war is a legacy peculiar to the Baltic. The frank admission in the *Livonian Rhymed Chronicle* that "to break a stubborn stone, one has to strike hard" invites the reader to assume the worst.[25] It was, after all, a rough world in which kindness was taken for weakness. In 1205, the citizens in newly founded Riga, offering hospitality to a passing Lithuanian army prompted the pagan leader, a Lithuanian war leader named Svelgate, to surmise, "if we conquer the places to which we are going, let us destroy this town and capture and kill its men. For the dust of this city will scarcely satisfy the fist of our people."[26] Svelgate made good on his promise only to die in the subsequent attack on Riga. The pagan Semgalls teamed up with the Christian Rigans and caught Svelgate sitting in his cart. He was speared and while still "quivering" beheaded with his head "put on one of their wagons which they had loaded only with the heads of Lithuanians."[27] The pages of the chronicles of the Baltic Crusades are blood-soaked with the routine violence of the project, by both pagan and Christian forces.

As a sampler, the pagan Kurs beheaded their own wounded at a battle on the banks of the Daugava in 1210, while the Esthonians roasted some of their Christian prisoners alive.[28] A later Christian Lettish leader named Thalibald was captured by a combined

Saccalian and Ungannian pagan army and was "roasted like a fish," causing his Christian sons to retaliate by burning "alive all the men they could capture in revenge for Thalibald."[29] Two years later a Christian army took the Saccalian leader Lembit's head back to Livonia as a war trophy, a counterpoint to the sympathetic magic of their opponents.[30] Having observed "how the pagans cut off and carried away the heads of the Brothers they slew,"[31] one gets the sense that the Christian forces succumbed to the urge to retaliate as a major part of their adoption of pagan Baltic war practices. Battle after battle produced not only the expected casualties of war—one battle account describing the carnage as "The enemy fell away from them on every side, just as hay falls to the ground before a mower"[32]—but excessively brutal behavior, as when the Swordbrothers beheaded all their prisoners "in order to take vengeance upon those lying and unfaithful nations."[33] The normalization of this type of violence was so well known after the fall of the pagan stronghold of Dorpat in 1225, that the surrounding villages hurried to make peace with the Christians, "for they feared lest the Rigans do unto them what they had done to the people of Dorpat."[34] And what was that? "Of all the men who were in the fort, only one remained alive."[35] This was a "knightly exploit" worthy of commemoration as seen by these ministers of shields and swords.[36]

As repulsive as these incidents are, they are not dissimilar to behaviors found in medieval Europe generally and in the Crusades specifically. Massacres, amputations, beheadings and the like were the unexceptional media of warfare across many cultures of this era. While we might expect better from Christian forces with the ostensible objective of protecting and spreading the Faith, such actions were not confined to the Baltic region nor to the era of the Baltic Crusades. It is not surprising that the accepted practices of war would be the "coinage of the realm" in these encounters. However, one might expect a sense of limitation on both the practice and the enthusiasm.

But one warmaking tradition popular among the tribal societies of the Baltic region might be employed to great effect in, as Bernard put it, "destroying either the rite or the people." This was the taking of women and children as captives. The taking of women and children, *mulieres et parvulos*, as well as horses, flocks, and any other moveable spoil of war was a commonplace among the tribally organized peoples of the Baltic, as among tribal peoples throughout

Europe generally. Torben K. Nielsen has noted the routine nature of the practice among the Baltic peoples and its utility for tribal victory: "Abducting women and children would effectively put an end to existing pagan dynasties in the area (and) initiate effective destruction of pagan kinship relations . . . and hereby destroy the former pagan societies from within."[37] William Urban believes this practice was reinforced by the nature of the German knights who comprised much of the Baltic crusaders. Noting that "race or ethnic origin was never a problem" but "all that was important was class," he points out that the knights were roughly equivalent in class to the *seniores,* or tribal leaders that they fought. So the intermarriage, after the women-stealing was finished, was a gateway to melding the two societies into one as "widows of prominent leaders . . . married newly-arrived German knights."[38]

This is an old tactic, as revealed in the Lombard origin story as recorded by Paul the Deacon. Writing in the late eighth century, Paul noted that during their formative years the Lombards absorbed the remnants of their defeated foes after killing the warriors. This was a type of tribal accretion whereby a group might increase its numbers via captives, and thus incorporate a former enemy into the tribe. It also has given us one of the most fascinating stories of the post-Roman West: when Lombard women were captured as war booty by the victorious Avars, only to escape defilement and possible execution by tucking rotting chicken flesh under their clothes. The Avars, thinking "that all the Langobard women had a bad smell," spared them.[39] We are often made aware of this practice of taking women as spoils of war only from the royal point of view as the sources frequently note the victorious king taking a family member of his dead opponent as a bride, as the sixth-century Lombard king Alboin did with Rosamond of the Gepids, or as happened to the future St. Radegund, a Thuringian royal, taken as war booty by the Frankish king Chlotar I, in the 520s.[40] But these types of examples misleadingly suggest only a merger at the top, when in fact the whole tribe was involved. It served a double purpose: effectively erasing the defeated tribe as an ethnic and political entity while adding to the size and influence of the victorious tribe. While this may have been common along the Baltic, it seems quite at odds with Christian notions of just war and even missionary war. Taking the women and children of the defeated people does not seem to fit the avowed objective of either.

Did the Christian crusaders borrow widely from pagan practice or was it a singular aberration? Just in Henry's *Livonian Chronicle* there are at least thirty examples of putatively Christian forces taking women and children, as well as the other spoils of war, as the rightful victor's share. At some points in the narrative the practice becomes almost a refrain attached to the verses of a battle description. And yet the same chronicler points out that the pagan Oselians were notoriously wicked for "visiting many hardships and villainies upon their captives, both the young women and virgins, at all times, by violating them and taking them as wives, each taking two or three or more of them."[41] These actions were called "unlawful" because "it is not right that Christ be joined with Belial, or is it suitable for a pagan to be joined to a Christian."[42] Yet in Henry's description of Christian forces dividing up women after battle, there is no word of censure. In the *Livonian Rhymed Chronicle* there is a seeming hint of disapproval. The anonymous poet described the merger negotiations between the Swordbrothers and the Teutonic Knights, by noting that, "they (the Swordbrothers) wish to embrace our order so as to improve their lives and I hope that they will stop those practices that harm their souls."[43] One is tempted to think that "those practices that harm their souls" might include women-stealing, but the further references in the *Rhymed Chronicle* that depict the Teutonic Knights enthusiastically participating in this practice give lie to that thought. Four years after the Teutonic Knights took over the operations in the Baltic, they boasted of their victory over a Lithuanian force that, "We have killed many men and captured wives and children and horses and cattle."[44] Perhaps the earlier criticism of the Swordbrothers was no more than political posturing in advance of the merger. Following the Swordbrothers' disastrous defeat and near annihilation at the Battle of the River Saule in 1236, Teutonic Knight chroniclers like the anonymous poet felt no need to devalue their rival, who would now willingly accede to absorption under the banner of the Teutonic Knights.

The question then arises as to what justification the crusaders might have for this flagrant disregard for Christian tradition. Their puzzling behavior has been treated in a variety of ways by contemporary scholars. William Urban well describes the uses of slavery among the pagan peoples as an explanation for the origins of the practice believing that "this type of warfare reflected the limited goals of the tribesmen, who wanted prestige, booty, and prisoners, not land or tribute."⁴⁵ This leaves unanswered the question of what the Christian forces actually did with the women and children. Did they sell them as slaves as well, or keep them for themselves as slaves or concubines? The *Rhymed Chronicle* gives us a hint, albeit one difficult to decipher accurately. A Christian Kur asked the Teutonic Knights for protection and to "let me and my wives and children stay with you."⁴⁶ Is this a testimony to the commonplace use of multiple wives taken in war, or an appeal to the Teutonic Knights for an exemption from their normal prohibition of this practice? The bulk of the evidence seems to suggest that the Knights absorbed many of these women into their own households.

Once again, the origins of this dilemma may lie in the early medieval days of Christian conversion among pagan, barbarian people. The late antique struggles along the northern frontier of the Roman Empire had created a paradigm for dealing with fragmented tribal peoples. Brent Shaw has outlined the problem by noticing that: "Any peace agreement on the Rhine or Danube was necessarily made with a finite ethnic group that covered only a relatively small geographic space."⁴⁷ Shaw thinks this encouraged a "genocidal aspect to this frontier warfare ... not ... in the sense of the physical extinction of all persons belonging to a given social group, but rather entailing the destruction of their social formations and identities."⁴⁸ He calls this "ethnocide" and it seems an apt interpretation of Bernard of Clairvaux's wish that either the people or the rite be exterminated by Christian crusaders. This might bring together the divergent views on the motivation for this practice: religion and economics. While noting that the taking of women and children was "not an uncommon feature of medieval warfare," Shami Ghosh sees a connection between the two in the multiple instances of "the capture of women and children" in the chronicles. He concludes it "indicates that in the mind of the chronicler the purpose of battle was far from solely the defense of the faith" but qualified as an offensive war that "provided gains that had no explicit religious value."⁴⁹

He is right to see the duality of the enterprise, but misses the unity of the motives for it. It is very much a closed circle where the economics, whether sale of humans, livestock, or any other valuable spoil of war, reinforces the religious objective and the religious reinforces the economic outcome. The connective is the cultural package that sees little or no separation among the two. In this context, Bernard's instructions to either wipe out the rite or the *natio* become sensible. Thus the taking of women and children becomes a function of missionary war and deserves, if not religious praise at least ecclesiastical absolution as a proper crusading effort. But this absolution came in the form of a benign silence from the ecclesiastical authorities rather than in a wholehearted approval.

Pope Innocent III, in an attempt to allow a gentle transition from paganism to the Faith, had sent a letter to Bishop Albert of Buxhövden in April 1201, suggesting that new converts "could not be expected to leave behind all their customs and practices on the acceptance of baptism."[50] The Pope hoped to prevent apostasy by lessening the shock of transition from one lifestyle to another. The expressed target of his statement was the Baltic practice of a widow marrying her deceased husband's brother, which led to a type of polygamy. Festively titling the letter *Gaudeamus*, Innocent held that arrangements of this type that predated the subject's conversion and baptism should be allowed to stand. As precedence for this stance, Innocent cited the famous letter of Gregory the Great, written to the successful missionaries in Anglo-Saxon Kent sometime around the year 601, that advocated the keeping of some pagan customs such as festival dates and worship sites if, and only if, they were cleansed of their pagan significance and consecrated to Christianity. Gregory had hoped that "If the people are allowed some worldly pleasures in this way, they will more readily come to desire the joys of the spirit. For it is certainly impossible to eradicate all errors from obstinate minds at one stroke."[51] More than a century later, in 726, this approach was still in vogue as Pope Gregory II (r. 715–31) allowed a loosening of strict canonical marriage rules for the Anglo-Saxons by saying "moderation weighs more with these savage people than strict legal duties."[52] Following this historic precedent, Innocent made, in William Urban's terms, "a liberal interpretation of the law in order to avoid endangering the soul of any potential convert," and thus the pagans were only bound by church law after conversion.[53]

Some legitimate controversy can still attach to this ruling, in that ritually cleansed pagan sites and the continuation of uncanonical marriage practices are not necessarily commensurate. But since this missive was sent fairly early in the Baltic enterprise before the regularity of taking women and children set in, it skirts the issue of most concern for the Christian crusaders and raises even more questions. What possible consecration could apply to the taking of women and "little ones," *mulieres et parvulos* by already baptized Christian forces? There were apparently no previous pagan unions to grandfather into legitimacy. One is left with the inescapable conclusion that, if the chroniclers are accurate in their descriptions, the Christian crusaders simply adopted pagan practices at will, and without apparent censure, leading to the evaluation that "Christian conduct did not, at least in this respect, differ from that of the heathens."[54] Nor is this confined to the Baltic Crusades. The monk historian Widukind of Corvey recounted the siege of the Slavic Wilzi stronghold of Lenzen by the Saxon king Henry in 929, by noting that after taking the fort "the slaves, and all of the money along with the wives, children, and goods of the king of the barbarians were carried into captivity."[55]

A complicating factor was the tendency to import the women and children stealing military gambit from a Christian v. pagan conflict to wars in general. The chronicler Henry notes that in 1216, after the Ungannians had finally agreed to baptism and affiliation with the Latin Christian side, the Russians of Pskov, also Christian, under their leader Vladimir invaded and "burned and despoiled the land, killed many men, and took the women and children captive."[56] Apparently it made no difference whether the opponents were Christian or pagan as to the use of abducting women and children. Quite apart from the Pope's liberal ruling on the matter, another justification for this frequent resort to pagan practice must be found other than prior ignorance of Christian principles.

The years of the Baltic Crusades were ones in which there was a confluence of two strands of thinking in Christendom: that the Christian warriors represented a chosen people and that the apocalypse was near; in Bernard's mellifluous Biblical borrowing, it was a *tempus acceptibile*, or "the acceptable time" for action. Therefore scriptural references that might apply to the ancient Hebrews were seen to pertain to current crusading. The standard description of the Christian use of the abduction of women and children was: "They seized many people, killed all the men, and dragged away the women and children as captives. They took away with them the flocks and much loot."[57] This forms an almost exact parallel to Deuteronomy 20:13-14:

> When the Lord your God delivers it (the pagan city) into your hand, put to the sword all the men in it. As for the women, the

children, the livestock and everything else in the city, you may take these as plunder for yourselves.[58]

As the new chosen people, serving in these last days, Old Testament instructions may have seemed to offer the crusaders sufficient cover for the adoption of a violent, pagan custom. But there was another, more recent development that provided justification for the syncretism of mixing in Baltic pagan war practices with Christian crusading: the growing presence of the Virgin Mary.

The Baltic Crusade became in time an enterprise firmly under the rubric of the Virgin, particularly as the Swordbrothers melded into the Teutonic Knights after 1236.[59] This naturally poses an interesting question: How can crusaders who take women as spoils in war elevate the most hallowed woman in Christian history to the position of leadership for the project? There seems to be a conflict inherent in such a usage. Yet the Virgin is not a mere woman. By the twelfth century, and particularly during the pontificate of Pope Innocent III (1198–1216) who revered her greatly, she had become the Queen of Heaven, a spiritual entity reverenced above even the normal coterie of saints. Therefore, while Jesus is given praise for the crusaders' victories,[60] the Virgin Mary is also routinely credited with whatever successes the crusaders achieved. Her involvement in the bloody business of war is unmistakable in Henry's *Chronicle,* as he lists the roster of vanquished foes and even includes the Mongols as agents in her hands to protect Latin Christian gains:

> Thus, even thus, the Lady of the world and the Empress of all lands always protects her special land. . . . Did She not rule when She afflicted the many kings who were fighting against Livonia? Did She not afflict them when She struck with sudden death the great King Vladimir of Pskov as he was coming into Livonia with his army? Did She not immediately deprive of his kingdom the great king of Novgorod who despoiled Livonia for the first time, and did She not cause him to be driven out shamefully by his citizens? Did She not kill through the Tatars the other king of Novgorod who devastated Livonia for the second time?[61]

This list goes on to include Swedes, Danes, and all the various opponents of the crusaders, only to end with the paradox of her tenderness to her followers and her brutality to her enemies:

> Behold how the Mother of God, so gentle to Her people who serve Her faithfully in Livonia, always defended them from all their enemies and how harsh She is with those who invade Her land or who try to hinder the faith and honor of Her Son in that land! See how many kings . . . and elders of treacherous pagans She has wiped off the earth and how often She has given Her people victory over the enemy![62]

Henry caps it all with the admonition: "Fear this gentle Mother of Mercy . . . Who takes such cruel revenge upon Her enemies."[63]

Even allowing for a fever pitch of religious hyperbole, a type of Marian triumphalism, it is inescapably obvious that the Virgin Mary was not seen as a benign, distant supervisor but rather, almost like the early medieval perception of the *Deus ultor*, "the vengeful God," a willing and active participant on the battlefield. The *Livonian Rhymed Chronicle* illustrates just how pervasive this Marian presence was on the contested fields of the Baltic Crusades. When going into battle against the Lithuanians on the Schenen River in Kurland in 1290, "For the sake of God, the Christians sang the song, *Saint Mary, help us to victory*"[64] and when losing in an earlier engagement, "the flag of Our Lady was cut down without mercy" by the victorious pagans.[65] A converted pagan, one Suxe by name, was eulogized for his brave death in battle: "Mother, Maid Mary, noble and pure, preserve his soul from all distress, for he died in Your service."[66] This pervasive Marian involvement provides more than sufficient cover for behaviors quite divergent from the normal expectations of Christian just war and place the Baltic Crusade firmly in the category of a holy war.

The tendency is to see this emphasis on Mary as a new development, and in many ways it was. Multiple studies on the emergence of courtly love testify to the fertility of this line of investigation. There did seem to be an efflorescence of interest in the Virgin during the thirteenth and fourteenth centuries. But the superstructure for the Virgin becoming the powerful military patroness over the expanding region of Christian crusading conquest may have other, earlier roots.

These roots may be found in the emergence of the Late Antique cult of the saints. While this is a belief system that is almost impossible to document, as evidenced by the misty imprecision of its origins, the cult of the saints became as pervasive as almost any

THE MINISTRY OF SHIELDS AND SWORDS 137

FIGURE 5 *The Mary Window at Marienburg Castle, Malbork, Poland. This huge stained glass window at the principal fortress of the Teutonic Knights was dedicated to the Virgin Mary, symbolizing the belief that the Virgin was their special patroness, thus creating a union of territorial claims with sainthood. (Photo by the author)*

feature of medieval Christianity.[67] Whatever the true inception of this practice, it is beyond dispute that the cult of the saints became closely associated with *loca sanctorum*, or "holy places." The tombs of the saints rapidly became centers of pilgrimage and so did their surrounding territories. Peter Brown has likened it to pools on a drying surface.[68] Despite this typically lyrical description, it may be said that Brown's model better serves to explain the process when it is reversed: "drying pools" implies an evaporation of the practice, whereas its true destiny was to seep relentlessly over the Christian lands of the West. This tendency was apparent from the inception of the cult of the saints. One of the earliest, and most influential, voices in this development was that of Paulinus of Nola (354–431). A Roman aristocrat and contemporary of St. Augustine, Paulinus was devoted to the expansion of his patron saint's power, penning a yearly "birthday poem" to St. Felix on the anniversary of his death. In one poem he likened the saints to the "bodily limbs" of the One God and held that "regions are apportioned to the bodies of saints." Foreseeing the almost endless expansion of this territorial metaphor,

Paulinus concluded that "the influence of an interred saint is not confined to the area where his whole body lies. Wherein there is a part of a saint's body, there too, his power emerges."[69]

As the number of saints multiplied and their shrines put out branches in the form of oratories, convents, monasteries and churches dedicated to them, the landscape began to fill with protected holy sites and their associated territories. This saintly territorialism was reinforced by the historical tendency on the part of Christianity to see the religion as based on discrete territorial enclaves. There was a physical, land-based, notion of Christianity apart from the winning of human souls to the faith. Taking root first in the cities, the Roman *urbs*, those living in the *pagus*, or surrounding countryside, were considered outside the fold. Indeed, the very word pagan, used in crusading context as a descriptor of all those, even Muslims, outside the Christian faith, comes from this use of the location, the *pagus*, to describe non-Christians. The location rather than merely the belief conditioned the term. The spread of Christianity, as well as the spread of saints' cults, had a territorially based common experience. So too did the incorporation of whole pagan lands such as that of the Baltic Crusades. The price associated with this territorial transaction would be the issue of administrative ownership. The making of and marking out of Christian pilgrimage sites, as the inclusion of lands into Christendom, would engender future disputes over proprietary rights.

As early as the sixth century, it became necessary to acknowledge the power of the local saint as one entered areas under his or her purview. A famous example is that of the aggressive Frankish king, Clovis, who was careful to restrict his soldiers from pillaging not merely the church properties dedicated to Martin, but the entire region of the Touraine as he progressed south to face the Visigoths in 507. When some of his troops violated his prohibition, Clovis exclaimed "And where will our hope of victory be if we offend the blessed Martin?" Clovis was rewarded for his circumspection by the desired victory and, when he also ordered his men not to pillage the property of St. Hilary of Poitiers, he was granted an Old Testament-style miracle: a pillar of fire to guide his army.[70] The linkage of saintly power with military victory would be normative in future crusading contexts. The use of warfare to expand Christianity would, of necessity, be a means of expanding the cult of the saints. But the question remains, how did saintly *praesentia* and *potentia*, typically localized and fragmented, evolve into a system that featured regional or even national patron saints, such as the use of the Virgin Mary as the patroness of the Baltic Crusades? The cult of the saints might well be a force for fragmentation in a land already separated "into natural districts, so that people sharing a common language nevertheless found it difficult to establish any government above that of tribal councils."[71] Students of medieval saints' cults have noted that it is "too simple . . . to juxtapose notions of a Gallo-Roman heartland against a recently converted periphery."[72] It would also be unrealistic to assume that the now centuries-old practice of saintly territorialism did not migrate into pagan lands, even if altered by the changed location and period. It would also be unrealistic to think that the periphery left those from the heartland unaffected.

The question on the nature and extent of this change, much less any serviceable answer, is a multifaceted one that must include things such as tribal consolidation into kingdoms, the supplanting of one popular saint in favor of a royal favorite (as occurred in France with the replacement of St. Martin by St. Denis), and other, more particularly local influences. But one line of suggestive development depends on what happened when most of the available villages, fields, and territories had already been assigned to individual saints. Was there a change in the cult of the saints that redirected their territorial authority away from these almost endlessly multiple holdings to an over-arching regional presence? Of course, as new pagan lands were added a saint could emerge as the patron, but the notion of regional and national saints had already been put in place before the main thrust of Christian expansion along the contested frontiers of Europe. This transition constitutes a portion of the prehistory of the "ministry of shields and swords" as practiced in the Baltic.

More than fifty years ago Gabriel LeBras advocated a sociological view on the emergence of the cult of the saints,[73] noting that worshippers tend to model their view of Heaven on what they observe on earth. Heaven's structure then became a type of mirror, faithfully reflecting the order of human society. This observation has sparked a bit of academic back and forth with Peter Brown wondering if rather than a mirror, this created a type of projecting screen where the hierarchy of Heaven was seen to represent what should be, not what is.[74]

While such a sociological construct is fair game for debate, it seems that the church used this structure to build its earthly, as well as heavenly, empire. The iconography of Christ in majesty not only portrayed Him in imperial garb and insignia, but his attendants as well. Even the popular stories reflected this structuring of heaven along earthly, Roman lines. The Christian mystic Dorotheus reported his dream that he was adorned with the uniform of an imperial official upon his arrival in heaven.[75] It appears obvious that a similar situation existed for the twelfth- through fourteenth-century Baltic crusaders and the agents of Christianization in the post-fall world of the fifth and sixth centuries. LeBras thought the post-Roman church was setting "itself to pour the ancient traditions into the new mold"[76] when they sought to establish the cult of the saints. Surely Christianity in general would seem to us to be "ancient tradition," but for the pagans along the Baltic littoral it would appear all too new. But novelty aside, the crusading activity there would be an attempt to pour, albeit quite forcibly, a tradition into a new mold. This approach took many forms, as LeBras admitted: "On the land it keeps or conquers, the Church plants its buildings. . . . everywhere there are little monuments—oratories, chapels, crosses—proclaiming the conquest of the land."[77]

The standard practice of apportioning saintly territorial control to the landscape region by region fits well with the ever-moving frontier of Christianity along the Baltic Sea. Mary, accepted as Queen of Heaven by this date, would be a proper patroness for a project much bigger than an occasional oratory or basilica in a village. As celestial queen she would rule over nations. Henry admits as much in his *Livonian Chronicle* when he credits Mary with rule over "all these newly converted lands."[78] Her overarching heavenly status mirroring the trans-tribal conquests of the Baltic crusaders.

The presence of residual pagan practices in the "ministry of shields and swords" scenario calls into question the transformative nature of the conversion for the pagans and the corrosive influence of native customs on the Christians. Arthur Darby Nock, nearly a century ago, believed that a better word for the conversion of the pagans might be "adhesion."[79] But adhesion implies that two items are joined almost in a type of lamination. The product of the ministry of shields and swords, baptism by treaty, by definition seems to be the union of two opposing peoples as a by-product of battlefield victory. Perhaps the adhesion of pagan Baltic practices and Christian ones provides an excellent syncretistic opportunity for the joining of customs that should be far apart.

As the adoption of the Virgin Mary as patroness of the Christianized Baltic lands naturally predisposes toward seeing Christianization as a matter of territoriality and sociopolitical control, the question of who should gain the lion's share of this new, and lucrative, territory inevitably arises. Further complicating this was the creation of spiritual nodal points—pilgrimage sites—that would draw worshippers and the attendant wealth and eminence they would bring. This issue would prove productive of tension and even war between the various parts of the new Baltic Christian communities.

Questions for discussion

What is apostasy and how did it fuel the Baltic Crusades?

If spiritual issues such as baptism become tied to war, how does this affect the use of syncretism?

How much, or how many, pagan customs can be incorporated into Christianity without doing violence to the religion?

What is the proper way to keep some of the old customs in a newly Christianized society?

What role does anomie play in all this?

What was the purpose of taking women and children as spoils of war?

What was the church's response to this?

How was this taking of women and children as war booty justified?

What is meant by the term "reisen"?

How is it possible to have crusading activity along the Baltic during the frozen winter months?

8

A new kind of pilgrim

As the weather gentled each spring, allowing a complement of Danish and German crusaders to form up for their yearly summertime *reisens* to the East, it became traditional to refer to the warriors as *peregrini*, or "pilgrims." This certainly seemed proper as crusaders in general had been called pilgrims since the days of the First Crusade, long before they were called *crucesignati*, or those signed with the cross. However, the use of the term for the Baltic Crusades raised more questions than answers. One surprising result of the practice of missionary war and the "ministry of shields and swords" along the Baltic involves the use of proper terminology for the participants. It seems it is one of the many peculiarities of the Baltic Crusades that these crusaders are called "pilgrims."

Criticism of the use of this term has taken several tracks: the fact that the crusaders' destination does not qualify as a pilgrimage site, that the terminology was slow to catch up to the new realities of these crusades, and that a mere transference of the term from the Holy Land experience caused them to incorrectly be labeled *peregrini*. William Urban has noted that this term presents a problem for scholars. His view of the problem is based on the first criticism. He argues that "those crusades could hardly be considered pilgrimages (though chroniclers called volunteers 'pilgrims')."[1] Diana Webb blames the terminology on a lapse between a changed practice and a suitably accurate term by judging that "so slow was a specialized terminology to establish itself that participants in the crusades against the pagan Baltic peoples were still sometimes called *peregrini* in the thirteenth century."[2]

While this observation might well be true, it is also not a surprising one. There is often a time lag between the emergence of an actual practice, or change in practice, and a properly descriptive term for it. John Headley has done much work on this very phenomenon, holding that *res*, "the thing," often precedes *verbum*, "the word."[3] Pope Eugenius III did avoid the terms *peregrinus* and *peregrini* in his enabling decree *Divina dispensatione II* that began the Baltic Crusades, choosing instead to use pronouns such as *quorum*, *illam*, or *illos*[4]—the later popularity of the term with chroniclers signifies that the intention to class crusaders as pilgrims generally was clear. Henry's *Livonian Chronicle*, probably written from 1224 to 1227,[5] does not use pronouns for the crusaders but routinely calls them *peregrini*. That these fighters were crusaders is attested by an exchange between the warrior-bishop Albert of Buxhövden and Philip of Swabia, Holy Roman Emperor (1198–1208). When the bishop asked the emperor if the goods of the "pilgrims" were protected as with the Jerusalem crusades he received a clearly affirmative reply.[6] The dependence on this type of pilgrimage for any progress in the Baltic Crusades was frankly admitted by Bishop Albert when he said, "he could not make progress among the people without pilgrims" (*sine auxilio peregrinorum*).[7] The *Livonian Rhymed Chronicle*, a principal source for the years after Henry's Chronicle, also terms the crusaders *peregrini*, noting in a somewhat chronologically confused passage that Pope Innocent III received "honorable pilgrims" from the Baltic and promised that he would also receive "in the future whatever pilgrims wish to come to Livonia."[8]

Was all this simply the misapplication of a standard term to a nonstandard situation, a mere continuation of terminology already established for crusading in general, or perhaps an onomastic conflation like the use of the word *barbarus* for soldier in the late Roman Empire?[9] The issue of Baltic *peregrini* is a multifaceted one. It features crusading only for a season, and not until the job was done, as well as a geographically elastic reach of indulgences and the question of how flexible, or inflexible, the crusade vow might be. These are lines of investigation that have fascinated scholars in the past and continue to do so. It may be, however, that a reappraisal of the basic characteristic of pilgrimage—its proposed destination and how, or if, a suitable substitute sacred site might replace the lack of such a holy place—could be the key to answering many of the ancillary questions about it. The mechanisms of crusading pilgrimage in the Baltic theater of operations might derive their unique contours from a change in the essence of pilgrimage. The

Baltic crusaders may well still be pilgrims, but of a quite different type. And, as we shall see, this change had a long prehistory as well.

Thomas Asbridge has noted recently that the interweaving of holy war and pilgrimage is at the very heart of the concept of crusade.[10] Once crusading became normative, it would be excusable to expect the term for pilgrim, *peregrinus*, to be automatically applied even in cases where many other essentials of pilgrimage were lacking. But there seems to be something novel in the use of the term *peregrini* for Baltic crusaders. While these pilgrims certainly fought to cleanse their penitential records, just as their comrades in arms did in the Holy Land, what holy sites were the targeted destinations of their efforts? Surely a pilgrim must have a holy site, or *locus sanctorum*, in mind whenever starting out on a journey so perilous as a crusade. Those venturing to the Holy Land were looking to Jerusalem and specifically the Church of the Holy Sepulchre as the destination of their physical and spiritual journey. Many crusaders to Palestine, when their combat was concluded, swam the Jordan River, received the traditional pilgrim's palm frond, and returned home.[11] How could this work in the Baltic region? Without that target destination of a spiritually lifting holy site, how might spiritual benefits actually accrue? This is the problem William Urban was noting: The Baltic Crusades offer little or nothing in the way of holy sites, *loca sanctorum*, for potential pilgrim warriors.

Peregrini in the Baltic Crusade context has thus often been dismissed as an aberration, or a misapplication of proper terminology in much the same way the Baltic Crusades themselves have been disqualified or deemed a misuse of the crusade definition. Perhaps a look at the long prehistory of pilgrimage will shed light on whether or not *peregrini* of the Baltic variety were truly an aberration.

The dismissal of Baltic *peregrini* is based in part on the received wisdom that the practice of pilgrimage has been an unchanging concept since its inception. It is hard to argue with this view, dating as it does from the very beginnings of Christian pilgrimage. The triumphant, and perhaps triumphalist, tour undertaken by the Augusta Helena (d. 329 AD) to the Holy Land in 325, fresh on the heels of her acquisitive emperor-son Constantine's conquest of the eastern half of the empire from Licinius, touched off a wave of pilgrimage to holy sites, notably, but not exclusively, in Palestine. Going to a *locus sanctorum* for spiritual benefit and then returning with some tangible token of sanctity to signify an upgraded spiritual state, as did Helena with her holy souvenirs, is at the heart of standard definitions of pilgrimage. Linda Kay Davidson and Maryjane Dunn-Wood provide a typical, if somewhat unwieldy, example when they define pilgrimage as

> the physical journey from one's normal place of residence, to a religious shrine in order to pay religious homage to a recognized holy being and through that religious activity to pay homage to or request special favor from God.[12]

This appears to be correct in that the same motives and techniques that animated Helena and those who followed her example seem to be in play in the minds of the first crusaders as they sought a military pilgrimage to the Holy City. If pilgrimage has always been an *idée fixe*, as a journey to a place for holiness, then the Baltic version is plainly a misuse. But pilgrimage was not always an immutable concept and may not have been so far our Baltic crusader-*peregrini*.

There had already been significant change in the notion of pilgrimage prior to the opening of the Baltic Crusades. The First Crusade of 1095–99 was noted for moving warfare from something requiring penance to something that was penitential in and of itself, thus permitting warriors to take armed pilgrimages to a *locus sanctorum* to gain a positive spiritual benefit: *remissio peccatorum*, "the remission of sins." This revolutionized the received image of what a pilgrim was to be. But most of the scholarly attention to this union of pilgrimage and warfare has focused on the "armed" part; how pilgrims morphed from being inoffensive chaps, forbidden to bear arms and thus equipped only with a knapsack, staff, loaf of bread, and jug of wine, into armored, weapon-wielding warriors intent on holy mayhem. While this is inarguably an essential line of inquiry, it presumes that the notion of pilgrimage was static. It presupposes the grafting of a novel idea, warfare, onto the stable and immemorially unchanging, body of pilgrimage. Views on holy war may have developed allowing this conjunction, but the idea of pilgrimage did not.

Yet all Christian pilgrimages were not the same. Giles Constable, in his seminal study on opposition to pilgrimage, has noticed the "ambiguity of medieval attitudes toward this characteristic activity,"[13] and ambiguity can encourage fluidity when attached to an institution or practice. Dee Dyas has provided a useful taxonomy for sorting out the differing manifestations of this pilgrimage ambiguity by drawing a bright line between place pilgrimage, that features a journey to a holy place and a subsequent return, and life pilgrimage, popular among the Celtic church, that viewed pilgrimage as being led by God to wherever He wished,[14] with no return sought or expected. During the eighth and ninth centuries these two viewpoints coexisted, and often competed for acceptance. Place pilgrimage ultimately won out, buoyed by decisions from church councils in 744 and again in 813.[15] This made what was normative in the Late Antique view of pilgrimage, journey to a place, once again standard. To borrow a phrase from the Arthurian legend, it was now *quondam peregrinatio et futurus*, "the once and future pilgrimage." The same motivating factors that produced place pilgrimage in the fourth century also activated *peregrini* in the high and later Middle Ages. But there had existed an alternative version of pilgrimage: Celtic life pilgrimage, often called *peregrinatio pro amore Christo*, or "pilgrimage for the love of Christ."

The origins of this type of pilgrimage are necessarily shrouded in the twilight of sixth-century Ireland, but are generally thought to have begun with the career of Columba (521–97 AD). Columba, having triggered a war concerning his unauthorized use of a manuscript, was chagrined by the carnage of the conflict. It was said that some 3,000 men died in the Battle of Cooldrevny. Vowing to make amends for his role in the slaughter, Columba left Ireland forever and established a monastery on an island called simply "insula." The foundation grew and became known as Iona, one of the bright lights of culture and religion in a darkening world. But the essence of Columba's journey, to go wherever God led and remain there, became a model for others. The concept was called "white martyrdom" in that it meant a type of death for the participant who would never again see his family, friends, or even his homeland.[16]

White martyrdom was brought to the Continent by the next generation of Irish monks, led by Columbanus (543–615 AD), and it formed a competing and somewhat adversarial model to place pilgrimage. Columbanus himself crowed that it was *potior peregrinatio*, "the better pilgrimage,"[17] and it grew in popularity to the point that the Continental church felt constrained to condemn it as too disruptive and ungoverned. The point of contention was the penchant among Columbanus and his successors to see this type of pilgrimage as a roadway. In his thirteen surviving sermons, preached in the great basilica of St. Ambrose in Milan in 613/14 AD, Columbanus used the roadway metaphor no less than nine times, as exemplified by this quote from Sermon VI: "By the Lord's help we have said of human life that it is in the likeness of a roadway."[18] But perhaps his best statement linking life pilgrimage to a roadway is found in Sermon VIII, where he makes a direct connection between white martyrdom and pilgrimage:

> Since we are travelers and pilgrims in the world (*mundi viatores et peregrini*), let us ever ponder the end of the road, that is of our life, for the end of our roadway is our home.... Let us not love the roadway rather than the homeland ... on the road we so live as travelers, as pilgrims.[19]

It was precisely this notion of undirected and unauthorized travel that caused the established Continental church concern. These Irish pilgrims were seen as *gyrovagi*, the unpredictable type of monastic wanderers that St. Benedict had condemned heartily in his Rule. Early on in the emergence of monasticism there had been some monks who left their isolated abodes and intimidated, and therefore influenced, church officials and policy with violence.[20]

The charge was misplaced when leveled against the Irish white martyrs of the seventh and eighth centuries. They founded enduring monasteries and only moved when impelled by a direct impulse from God. However, in the perception of the official church they were not only transient, but independently so. A series of rulings condemned the practice and, consequently, the *peregrinatio pro amore Christo* soon died out and notions of pilgrimage returned to their previous structure of travel to a holy place with a subsequent return. Oddly, the chief opponent of this white martyrdom type of pilgrimage was the English missionary Boniface (680–754 AD). The Anglo-Saxons of Boniface's homeland had been brought to Christ in equal part by the efforts of Irish *peregrini* and Roman ecclesiastics. But Boniface was supremely interested in church organization and control. The tendency toward autonomy that the Irish monastic foundations exhibited threatened the orderly functioning of bishoprics and the burgeoning parish system. However, it is one of the many ironies of history that the principal antagonist to *peregrinatio pro amore Christo*, Boniface, should be remembered as one who blended both the Irish and Roman perspectives into a highly successful process. As Peter Cramer credited the great success of Anglo-Saxon missionaries to the Continent in the eighth century, to their "combination of missionary thrust and administrative efficiency" uniting "the old Irish tradition of the missionary in exile and the ... ancient principle of centralization of Rome."[21] At length even the Irish made peace with this place pilgrimage victory. One scribe wrote that it was actually better to find Jerusalem in one's heart while at home rather than seeking it far afield, even to Rome itself: "To go to Rome, much labor, little profit; you will not find the King whom you seek here unless you bring Him with you."[22]

What does the long ago, and forgotten, struggle between two competing visions of pilgrimage have to do with the Baltic Crusades? The fact that there was once an alternative pilgrimage style invalidates the unchangeable nature of pilgrimage and, more importantly for our purposes, opens a door of understanding for the vexed Baltic form of *peregrinatio*. It means that European Christians were not averse to change in the fundamentals of pilgrimage. A static view of pilgrimage that omits a struggle against a competing version that was won at great cost in the eighth and ninth centuries gives the impression that pilgrimage was immutable from its inception. Yet it would not be unthinkable for Christians to accept a changed model of pilgrimage, even as it might be associated with the crusading variety. In fact the union of holy warfare with pilgrimage accomplished by Pope Urban II at the Council of Clermont in 1095 may be seen as another turn in the ongoing diversification of pilgrimage. The prior view on pilgrimage, whether place pilgrimage or life pilgrimage, featured prominently the requirement that they be unarmed. The received image of a pilgrim was one of an inoffensive chap, forbidden to bear arms, and thus equipped only with a knapsack, staff, loaf of bread, and jug of wine, with perhaps a special badge marking him as a person on a spiritual journey. Yet the lance-bearing, mailed participants in the First Crusade were novel *peregrini* in their warlike function, their bellicosity, marking a real departure.

While the crusaders may have been a new breed of pilgrim due to their fighting ability, they were not new in their fervent place pilgrimage. The lure of the holy sites in Jerusalem and surrounding territories was a major, perhaps the major, recruiting tool for crusaders. And one of the recurring problems during the

Crusades was the constant lack of fighting manpower due to the uncomfortable fact of the survivors of the campaigns, having fulfilled their pilgrimage vows, promptly returning to their Western European homelands.

If crusading *peregrini* in the Holy Land represent a new version of pilgrimage in their warlike status, perhaps the Baltic pilgrims were simply another alteration of the concept as well. Rather than being a mere misuse of the term "pilgrim" for Baltic crusaders, these *peregrini* signify a type of return to an earlier view of pilgrimage, at least in part. This would constitute a prehistory of Baltic crusading pilgrimage and help to contextualize the seemingly odd behavior of this "edge crusade." Baltic crusaders may not have seen their pilgrimage as a journey to a holy place, but rather a commitment to a holy activity, much like the Celtic version of life pilgrimage. Crusaders in the Holy Land, understanding the point of conflict with their Muslim opponents theologically to be the status of Jesus as the Son of God, were keen to quote him as recorded in John 14:6: "I am the way, the truth, and the life. No one comes to the Father except through me."[23] Included in that verse is the notion that following Christ is a journey—He is the way, *Ego sum via*—so the earlier Celtic view of life as a journey could resonate among those embarking on a crusade. Pilgrimage would be more than travel, as Henry's *Livonian Chronicle* reveals: "After these events ... the pilgrims (*peregrini*), who had soldiered under the cross for their God throughout this year in Livonia, returned to Germany."[24]

As the Baltic crusaders were not journeying to a *locus sanctorum*, but fighting their way into pagan lands, what was the spiritual benefit and how could they realize it? If it were only a matter of fighting, that could be, and was often, done at home. What were they actually doing in the field and how did they qualify as pilgrims? Recently there has been a flurry of scholarly activity concerning the Baltic crusaders making sacred pagan lands and sites as they conquered. Perhaps taking their cue from the groundbreaking work of John Howe,[25] on creating a Christian landscape in formerly pagan territories, a bevy of medievalists, mostly from Denmark, have examined the growing trend of establishing Christian markers, or *tropaea*, in the Baltic lands. Carsten Selch Jensen, using arguably the most important primary source for the early Baltic Crusades, Henry's *Livonian Chronicle*, has observed "no place in Livonia was in itself sacred (in contrast to the beliefs of the local pagan population), but places were made sacred."²⁶ As the crusading era brought in its wake a near obsession with the sacred places of the Holy Land, particularly the Church of the Holy Sepulchre in Jerusalem, any newly created *loca sanctorum* in the Baltic lands could not be confined to the few sites of Christian martyrdom, as in the rest of the continent. As a function of historical necessity, these spots were increasingly scarce the farther eastward the crusaders ventured.

What was possible, lacking suitable ready-made holy sites, was the physical replication of structures associated with salvation history, making "the Holy Land as a part of salvation history also physically present."²⁷

The presence of the Holy City of Jerusalem is pervasive in medieval life, whether in an allegorical or material sense. Norman Housley identified at least three uses for the concept of "Jerusalem" in crusade studies: "Some of the 'Jerusalems' that this entailed—the allegorical (representing the church), anagogical (prefiguring heaven) and tropological (symbolizing the individual's soul)—overlap and defy precise analysis."²⁸ There may be an

FIGURE 6 *Church of the True Cross, Segovia, Spain. This view, taken from the tower of the nearby Alcazar, shows the architectural outline of the church, built in 1208 by the Knights Templar, as it mimicked the Church of the Holy Sepulchre in Jerusalem. (Photo by the author)*

architectural use as well. Once again this development may trace back to Constantine's influential mother, the Augusta Helena. Her arrival in Jerusalem in 325 touched off a rebuilding of the city, radically reduced almost two centuries before by the Emperor Hadrian's decree that it be renamed Aelia Capitolina and purged of Jewish sites. The Augusta's building program helped to offer "Christians an alternative to a simple narrative of Christianity's movement away from the terrestrial Jerusalem and towards a more spiritual and figurative understanding of the holy city."[29] This new perspective could open the door for "Jerusalems" elsewhere, some reaching levels of structural imitation that resembled, in the words of Guy Strousma, "a 'theme park' of sorts, the first Eurodisney, offering a reproduction of Jerusalem."[30] This impulse only grew after the turn of the millennium with careful measurements of the holy sites providing a means for recreating Jerusalem allegorically.[31]

Near some Livonian cities or castles there were chapels built and designated as "Jerusalem" with architecture that scrupulously imitated the Church of the Holy Sepulchre in Jerusalem.[32] So prevalent was this move to create "Jerusalems" that scale models of this holy church appeared throughout contested Europe from Segovia in Spain to Eichstatt in Bavaria and Schleswig on the Wendish frontier. Taking a cue from the vexed document known as the *Magdeburg Appeal*, probably composed in 1107–08 but seemingly never acted upon, the Slavic frontier along the Baltic was styled "our Jerusalem" to the intended audience of would-be crusader pilgrims.[33] A climax was reached at the Fourth Lateran Council in 1215, when the martial bishop of newly founded Riga, Albert von Buxhövden, gained conciliar agreement that Livonia was rightly to be seen as the land of the Virgin Mary and thus of no less importance than the Holy Land itself.[34] This seemed an appropriate and logical sequel to the papal ruling some fifteen years earlier that made crusading in Livonia the "equal with that to Jerusalem."[35] The popularity of the notion is today attested by the title of a fine study of Baltic conversion by a collection of Scandinavian scholars titled *Jerusalem in the North*.[36] As John Howe remarked for Christendom in general: "As Christianity expanded, demonic territory contracted (and) in churches, shrines, and sacred places, western European churchmen made the kingdom of God immanent to their congregations and themselves."[37]

One might add "to the newly conquered and converted Baltic peoples" as well. In this, Baltic crusaders are partaking of an old Christian approach, albeit with the added factor of military violence. Noting the "spiritual importance of the Levant," Nicholas Edward Morton provides the linkage of spirituality and warfare by citing the Teutonic Order's directive that, after the 1271 fall of the key castle of Montfort in Palestine, "they build a castle on the borders of Kulm and Pomerania . . . calling it Starkenburg that is called Montfort in Latin."[38] It would not only be Christian shrines that would be duplicated along the Baltic, but military structures as well. Realizing the enduring spiritual appeal and importance of the Holy Land, there would be an undercutting of Palestine's significance when the Baltic lands are viewed as an equivalent. While the proliferation of structures modeled on *loca sanctorum* in Jerusalem might seem only to enlarge the impact of the Holy Land for Baltic *peregrini*, we may also choose to look at this mimesis from an alternative angle. Have we focused too much on these models as copies of Holy Land sites and not enough on how these models elevated their new locations spiritually? As crusaders copied

FIGURE 7 *Church of the True Cross, Segovia, ground view. As Segovia was near the reconquest line between Christian and Muslim territory, this church is an example of the tendency to erect holy sites along the contested borders of Christendom. (Photo by the author)*

the Holy Land they blurred the lines of distinction and significance between the two, with a replication of sites both holy and military.

This consecration of formerly pagan locations has a long history in the Christian West. Gregory the Great, pope from 590 to 604, is famous for instructing his successful missionary team in the Anglo-Saxon kingdom of Kent to create new Christian sites of worship out of formerly pagan cult centers, concluding that

> the temples of the idols among the people should on no account be destroyed. The idols are to be destroyed, but the temples themselves are to be aspersed with holy water, altars set up in them, and relics deposited there.[39]

While it is a different undertaking to cleanse a pagan temple to make it suitable for Christian use and to construct new holy sites for pilgrims, the notion exists that pagan locations can be reclaimed and that the creation of a new worship site would not be an unheard of idea by the era of the Baltic Crusades.

Christianity, unlike some pagan religions, has been independent of specific physical sites for its doctrinal beliefs, but it has "always had a sacred geography of its own with a variety of holy places" for the practice of these doctrines.[40] Therefore, pilgrimage sites were frequently made during the Middle Ages as events and the discovery of holy remains dictated. A good example is St. James, whose tomb was discovered in northwestern Spain at Compostela (perhaps derived from *campus stellae*, "field of stars") after he had miraculously ridden out of the sea on a white charger to aid the Christian victory over the Moors at Clavijo in 844.[41] Regardless of the authenticity of the battle and James' participation, the tomb became an early success as a pilgrimage destination, a fact validated by the conquering Muslim emir Al-Manzor who made the conquest of Compostela a prime objective in his 997 push into northern Spain. Another, perhaps better known, example is tied to the political give-and-take of the twelfth century: the tomb of the martyred Archbishop of Canterbury, Thomas á Becket. Becket was murdered within the supposedly sacrosanct walls of Canterbury Cathedral in late December 1170 due to his opposition to King Henry II. His grave became an immediate pilgrimage site of great popularity as Geoffrey Chaucer's fourteenth-century literary masterpiece, *The Canterbury Tales*, attests. All in all, while many may believe that place pilgrimage was always the only type available, the creating of new places for pilgrimage continued apace. Therefore, the Baltic crusaders who were creating new *loca sanctorum* in formerly pagan lands would not be doing the unthinkable.

It is now time to apply these new insights on the sacralization of formerly pagan sites to the notion of what constituted crusading *peregrini* in the Baltic context. If there were no traditional pilgrimage sites available, and the pilgrims created their own replicas of *loca sanctorum* while on crusade, did the act of creating these holy sites become the new essence of this pilgrimage? If that is true, how can this new model be categorized? It can only be place pilgrimage upon the completion of the campaign and the construction of the holy site replicas, not at the beginning of the "pilgrimage." Yet it cannot be classified as a revivified version of life pilgrimage, the *peregrinatio pro amore Christo* of old Irish provenance, in that the crusaders fully expected, barring the lethal vagaries of war, to return from their *reisens*, or yearly crusading journeys. In fact, the "pilgrim's year" was developed exactly to delimit the duration of these crusading commitments; to put a time constraint on the military service to Christ and the besieged Christian outposts that this type of missionary war was designed to protect.

Place and life pilgrimage are often concentric in their actual application. Both take the pilgrim to a place, although for the life pilgrim it will be unknown at the outset and may change over time according to God's will. Both place and life pilgrimages are task-oriented pilgrimages as well, the first episodic and the second a permanent continuation. The various forms intersect much like a Venn diagram and yet in specific situations one can clearly label them as separate. The Baltic *peregrini* are place pilgrims in that they are actually creating *loca sanctorum* that may then stand as pilgrimage sites for themselves as well as future travelers. In this instance the task of conquering and consecrating pagan lands becomes the overriding feature of crusading pilgrimage along the Baltic. Yet the act of creating pilgrimage sites tends to move the concept more toward the life pilgrimage model in that the emphasis is not on the journey alone, but on the activities that compose it.

Is it then accurate to classify the Baltic *peregrinatio* as a "task pilgrimage"? Such a category is difficult to pin down. All pilgrimages are to some degree task pilgrimages, from the task of traveling to and returning from a holy place or the life pilgrimage idea of living one's life day by day at the direction of God. But the Baltic *peregrini* model provides a subtle shift from doing to being. These pilgrims are indeed traveling on a spiritual journey, although that is often hard to discern amid the red haze of war, and even creating their own holy places as a by-product task of their swordplay. The actual pilgrimage, however, is more a state of being crusaders than simply executing an armed holy itinerary. In this they are hearkening back to a portion of the Celtic-style heritage. Like Columbanus, they are on a roadway of their own, and God's, making with no fixed destination apart from what they can create in view.

The major difference, of course, is that these Baltic *peregrini*, unlike their Celtic predecessors, are not on this pilgrimage for life, but only for a crusading season. However short the armed pilgrimage for these pilgrims, lacking a holy destination, it is their warmaking that validates any spiritual benefits they may attain. War has thus moved from an enabling method for pilgrimage to holy places to a role as the action that produces spiritual rewards. Perhaps that is why the bulk of the leadership, and even in most cases the rank and file, of the Baltic crusading forces were so often comprised of members of the military orders such as the Swordbrothers and later the Teutonic Knights. Bernard of Clairvaux, so instrumental in the beginning of what would develop into the Baltic Crusades, had argued at the Council of Troyes, and later penned in his *De laude novae militiae*, a defense of the union of warfare and spirituality that these monk-warriors represented.[42] Warfare had moved from an aid to spirituality to a spiritual act in and of itself and through the physical erection of churches modeled on Holy Land sites, a lasting imprint of this remained even as the *peregrini* moved on.

In this the Baltic pilgrims are well connected to the Christian past. Aside from arguments about the condign punishments of apostates, owing to the checkered relationship of the Slavic and Baltic peoples with earlier Christian missionaries, when entering and conquering previously non-Christianized lands and peoples these crusading pilgrims were not merely doing *dilatatio Christianitas* in the normative sense. While they were certainly expanding Christendom by regaining lost bishoprics, their pilgrimage was not solely an act of reclamation, but establishment. The copies of Jerusalem churches they left as new *loca sanctorum* were akin to the traditional growth of Christian territorialism most obviously manifested in the growth of the cult of the saints. It is instructive to note that the same word used to describe the tomb of St. Martin at Tours, *condita,* or "founding," was the same word traditionally used to describe the establishment of the city of Rome. After his death, Martin was, as Peter Brown has reminded us, fully at Tours as well as fully in the hand of God, *Cuius anima in manu Dei est, sed hic totus est,*[43] a duality of presence that is very much like the foundations of replicas of the Church of the Holy Sepulchre throughout the Baltic lands. If Christianity had the tradition of this simultaneous presence then "our Jerusalem" makes sense. And the spreading establishment of oratories, once dedicated to these "fully here" saints and now in the Baltic to a sacred Jerusalem church, represents a continuation of expansive sacralization of newly won territory.

Baltic *peregrini* were pilgrims not because they were going to a holy place but because they were fighting and thus creating holy places. Their warmaking, not their destination, certified their status. This seems only a logical extension of the standard crusade premise of the interrelation of warfare and pilgrimage but can increase greatly the elasticity of the application. If warfare can create holy places as instant pilgrimage sites, then where could it not? This might explain why the replica churches appear along the contested fringes of Christendom far from the Baltic, whether on the Muslim-Christian frontier in Spain or on the eastern march in what would be Austria. The conquest and consecration of pagan shrines and territories, done at the point of a sword and lance, created new, sufficiently holy, *loca sanctorum*. The act of crusading and the subsequent sacralization of new, once pagan sites therefore constituted a form of task pilgrimage, but with a significant alteration in the understood concept of pilgrimage.

How then are we to classify the "problem" of the Baltic *peregrini?* They do not fit readily into accepted models of pilgrimage, yet the growing body of research on the Christian sacralization of the landscape offers a useful clue to their status. Further complicating their classification is the fact that fresh waves of Baltic *peregrini* would not be on pilgrimage to a newly-founded "Jerusalem church," say, in Schleswig on the western rim of the Baltic, but would always be pushing eastward into unconsecrated territory. The practice created an ever-expanding arc of Christian shrines suitable for visitation by other, later pilgrims. But the crusading, advancing *peregrini* who earlier established them while on the march would have moved on, pushing the frontier even deeper into pagan territory. Baltic *peregrini* seem novel to those who do not take the backward glance at the prehistory of pilgrimage. There one finds a paleo-phase in early place pilgrimage, a meso-phase in the Celtic option of *peregrinatio pro amore Christo*, and a neo-phase that altered pilgrimage again via the union of warfare with that penitential rite. The process was dependent on the expansive acquisition of territorial control as much as on the gaining of an enhanced spiritual status. As the practice played out, the question of who governed these newly won lands rose in importance and led to unseemly conflict between Christian coreligionists.

Questions for discussion

Has Christian pilgrimage always been a matter of journeying to a holy site?

Why did the crusading objectives of recovering formerly Christian sites present a problem for the Baltic Crusades?

How did the Baltic Crusades alter the nature of pilgrimage?

Was Baltic crusading pilgrimage a form of life pilgrimage, task pilgrimage, or something new?

Why was the Church of the Holy Sepulchre imitated in the Baltic lands?

How did the focus on holy places play into the notion of territorial conquest in the Baltic Crusades?

How did this territorialism feed into taxation and tithing requirements?

9

Christian on Christian violence

In 1225, a contingent of German crusaders from Odenpah entered the province of Wierland and "expelled the Danes, saying that this land had first been made subject to the Christian faith by the Livonians with the banner of the Blessed Virgin."[1] This touched off a chain reaction that included the sending of a papal legate, William of Modena, to negotiate a peaceful resolution in this dispute between two Christian parties. When the shaky ceasefire was broken in 1227, the papal legate's trustee, styled Master John, assigned to govern the disputed territories (Wierland, Jerwan, and Rotalia) launched a punitive campaign against the offending Danes. As they had plundered Rotalia, they were tracked down, suffering fifty dead, and penned up in the stronghold of Maianpathe. After three days of siege, the crusaders "had mercy upon them because they were Christians and sent them away."[2] The papal legate then dispatched a sizable force of Germans to fight "against the savagery ... of the Danes."[3] The denouement was that the crusaders decided to make peace with the Danes in order to "be better able to fight against" the neighboring pagans.[4]

To the reader of the Baltic Crusade chronicles, accustomed to following the saga of Christian versus pagan missionary war, the account of Christian on Christian violence is jarring. Yet is it not unique. Relations between the crusaders and their Russian neighbors deteriorated to the point that Henry's *Livonian Chronicle* ominously observed that "a big war with the Russians was threatening" in 1216,[5] and the anonymous poet of the *Livonian Rhymed Chronicle* accused these Orthodox coreligionists of wanting "to obstruct Christianity just as before, and their godlessness caused much harm."[6] In 1240, a Christian army "went happily into Russia" and took a castle by storm letting "not a single Russian escape, killing or capturing all the defenders"[7] The Danes fared no better, as we have already seen. Both Christian opponents, the Russians and Danes, were routinely identified in the sources as "enemies of God."[8] As the crusaders pushed ever eastward, the incidence of combat encounters against Danish and Russian coreligionists seemed to increase in both intensity and number. Since these same chronicles describe missionary war as being necessary to defend Christian fellowships from pagan attacks, how are we to respond to the many times these wars are used to defend against other Christian, rather than pagan, forces?

It was not always so in the Baltic Crusades. Early on in the enterprise, the Christian missionaries and even the armed crusaders had a good relationship with both the Danes and the Russians. When Bishop Meinhard sought to extend his missionary efforts in Livonia around 1184, he asked permission of King Vladimir of Polozk, the nearby Russian lord, "to whom the Livonians, while still pagan, paid tribute."[9] Permission was granted. Perhaps the cordiality was based on the mistaken belief that the new converts would simply add to Vladimir's control, but the fact remains that he did nothing to impede the missionary efforts. In 1199, after a rocky and violent start to the Livonian mission, the newly consecrated bishop Albert of Buxhövden successfully recruited some 500 crusaders in Gothland and, "Afterwards, crossing through Denmark (*per Daciam transiens*), he received gifts from King Canute, Duke Waldemar, and Archbishop Absolon."[10] Seven years later, a "great army" that the Danish king had mustered to help "take vengeance on the pagans and subject the nations to the Christian faith" came to the crusader stronghold of Riga and were received "most devotedly" by all there.[11] Additionally, King Valdemar of Denmark has been called a "crusading king" by modern scholars due to his success in conquering the cultic citadel of Arkona on the island of Rügen in 1168. The later bitter enemies were co-laborers in the early days of the Baltic campaigns.

What are the reasons for this reversal? Why did co-laborers transform into deadly antagonists? The conflict between these co-religionists may not lie fully with religion. William L. Urban has done an excellent job of placing the issue in a geopolitical context. He believes "the situation reflected the greater conflict among the foremost members of the ruling dynasty in Russia" and sees the Danes "entering the competition, coming to make good their claims on Estonia."[12] This is a necessary evaluation of the give-and-take of politics once Russians, Danes, and even Swedes had become opponents of the crusaders. The question for us is how they became opponents in the first place. What were the points of conflict that could be so serious as to lead to war? And, what were the antecedents for this in earlier medieval history? The chronicles of the Baltic Crusades offer at least three possible points of conflict that ripened into outright war between Christian coreligionists.

The first appears in Henry's *Livonian Chronicle* and concerns a misunderstanding that derived from jealously and falsehood. This might be expected in an age based more on the personalization of government rather than the existence of abstract states. Personal relationships are fragile and fickle things by definition, all the more so when masquerading as government policy. The issue at hand was a prize warhorse given as a gift by Bishop Albert of Buxhövden to King Vladimir of Polozk in 1206. The gift was, in true medieval fashion, to cement good relations between the two as had been enjoyed by Albert's predecessor, the aforementioned Bishop Meinhard who had asked and received permission to evangelize among Vladimir's pagan subjects.[13] However, the plan was foiled when the Livonians promptly stole the horse and told the Russian lord that Albert had insulted him. Instead of the issue resolving in an act of confession or verbal confrontation, it was productive of war. Ironically, a future opponent of the German crusaders, the Danes, came to their aid and helped defeat the Russians. Today's friend is tomorrow's enemy, yet there must be more than an occasional hurt feeling and the misunderstanding it produced to rotate the kaleidoscopic political reconfigurations that existed in the Baltic Crusades. Duplicity can be smoothed over and one wonders if the incident were more of a pretext than an actual cause.

Another reason put forward by the chroniclers, especially Henry, is that there were practical differences in the two parties that involved the interplay of religion and government. The matter of baptism was central in this disagreement. Henry tells us of an argument between the Russian king of Polozk and Bishop Albert in 1212, concerning the ongoing baptisms in Livonia.

> The king maintained that the Livonians were his servants and that it was in his power to baptize them or to leave them

unbaptized. It is, indeed, the custom of the Russian kings not to subject whatever people they defeat to the Christian faith, but rather to force them to pay tribute and money to themselves. The bishop, however, thought one should obey God rather than men, the heavenly King rather than an earthly king. . . . He steadfastly affirmed, therefore, that he would not quit what he had begun.[14]

Henry seems oblivious to the hypocritical nature of his complaint. The German crusaders were every bit as keen to mulct payments from their conquered and baptized peoples. But once baptized, the payments were sanctified as tithes rather than simple extortions.

The Russians apparently chose not to baptize their pagan subjects thereby avoiding much trouble with lightly baptized people washing off their baptism. This reluctance to baptize first and instruct later was one of the lines of discord that developed in the earlier Middle Ages and led up to the rupture between Catholic and Orthodox communions that hit critical mass in 1054. The differences were illustrated by the Orthodox Church's treatment of the Serbs. Describing something politically like the conversion model called "adhesion," Jonathan Harris discusses a Byzantine-Serb treaty from 874.

> The main terms of the treaty were that the Serbs would accept Christianity from missionaries sent from Constantinople and consider themselves to be under the authority of the Byzantine Emperor. They would, however, continue to be ruled by their own princes. Recognition of the Byzantine Emperor's theoretical claim was enough: no attempt was made to annex the lands of the Serbs.[15]

There was no baptism by treaty, only a political affiliation that allowed Orthodox Christian missionaries to work, and presumably baptize the peoples as they were instructed. The Russian lords of Polozk, Pskov, and Gerzika used this model with the Balts, preferring hegemony over them and their satellite rulers. Later in the Baltic Crusades, the Saxons would use the baptism by treaty model that was the instrument of their inclusion in the faith and the Russians the Byzantine model that was used in their religious past. Different prehistories brought about contemporary conflict.

The crusaders seem to have seen the baptism of pagan peoples as more of a governmental incorporation than a matter of personal salvation. Therefore the reluctance, or refusal, of the Russians to baptize their subject peoples was seen as a failure on their part to expand the church. More ominously, it further meant that since these people were not baptized by the Russians, they could be washed in the font by the crusaders and thus made part of the Livonian church. This had the effect of creating a collision course between German and Russian Christians over territorial control. The German crusaders saw an asymmetry when the population had one faith, but another master. Concerning the Russians, the issue was a sacramental and theological one with strong overtones of political power. They viewed baptism as an inward regeneration. They had no counterpart to Augustine's interpretation of original sin that required baptism for infants. It appears that as "for the East, it is the effects of the fall that are inherited, not original guilt." Taking this position meant "the Eastern churches had a more ambiguous approach to the problem of babies dying without baptism."[16] But this is equally an issue for pagan adults. As there was not a pressing need to baptize babies to prevent damnation, there was no pressing need to baptize incorporated pagan peoples. The German crusaders saw this as a failure of the Christian mission, while the Russians saw it as allowing time for proper instruction to precede the baptismal rite. The Western perspective that informs this work, as in so many others, focuses on the activities of the German crusaders as they pushed eastward. This is undeniably correct, but we must be careful not to overlook the rather piecemeal push westward by the Russians in behalf of Orthodox Christianity. The local Russian lords, styled "kings" in the sources, were a countervailing force of significance. Because the Russians were not as unified, they are ignored—a forgotten, demi-crusade—yet from the ground level view of our Baltic crusaders, the Russians were a continuing counterpoint to their crusading efforts.

However, this issue of baptism does not explain fully the quarrel that the crusaders had with their non-Orthodox opponents, the Danes. Danish churchmen were fully in favor of baptizing all those they subdued in war, as were the crusading priests. This created a fierce competition for the souls and soil of the Baltic peoples. In 1220, the inhabitants of Wierland, believing "the Christians had one God, both for the Danes and the Germans, and one faith and one baptism," innocently accepted Danish baptism. The crusaders of Riga "held that Wierland was theirs, since it had been subjected to the Christian faith by their men" and responded with an onslaught of baptizing priests to undercut the Danes.[17] This led, inevitably, to an encounter between some now-Christian Lettish priests, representing the crusaders, who offered baptism to the inhabitants of a village called Reinewer. The villagers replied that they had already been baptized by the Danes and said, "Since we have been baptized once, we will not receive it again." The confounded Lettish priests simply "smiled a bit and, shaking the dust from their feet at them, they hurried to the other villages."[18] Lest one think this is a simple matter of competition for parishioners, it must be noted that the Danish-Rigan dispute turned violent and remained so. A man named Tabelin, who was apparently a leader in the small province of Purdiviru, got caught up in this rivalry. Accepting baptism from the Rigan crusaders and sending his son as a diplomatic hostage to the Swordbrothers deeply offended the Danes when they annexed his province. They hanged Tabelin shortly after 1220.[19] It got so bad that the understandably confused natives wondered if the Christian faith was as changeable as the political situation in their land. When, in 1221, Esthonia and Livonia fell under Danish hegemony, Christian Letts and Livonians protested their re-assignment, saying "that hitherto they had fought the Lord's battle against the pagans for the honor of our Lord Jesus Christ and His beloved Mother, not for the honor of the king of Denmark."[20] But the issue here was not so much about the sacrament as the control that sacrament conferred. This inevitably brought matters of revenue and lordship into play. The *dilatatio Christianitas* was a fervent heavenly goal, but also an earthly territorial one with all the rights and privileges that accompanied it. The traditional existence of the *adelskirche*, or "church of the nobility," so much in vogue in the Christianization of earlier pagan peoples assisted in this territorial obsession. Since aristocracy is land based, and kingship is by nature territorial, the association of religion with specific land boundaries is virtually unavoidable. Christianity can be, after all, a religion of a specific place, as the Jerusalem focused Crusades testify. The places available in the Baltic for religious and territorial control would become hotly contested prizes.

The nature of these prizes could vary from the particular to the general. In 1212, a dispute between the Swordbrothers and the now

FIGURE 8 *Moat at Marienburg Castle, Malbork, Poland. This fortress, largely completed by 1300, was the redoubt of the Teutonic Knights as they pushed ever eastward along the Baltic. Built of brick, it is arguably the largest castle in the world and was the nerve center of the Knights' monastic quasi-state. (Photo by the author)*

Christian Letts rose to the level of warfare that "wounded" several participants. The issue at stake was the disposition of "bee trees," apparently a reference to the valuable beehives of the territory. When the Letts received a ruling not to their liking, a war broke out. Finally, after multiple attacks on each side's fortifications, a settlement was brokered by Bishop Albert of Buxhövden that restored the bee trees to the Letts but permitted the Swordbrothers to keep some of the adjacent fields.[21] Christian on Christian violence even among coreligionists often turned on the issue of land, wealth, and territorial control. In a larger sense, the ongoing dispute about the division of conquered lands between the Bishop Albert and his own creation, the Swordbrothers, puts territorial control in the forefront of the story. They "vehemently begged the bishop for a third part of all Livonia" since their numbers were growing and their role in this missionary war was expanding, "so ought their possessions and goods increase." Bishop Albert, wishing to mollify his men, granted them a third of all Livonia "since he had received Livonia from the emperor with every right of lordship and law," also wisely acknowledging that he could not divide any "lands not yet acquired or converted."[22] As reasonable as this sounds, in practical terms it meant that as the Crusade progressed geographically there would be continuing strife among even the crusading forces as to the disposition of each new conquest. Thus in 1209, the newly reconquered fort at Kokenhusen was divided by the bishop among the Swordbrothers and a nobleman named Rudolph of Jerichow, and fifteen years later Esthonia was divided similarly.[23] The proprietary and almost cavalier way entire provinces as well as specific valuable agricultural properties were parceled out provides great support for the notion that the Baltic Crusades were nothing more than lightly baptized land grabs.

A third reason presented in the sources, and one closely intertwined with the second, was the issue of heresy. As we have seen, the issue of heresy is an elusive one to pin down. At what point does a difference in doctrine rise to the level of a rejection of the whole? The pagans washing their baptism away in the river were apostates, walking away from Christianity to another system of belief that was entirely different. This clearly rose to the level of apostasy. But fellow Christians, if perceived to hold widespread deviancy from orthodoxy, are heretics who deserve the same condemnation and punishment as apostates. Perhaps the punishment necessary should be even more severe in that their behavior undermines the true way of the faith. It is no accident that crusaders loved the scriptural passage found in the Gospel of John 14:6, where Jesus is made to say: "I am the way, the truth, and the life. No one comes to the Father except by me."[24] The exclusivity of the claim can be interpreted to require strict adherence to even the most delicate and nuanced forms of theological interpretation.

During the heyday of the Baltic Crusades, the Western church was more and more given to this point of view. Innocent III, pope from 1198 to 1216, who was repeatedly instrumental in authorizing and expanding the Baltic enterprise, is also noted in history as the pope who pushed for crusading within Europe against heretics. Is it coincidence that his pontificate covers the period of transition from Danes and Russians as colleagues to enemies along the Baltic? That the issue of was great importance to this pope is attested by the *Gesta Innocentii III*, or *Deeds of Pope Innocent III*, an account of a portion of his reign dating from 1204 to 1209 AD. The anonymous author dedicated 151 out of a total of 265 pages to the topic of "Crusade and Church Unity."[25] Typical of the pope's approach, framed in the wake of the devastating Fourth Crusade (1202–04), was his admonition to the emperor in Constantinople to "lead the Greek church back to the obedience of the Apostolic See, its mother, from whose *magisterium* it had withdrawn, persevering for a long time in its contumacy."[26] The goal was obedience and unity of doctrine, as Innocent sought to purify the church universal from "contumacy" as well as improper doctrine.[27] Christopher Tyerman has wisely observed that "heresy became reform's inescapable companion" as key issues of faith, observance, and authority were worked out. The age of reform was "also its great age of heresy."[28]

Conflict with aberrant Christian communions was therefore all in the air during the thirteenth-century Baltic Crusade era. Compounding the problem and providing a bridge between the punishment of heretics and crusading proper was the tradition of seeing Islam as an aberrant form of the faith rather than an entirely new religion. Richard Fletcher has noticed that in the early Middle Ages, "the very thought" of seeing Islam as a new religion was "probably unthinkable to contemporary Christians." It was seen as "a particularly dangerous heresy."[29] Thus it was that papal decrees of ninth-century popes providing "an heavenly reward" for those dying in defense of the faith used the term *pagani* indiscriminately for Muslim and non-Christian foes alike.[30] Since the Muslims were regarded as a type of heretic, as were the Russian opponents along the Baltic, it may be fair to say that crusading against heretics was congenial for the idea of the crusade.

The peculiar sight of Christians warring against Christians in a missionary war also produced several practical problems. It brought about a collision of at least two strands of missionary war development: the baptism by treaty model and the punishment of apostates. Even when a pagan leader did not apostasize, there would be the sense that their baptism foreclosed further territorial gains. When the pagan Lithuanian king Jogaila was baptized and wed into the Christian Polish royal house in 1386, the Teutonic Knights protested loudly that the baptism was false. Their reasoning, as with so much in the Baltic Crusades, was twofold, both theological and material: first, they knew Lithuanian kings had been baptized before and then lost the faith. Mindaugas, the first king of Lithuania (r. 1253–63 AD), had been baptized, apparently at the urging of his wife, Martha, or Morta, in 1251/52, only to apostasize later. After his assassination in 1263, his son, Woischleg, remained Christian,[31] but it became common for Lithuanian kings to use baptism as a bargaining chip in political and territorial negotiations.[32] However, the Knights' complaint contradicted their baptism by treaty model in that they found themselves warring against a baptized Christian king under the assumption that his baptism was invalid. Of course, the secondary, although probably more essential, goal for the Teutonic Knights was the continuation of their conquests and the expansion of their growing state. The theological matter of baptismal renunciation provided useful and legitimate cover for their flagrant territorial desires. It also provided a rationalization for war.

There is one more issue in the Christian on Christian conflicts of the Baltic Crusades that was treated only lightly by the sources, yet made to bear great weight in most modern analyses: the financial gain accruing to territorial control. The territorial acquisitions among the crusading forces have produced the most trenchant criticism of the Baltic Crusades. The standard approach is to condemn the Crusades not only for their internecine squabbling over land and even bee trees, but also for their avid mulcting of the natives via required payments. Much of the discussion revolves around the tithe, which was payable upon conversion to the Christian faith. These payments, a type of theological tax, were the *zehnte* and the *zins*. William Urban has determined that the *zehnte* was twice the amount of the *zins* and was punitive in that it was applied only to tribes who had rebelled or been untrustworthy in the past. He calculates that the average *zins* would amount to some three to six bushels of produce per farm.[33] Many modern scholars view this as a trigger point in pagan-Christian relations as well as a *casus belli* for war between ostensibly Christian forces. Marcia Colish credits the "heavy and unanticipated fiscal demands" of the tithe as "leading to (the Livonians') revolt" and believes Bishop Meinhard "imposed heavy fiscal demands and forced labor for the upkeep of the fortress" at Uexküll.[34] The imposition of a tithe, whether punitive as with the *zehnte*, or normative as with the *zins*, forms much of the basis for condemning the crusaders as rapacious conquerors. This line of reasoning is based largely on the behavior of William of Modena, the papal legate who arrived in Livonia in 1225 with a full complement of pilgrim crusaders. Henry includes several of

William's preaching points as he visited the mission stations in this newly won land. But the complaint most often featured by the *Livonian Chronicle* is that the Swordbrothers were exacting too much in the way of payment from their new converts. On at least four occasions cited in Henry's *Chronicle*, William admonished the crusading knights to treat their Esthonian, Livonian, and Lettish subjects fairly, focusing especially on the tithe.

> He always took special care to warn the Brothers of the Militia and the other Germans in other provinces that they should teach the Christian faith to the Livonians and Letts and other converts . . . and that they should be sparing toward them, both in the matter of tithes and in everything, lest if too heavily burdened they should return to infidelity.[35]

It would seem that the crusaders squeezed the hapless natives dry. While this tendency to over-tax may well be true, there was precedent for the pagan peoples to pay a yearly tribute to their gods. The offense of the crusading churchmen may have been one of degree rather than novelty. As with most taxation systems, it could be subject to overreach. Thus, the problem with this narrative is its incompleteness. While we have no reason to doubt Henry's account of the papal legate, it gives the impression that the payment of religious duty was unknown in the Baltic until inflicted on the victim population by the crusaders. This is not the case. Pagans in the Baltic were accustomed to a temple tax for their gods. Noting that there was an ostentatious display of wealth in the pagan temples, much like the scene in larger Christian churches of the day, Richard Fletcher believes, "This wealth came in part from voluntary offerings to their gods. However, at Szczecin (Stettin) it also came from a sort of tax . . . it was customary for the worshippers of Triglaus to offer him a tenth of the spoils of war."[36] Likewise, Helmold of Bosau recorded that a type of statutory tax was sent every year from all the provinces of the Slavs to the shrine of the great god Svantovit at Arkona on the island of Rügen. And the late twelfth-century Danish historian, Saxo Grammaticus, reported that "a coin was paid annually by every man and woman as a contribution to the worship" of Svantovit's image.[37]

The payment of religious fees was known in the Baltic, but the real sticking point might be the change in masters rather than the actual sum required. There is also a change in purpose. The wealth presented to Svantovit or Redigast or any of the pantheon of pagan deities in the Baltic world was to ensure good harvests, victory in war, and the like. Little, if any, circulated back to the people. The view that the tithes collected were used to fatten the coffers and the waistlines of the Christian clergy is spurious and forms part of that caricature mentioned earlier of the corpulent missionary bishop "dabbing the meat juice" from his mouth. It may strike many as excess that tithes were used in part to arm military orders such as the Swordbrothers, and it may be unseemly that some clerics did in fact live much better than their parishoners. But Christian monies were also used for the upkeep of the poor and vulnerable as well as to provide a suitably impressive worship site to compete with the now displaced pagan shrines. The caricature may be only true in part. The reality may lie somewhere between material gain for the crusaders and material support for their new fellow Christians.

These are the problems of the Christian on Christian violence of the Baltic Crusades, nuanced much more than expected. But they are not novel. There is a prehistory to these issues that is not unique to the Baltic.

First, let us examine the issue of warfare among Christians. Carl Erdmann believed that following the early medieval victory in the West of Trinitarian Christianity over Arianism there were not serious Christian on Christian issues until the emergence of a spate of heresies in the eleventh century and thereafter, concluding that "in the interval the idea of war against heretics was irrelevant."[38] The lurid particulars of the Cathar heresy in the thirteenth and fourteenth century, that triggered Pope Innocent III's expansion of crusading into ostensibly Christian lands, tend to overshadow previously experienced conflicts. This view depends on a larger geopolitical perspective that credits the barbarian successor kingdoms, many were Arian, with supplying the *casus belli* of intra-Christian violence. While this is true, it is also incomplete. There were many conflicts between Christian polities quite apart from the theological issue of Arianism. As some of these were simply depredations, the general classification for Christian on Christian violence was civil war.

St. Patrick, in one of his few surviving written records, complained bitterly about the brutal depredations visited on his new flock in

Ireland. These were inflicted by a putatively Christian king from western Britain named Coroticus. Patrick wrote to Coroticus and his soldiers calling them "fellow-citizens of the demons, because of their evil actions" and declaring that they "live in death, as allies of . . . apostates." They were "blood-thirsty men . . . bloody with the blood of innocent Christians." When the appeal for the restoration of the enslaved survivors was received by Coroticus, it was greeted with "roars of laughter."[39] A vicious raid like this may well be only a manifestation of an unvarnished lust to dominate, or *libido dominandi,* that Augustine condemned. Such behavior occurs throughout the medieval West and was on display in the Wendish Crusade of 1147 when the Christian crusaders besieged the Christian city of Stettin (Szczecin), only stopping when the citizens displayed Christian insignia on their walls.[40]

The more common example of Christian on Christian violence during the meso- and neo-prehistory period of this phenomenon was straightforward civil war. The *Ten Books of History* by Gregory of Tours is replete with wars fought between rival Christian Frankish kings. This triggered a furious rebuke by the bishop-historian in the preface to Book Five of his work. The same situation applied in Visigothic Spain, after it moved to Trinitarianism away from Arianism, all the way through to its conquest by the Arabs in the early eighth century. One of the weakening factors in the Visigothic defense against the Muslim invaders was a civil war between King Roderick and a pretender named Paul. But the dispute about theology, as featured in the Arian-Trinitarian conflicts, was not the only issue driving Christian on Christian violence in the centuries leading up to the Baltic Crusades. These nontheological encounters were frequently labeled as civil wars.

Conflict between ostensibly Christian forces has a long, and disapproved, history in the West. It seems also to be one of the points stressed by Pope Urban II at Clermont in his call for the First Crusade. While there are several accounts of his famous speech, each written down several years and much potential memory erosion later, all stress his plea that Christian on Christian violence must cease. Fulcher of Chartres gives perhaps the most complete rendering of the idea when he makes Urban say, "Let those who are accustomed to wage private wars wastefully even against Believers, go forth against the Infidels in a battle worthy to be undertaken now and to be finished in victory."[41]

That this was no quirk of Fulcher's is attested by Baldric of Dol's account that has the pope warning his hearers that they "should shudder . . . at raising a violent hand against Christians," with the proviso that "it is less wicked to brandish your sword against Saracens,"[42] while Robert the Monk remembered Urban admonishing the assembled knights to "let your hatred and quarrels cease, your civil wars come to an end."[43] Apparently the pope included somewhere in his address the productive notion that Christians should cease destroying Europe with their internecine wars and redirect their martial efforts to the East.

This, too, has its own prehistory. Writing in the 580s, the bishop-historian Gregory of Tours sounded a note eerily predictive of the crusading call at Clermont. Addressing the fratricidal Merovingian descendants of Clovis, he opens his preface to Book V of his *Histories* with a sigh of frustrated sadness: "It gives me no pleasure to write of all the different civil wars (*bellum civile*) which afflicted the Frankish people and their rulers."[44] After a long account of the destructive nature of such conflicts, Gregory concludes:

> Beware, then, of discord, beware of civil wars, which are destroying you and your people. As things are, what else can you look forward to, except that your army will be beaten and that you yourselves will be left without support and will fall into ruin, conquered by enemy peoples.[45]

While one might argue that Gregory is condemning political civil discord, the religious nature of the issue is at the forefront. It is the other end of the spectrum from the mandate given by Avitus of Vienne to Clovis to use his military might to expand the faith. Christian king fighting Christian king does not accomplish this. Neither does, in the Baltic context, crusader forces fighting other crusader forces or even rival Christian creedal communities such as the Danes or the Russians.

The proliferation of apostasy only clouded the issue further. The outcome of missionary war in the Baltic created much the same result as the earlier efforts against pagans. J. M. Wallace-Hadrill summed it up in his evaluation of "the making of the German Church" by judging that "the essence of the whole story was this: the initial missionary field turned out to be a demi-world of lapsed Christians, lost communities practicing what had survived of Christian cultures in isolation."[46] This description is reminiscent of the situation following the great late Roman persecutions that led to Vincent of Lerins' penning his *Commonitorium*; a manifesto designed to establish true doctrine and practice.[47] Faith communities in isolation, tend to diverge from orthodoxy, particularly if there is a strong current of syncretism present. Therefore, Wallace-Hadrill's judgment may be even more accurately applied to the Baltic experience than to Merovingian or Carolingian missionary wars. The use of the baptism by treaty formula virtually guaranteed mass apostasy requiring the repeated administration of the "ministry of shields and swords."

These instant apostates could not be allowed to coexist, nor could competing versions of the Christian church. Neither recalcitrant pagans washing off baptism nor Russian Orthodox at odds with Rome would avoid punitive campaigns at the hands of the crusaders. As Henry's *Livonian Chronicle* reports the pagan belief that only unanimity of religious practice can ensure "true peace," differences in practice, whether blatant rejection or alternate theological and liturgical understandings, cannot produce amity among the two camps. Why might that be? Cannot a peaceful coexistence govern the relationship between these antagonists? We have already seen how Philip W. Gray, examining Augustine's use of *per molestias eruditio*, or "teaching by inconveniences," describes a rationale that, while not necessarily pertinent for all points of conflict between Christians, may describe the Baltic situation: schismatics prevent peace in the heavenly city and thus forestall any attempts at earthly peace.[48] The inconvenient *molestias* that the Baltic crusaders applied to obtain the unity that would provide peace was war itself.

Yet when all the battles had been fought, the women and children taken as spoils of war, and the defeated duly baptized, one question remained: What kind of government, political and ecclesiastical would be in place? The end result of baptism by treaty is not an answer to hostilities but a transfer of problems to another level, that of territorial control. Thus this use of war between Christian forces inevitably revolved around the control of territory, and that territorial control depended on the notion of frontier. While we are accustomed to linear frontiers complete with passport control, monetary exchange, and the like, the situation was different in the Middle Ages. In recent years, scholars have increasingly turned their attention to the existence and nature of borders and frontiers for the ancient and medieval worlds.[49] Much of the analysis has concerned the question of what constitutes a frontier. This issue would be of paramount importance when defeating and incorporating tribes of pagans. What were the reaches of their territory? How may one establish a line of demarcation between the newly Christianized tribes and those beyond? Ian Wood notes that "frontiers are essentially matters of perception," and describes the relationship of missionary war with frontiers: "On the whole it was not the pagans they met that alarmed the missionaries, even when they threatened their missionary achievements, but the peoples who lived beyond the horizon."[50] The looming presence of hostile people groups beyond the horizon of these newly converted and incorporated territories ensured that the edge of this "edge crusade" would remain elastic. Establishing this "horizon" more often than not also meant that territorial boundaries were hardened.

As modern opinion is that a frontier, perhaps often seen as a barrier, was more of a connective—a permeable zone of cultural exchange—there is a double effect to this linear demarcation and the almost intangible cultural flow over the line. Of course, the Roman word for frontier, *limes*, does originate in the word *lima*, or "threshold,"[51] but threshold can be as much a point of entry as a bar. In the Baltic, there loomed a clash of interpretation between the belief frontier of the Christian and pagan world with the physical frontier of political and military control. Where missionaries saw religion and culture, rulers saw property. The union of the two is one of, if not the, defining tensions of the Baltic Crusades. Which version of a frontier, religious or political, works when dealing with tribes that saw a union of religion and government? Conquest would be required for conversion and that would mean territorial control and taxation. A unity of religion with territory, apparently held by both sides in the conflict, would validate the use of missionary war.

Complicating matters would be the rather fluid nature of frontiers between the previously existing pagan tribal groups. How far did the land of the Samogitians extend, and was that extension reasonably constant? Tribal conflicts between Baltic peoples were endemic and immemorial. The conquest of these territories by Christian forces may have done much to establish a firm demarcation between these peoples even as they were supposedly joined to a larger unity called "Christendom." Once again, however, the emphasis on individual crusaders and their transitory participation in the Baltic Crusades creates as much of a problem as it solves. It leaves the impression that the whole process was nothing more than a series of forays, almost a military lark under the rubric of the "crusading year." This tends to mask the relentless progress of conquest and incorporation of multiple territories and peoples. The continual, rather than sporadic, nature of the crusades may explain why there were not new crusading authorizations every year. As much as they resembled them, these were not raids but permanent acquisition, and as such were based in the physical taking and holding of land.

But the winning of the land, despite its violent nature, was in many ways easier than winning the peace. And in these cases, the conflict between the winners went far beyond arguments over baptism. The old myth that has been exploded, to use Thomas Madden's term, of the disinherited younger sons comprising the bulk of crusade forces and thus creating an abandonment of the "faith and fiefs" rationale for the Crusades may be stood on its ear in the Baltic. Here the fiefs gained are not so much the personal property of the participating lords, although one suspects as much in the inaugural Wendish Crusade of 1147, but holdings by a body, whether the church as in the case of Bishop Albert of Buxhövden, or a religious order such as the Swordbrothers, or later the Teutonic Knights. Further, the disastrous cost of crusading, as shown for the bankrupted survivors of the Holy Land Crusades, does not serve as forcefully in an edge crusade where the distances are manageable. Certainly the prosecution of war with its very real, and unpredictable, nature is the most expensive undertaking in human existence, but the propinquity of the theater of operations in the Baltic region lessens the burden somewhat.

This different expenditure requirement may also explain the tendency toward negotiation in what would seem at first blush a zealously nonnegotiable religious conflict. Crusaders were often tempted to bargain a monetary settlement to their campaigns, preferring the immediate gain of treasure to the uncertain outcome of the battlefield. Perhaps the awareness of this dynamic was what prompted Bernard of Clairvaux to prohibit a monetary settlement to the Wendish Crusade, a sentiment echoed by his confrere Pope Eugenius III in his enabling decree *Divina dispensatione II*.[52] There was, sadly or salubriously depending on your viewpoint, a long prehistory of this type of financial settlement ending a religiously based military campaign. As early as the first religious invasion by an authorized Christian king, Clovis of the Franks, the tendency to negotiate ended the effort. When Clovis sought to conquer Arian Burgundy in 500 AD, the result of mixed motives to be sure, but at least partly for the sake of theological conformity, his victorious march against the Burgundian king Gundobad was stalled at Avignon. Besieging the city, Clovis was persuaded to settle for tribute rather than victory by a smooth-talking Roman double agent named Aridius. The rationale presented to Clovis was an adumbration of the same line of reasoning used by the participants in the Wendish Crusade of 1147.[53]

> You are destroying the fields, spoiling the meadows, cutting up the vineyards, ruining the olive groves and ravaging the whole countryside, which is a very fruitful one. In doing this you are causing no harm whatsoever to Gundobad. Why don't you send an ultimatum to him to say that he must pay whatever annual tribute you care to exact? In that way the region will be saved and he will have to submit to you and pay tribute to you forever.[54]

Military historians will correctly point out that Clovis' troops were probably running out of handy forage and food during their encirclement, while the assertion that the Frankish king's siege was "causing no harm whatsoever to Gundobad" cannot have been true. It is always a game of military chicken between the besieged and the besiegers as to who runs out of supplies first. But the tendency to cut a deal, take the wealth, and go home was real as well as of long historical standing and is repeatedly mirrored almost exactly throughout the twelfth century. Cosmas of Prague, writing before 1120, recorded an invasion of the Czech duke Břetislav's lands by the Emperor Henry III in 1042 in which the duke, fearing imminent defeat, sought to buy off the imperial forces.

> He tried to deflect the terrible anger of the emperor with these words: "The wars you make, Caesar, will have no triumphs. Our land is your treasury; we are yours and wish to be yours. He who rages against his own subjects is known to be more cruel than a cruel enemy."[55]

Likewise the Wendish crusaders, in 1147, seem to echo the same thoughts. Helmold of Bosau, writing some twenty years later, put this speech in the mouth of the crusaders at the siege of Dobin:

> Is not the land we are devastating our land, and the people we are fighting our people? Why are we, then, found to be our own enemies and the destroyers of our own incomes? Does not this loss fall back on our lords?[56]

The end result, as Helmold reminds us next, is that "from that day, then, uncertainty of purpose began to seize the army and repeated truces to lighten the investment."[57] A negotiated settlement works against the kind of zealous obsession needed for crusading.

At the heart of the problem of territorial and property control was the blurring of the line between lordship and religion. A prime example, as Henry recounts, was one Daniel. Not to be confused with a secular knight of the same name, Daniel of Lennewarden, this Daniel was a priest who earned his standing in the hard fought defense of the fort at Holm. He was sent with supplies and, most telling, a company of *ballistarii*, missile warriors, "and certain others to take over the aforesaid fort of Holm."[58] Both crusaders and their clerical comrades were avid to gain lordship over the newly won lands of pagan tribes. But was this something new, or did it also have a formative prehistory? As with many of the elements of the Baltic Crusades that had a contentious influence, both for the actual participants as well as modern historians, it may have begun with the best intentions.

Christianity from its beginning had shouldered the burden of caring for the material needs of the less fortunate.[59] By the time the church coalesced organizationally into the Episcopal system, the caring for the poor, widows, and disabled had devolved to the responsibility of the bishop.[60] In the fourth through the sixth centuries, coincidentally the same time frame as the early, paleo-phase of our prehistory, bishops were expected to offer food and material assistance regularly. To avoid the creation of a floating class of professional poor, those receiving assistance were to be enrolled in a register, the *matricula pauperum*—they were called *matricularii pauperi,* or "matriculating poor"—with their local bishop.[61] This was affirmed in church councils. The Council of Orléans, sitting in 511 AD, explained the situation with Canon 16, instructing that "the bishop shall distribute, *as far as his means allow*, clothes and food to the poor or sick."[62] It was a natural incentive for each bishop to expand his "means" and solidify his popularly granted title of *pater*. It is tempting, when surveying this drive for wealth, to focus on the glittering cross pectorals and shot silk finery worn by some bishops and assume ostentation. Wilfrid, later the controversial bishop of York, was "borne aloft on a golden throne" at his consecration in Gaul in 664 AD.[63] But for every ostentatious, and highly symbolic, show of wealth there was also an expensive, and increasing, need of the flock.

Therefore bishops were keen to exercise control over any and all religious establishments in their see, including monasteries. The same council, Orléans, that regularized aid to the poor also established official Episcopal control of monasteries and convents: "Abbots, because of the humility of religion, shall be under the control of the bishops, and if they do something outside their Rule, they shall be corrected by bishops."[64] Episcopal control of monasteries became a sticking point in the foundation of St. Radegund's famous Convent of the Holy Cross at Poitiers. When the married queen wished to become a nun and establish a convent, she needed a bishop to sponsor it. She approached Bishop Medard of Noyon, who, fearing the jilted king, only reluctantly became her overseer.[65]

Control of the monasteries became even more imperative once an Irish custom, popularized by Columbanus and his followers, encouraging laymen to deposit their movable wealth in the hands of the monks for safekeeping took hold. The "monastic banks" were mentioned by Paul the Deacon in his *History of the Lombards*.[66] The growing value and number of monasteries contributed to strife among differing branches of the church.[67] The establishment of "princely" bishops, complete with finery, armed retainers and all the trappings of grandeur was not uncommon. Richard Fletcher described the entourage of Wilfrid, the controversial and celebrated seventh-century bishop of York, as "in several respects akin to the retinue, or *comitatus*, of a secular nobleman or king."[68] Typically, Wilfrid had 120 in his group and they fought upon occasion (when attacked). It was more than simply a display of wealth, as these members of Wilfrid's party swore "that no one should turn his back and flee in battle but that each should either die with honour or live in triumph,"[69] a sentiment that echoed perfectly the ethos of the Germanic warband and provided a chilling connective between the display of wealth and martial valor. When attacked in Sussex in 666 AD, Wilfrid's men proceeded to vanquish "a fierce and untamed pagan host ... with no mean slaughter."[70] Competition for wealth and the accoutrements that accompanied it could transfer easily from the serene precincts of church property to the battlefield. The resemblance to the Germanic warband is telling for the Baltic. High-ranking Christian clerics, even up to the papal legate, William of Modena—who felt constrained to take revenge upon the recalcitrant Oselians as he left Livonia in 1226—would feel free to make war on other Christian groups led by equally bellicose prelates. There is, of course, no predetermined reason that concerns for the material sustenance of the flock should result in mimicry of secular lordship, but the avenue leading to that destination was paved by competition over property and the protection of the same. When coupled with the use of military force, accusations of heresy and the like, the acquisition of property can easily conjoin with missionary war.

Questions for discussion

Once pagan lands were Christianized, who was in control of them?

How did issues of church and state play into these newly Christianized lands?

What role did preventing civil war play in the Baltic Crusades?

What was the issue between the Germans and the Danes? How was it resolved?

Why were the Germans and the Russians at odds in the Baltic? Was there a resolution for this conflict?

How did the Baltic crusaders rationalize making war against fellow Christians?

What was the church's response to war among opposing Christian sides?

What was the nature of the frontier between Christian and pagan lands? Were there fixed territorial lines between the two?

10

The legacy of the Baltic Crusades

As the noise of battle died down and "a light, mild rain (that had) sent up a powerful swirl of dust that covered the battlefield and fighters" dissipated, some twelve thousand dead or wounded covered the field of conflict at Tannenberg that fateful July day in 1410. The losing Teutonic Knights were devastated, with their grandmaster, the marshal of the Order, grand commander, treasurer, several sub-commanders, and at least 400 of the brothers dead. The rest of their forces were captured or chased back to their stronghold at Marienburg.[1]

For all intents and purposes, it would seem that the Teutonic Knights were finished, thereby signaling an end to these "eternal" crusades. And indeed, the Battle of Tannenberg is viewed generally as the end point of the Baltic Crusades—but not for the obvious reason. The Teutonic Knights were able to successfully withstand a siege of their redoubt at Marienburg for nearly two months and despite ceding the province of Samogitia and Dobrzyn to Poland-Lithuania survived the calamity of military defeat. What wore them down in the coming years were the devastating costs of the war. The Order owed an indemnity equivalent to ten times the typical yearly income of the king of England as well as a staggering fee to ransom their prisoner-of-war brethren.[2] That the loss at Tannenberg did not serve as a dramatic end to the Baltic Crusades should not surprise. In 1236, when the Swordbrothers had suffered an even more terminal defeat at the Battle of the Saule River, their role was filled by a replacement order: the Teutonic Knights themselves. But this time the Knights would have no replacement and would spiral toward extinction rather than vanish all at once. In spite of the crippling provisions of the Peace of Thorn (February 1, 1411), the Order would exist as a territorial state until 1525, experiencing several intervening wars and political realignments.[3]

If Tannenberg was not as decisive as it seemed, what did end the Baltic Crusades? The answer may lie more in the court of public opinion as expressed at the Council of Constance (1414–18), rather than in the aftershocks of the slaughter at Tannenberg.[4] An appeal by the Order to the Pope to provide a justification for their actions and vilify the Polish-Lithuanian position arrived at a supremely confused and fractured moment in the history of the church. These were the last days of what would be memorialized as the Great Schism, a period from 1378 to 1415 that featured first two, then three rival popes. The Council had been called to solve this dilemma and decide who among the three candidates, a pope in Avignon, one in Rome, and one representing an earlier failed conciliar effort at Pisa, was the true pope. Greatly complicating the proceedings was the church provision that only a pope could call a council into session. Since all three rival popes feared deposition at the hands of a council they might authorize, none would legitimate the already sitting Council of Constance.

At length the Roman pontiff, Gregory XII, chose to subordinate his own position to the well-being of the church and officially approved the Council on July 4, 1415. The newly official Council promptly removed all three papal candidates, even Gregory, in order to avoid any appearance of collusion. Gregory was rewarded for his magnanimous work with a cardinal's hat, making the 88-year-old a rarity: a man who went from pope back to cardinal. The next order of business would be to elect a new, unified pope. But the Council demurred, choosing instead to govern the church from July 1415 to November 1417, with a chief presiding officer rather than a supreme pontiff. Only after realizing that much, if not all, Catholic theology had been contextualized through the office of the papacy, did the Council move to elect a new pope, Martin V (r. 1417–31). In the midst of all this drama, the appeal of the Teutonic Knights was examined and discussed, beginning on July 5, 1415.[5]

The argument against the order was framed by Paul Vladimiri, the rector of the University of Krakow and a spokesman for the Polish-Lithuanian king Jagiello. Replying for the Teutonic Knights was John of Falkenberg. But the discussion soon veered away from the specific grievances between the Order and the Polish-Lithuanian crown to a general debate on the validity of crusading. As the contest developed, Vladimiri even produced a more fulsome attack on the Order with the telling title *Articuli contra cruciferos*, or "The Articles Against the Crusaders." Eric Christiansen has noted wisely that this turn of events put crusading in a rather weak defensive position, since the passage of two centuries of legal analysis had strengthened the standing of natural law and just war doctrine had gained "far greater precision."[6]

This process of "precision" changed just war from the Augustinian position that war can be a necessary and even positive effort if pursued for the right cause to the belief that war was always an evil regardless of whether it was pursued for a good cause or not. Jonathan Riley-Smith writes: "Modern just war theory presumes, unlike Augustine, that violence is indeed an evil, but also that disorder can be a greater one."[7] This has its modern expression in the "dirty hands" view of warfare, popularized by Reinhold Neibuhr: It is sometimes needful but always polluting.[8] Both these developments, the growth of natural law popularity and just war theory refinements, militated against the rough-and-ready behaviors of the Baltic crusaders, casting the whole enterprise in an unfriendly light. It seems that crusading, although still advocated by Pope Pius II as late as the 1460s, was drifting into conceptual obsolescence. Certainly efforts against non-Muslim opponents who were Christians to boot seemed out of step with the times. But even the earlier efforts against pagans in the name of Christianity were impugned in the ongoing debate.

The question revolved around the issue of defensive versus offensive war. Both pope and emperor had no right to attack, as Eric Christiansen has pointed out: "Any infraction of the property rights of any unoffending neighbour, be he pagan or Christian, was a violation of natural law which not even the papacy could sanction."[9] The papal bulls that authorized the Teutonic Order's crusades were only held to be valid, in the Council's view, if they permitted the waging of a defensive war against pagans, using the Augustinian maxim of *vim vi repellare*, "force may repel force." The crusaders were justified in defending church lands and congregations with the same violence used against them. But the Baltic crusaders were judged to be using this right of defense as a pretext for their continuing offensive campaigns against pagans, a perspective that tended to overshadow the evidence of repeated attacks on Christian communities. This position also gave little weight to the notion that once-baptized pagans who renounced Christianity were apostates and as such still subject under church tradition to violent punishment. Perhaps the pagans were not always as peace-loving nor as innocent as the argument assumed. Additionally, the permission for defensive action needs further clarification. Does it mean that crusaders were only justified in their military response when attacked by pagans, or does it mean that crusaders could attack to defend and protect a Christian enclave in pagan territory that was under threat? The use of terms like "unoffending pagans" and "peoples living in peace" to describe the targets of the crusaders presumed that only the former was just. The other actions were simply naked attempts to "annex territory."[10]

Further clouding the debate was the conflation of the motivation for the wars with the practice of the same. Vladimiri came to the conclusion that "not only their (the crusaders) political powers were unjustified, but also that their scandalous conduct was inconsistent with the profession either of knight or of monk."[11] The double-sided question of whether the crusade was for the defense of fellow Christians and if so, was it conducted rightly or not, was blended into one condemnation. There seems to have been no effective way to separate the *ius ad bellum* concerns from the *ius in bello* misbehavior of the Order. In fairness, one might say that it is quite difficult to separate the two. Behavior informs theory and leaves the most tangible aftertaste in the historical record. The debate at the Council of Constance established a part of the negative legacy of the Baltic Crusades, seemingly closing a chapter in crusading history. Yet while the Baltic Crusades may have ended, the concept and practice of missionary war did not. A continuing legacy remained.

The "legacy" of the Baltic Crusades may seem an odd topic for inclusion in a study on the prehistory of that crusading movement. But, as prehistory suggests continuity, one cannot expect a total and sudden disconnect between Baltic crusading practice and theory and that which continued beyond the Battle of Tannenberg in 1410. The legacy of the Baltic Crusades and missionary war might include the implementation of these practices elsewhere, at least in part. What then is the legacy of missionary war as practiced in the Baltic Crusades? The components that were involved, whether it was the use of baptism by treaty, or the Christian on Christian violence, or the like, had divergent usages in the years after 1410. Far from missionary war being inflicted on pagan peoples guilty of apostasy, the Christian on Christian encounters morphed readily into the doctrinal warfare of the Protestant Reformation. But there were still pagan peoples to baptize and then punish for apostasy. Only these peoples no longer inhabited the shoreline of the Baltic, but rather the mainland of an entirely new world.

An attractive case can be made that the legacy of the Baltic Crusades, especially as it related to missionary war, is found in the experience of the Spanish *conquistadores* in the Americas. The similarities of intent and action between the Baltic enterprise and that in the New World convince many that the two are cut from the same cloth. As the noted American scholar, William L. Urban, has written in his fine history of the Baltic Crusades, "The Spanish conquest of the New World also exhibited the spirit of the crusades and lacked only the formalities of a papal bull and the assent of historians to be called by such a name."[12] The conjunction of two facts, the multi-century *reconquista* of the Iberian Peninsula from Muslim forces and the entry of European Christian forces into pagan rather than Muslim lands, supports the assumption that the conquest of the Americas was a geographically transferred epilog of the Baltic Crusades. Having completed one crusade, the Spanish merely moved on to another field using justifications and methods already established in the Iberian Peninsula years earlier. It was the continuation of the pattern developed in the north with a slight Spanish twist. In this view, the Spanish "crusade" moved westward, rather than east as in the Baltic, until it encountered actual Muslim native opponents in the Philippines.[13] By this time, the 1560s, the Spanish had lost the knack of warring with Muslims, now being more familiar with "plain unvarnished infidels" than their former Islamic opponents.[14]

In a way, a circle was being closed—there had been crusading in the Holy Land against Muslims, then there was crusading in pagan lands along the Baltic and the Americas, and finally crusading in Muslim lands in East Asia.

While there are many similarities between the Spanish and Baltic experiences, there are also important differences between these two religio-military entries into pagan lands. This should not surprise those conversant with the survival and almost inevitable mutation of institutions. The practical and theoretical legacy of the Baltic

Crusades of necessity conform to changing situations, much like how Augustine's just war theory survived only in part in the post-invasion world of the barbarian successor kingdoms. Yet the notion of missionary war, utilized along the ever-expanding arc of the Christian-pagan frontier in Europe, would have a useful, if altered, second life in the Americas.

Before analyzing the utility of the Spanish experience in the Americas for the legacy of the Baltic Crusades, the nature of the sources must be evaluated. Much like the "eternal crusades" along the northern edge of pagan Europe, two very different points of view on the enterprise jostle for dominance. On the one hand is the point of view of Bernal Díaz del Castillo, an actual participant in the conquest of Mexico under Cortes' leadership. Díaz tends to justify the motives and actions of his fellow conquistadores. He repeatedly portrays the conquistadores as men moved by deeply religious motives, although admitting that they came to the New World also to grow rich.[15] The other extreme is represented by Bartolomé de las Casas, whose *Brief Account of the Destruction of the Indies*[16] became the popular foundation for the *leyenda negra*, or "black legend," of Spanish atrocities in the New World.[17] Las Casas was no armchair critic, taking his ease back in Spain. He also participated in the affairs of the New World, ministering there in various countries for decades. Where Díaz generally sees no wrong in Spanish policies, Las Casas sees no good. Las Casas wrote of "the boldness and the unreason of those who count it as nothing to drench the Americas in human blood," blithely reckoning that the Spanish had killed "a thousand million."[18] It may seem an act of moral equivalency to believe the truth is somewhere between these two poles, but critical judgment must be exercised when using these appositive sources. Sverre Bagge has decried the modern scholarly trend to distrust narrative sources in early medieval studies owing to the relative paucity of the evidence.[19] But the relative size of the corpus of sources, while important, does not solve the problem of potential bias. A larger body of evidence, such as we possess for the Spanish encounter with the Americas, still does not answer the fundamental question about the information contained therein: "whether this is the expression of a deliberate ideology or a reflection of actual conditions."[20]

Making whatever allowance we can for these issues of bias, the most obvious similarity between the Baltic Crusades and the Spanish conquest in the Americas lies in the target population of these incursions. Both in the Baltic and in the New World, the opponents were pagan peoples, not Muslims. But the similarities here are categorical and not specific. The targeted pagans in the Americas were completely alien, and previously unknown to their European invaders. As such they were unaware of Christianity's existence, thinking the conquistadores and their strange customs god-like. Conversely, the Slavic and Baltic peoples were quite familiar with German and Christian customs via the rather culturally permeable trading frontier that they shared. The god Svantovit, whose cultic center on the island of Rügen was taken by Christian Danish forces in the first decades of the Baltic Crusades, is thought to be a syncretistic mix of Christian and pagan beliefs.[21] In the Americas, the native populations might eventually blend local religion with Christianity, but only after the conquest was complete. The initial encounter was between two cultures completely unknown to one another with no traditional shared frontier.

Another similarity that masks an important difference between the two is the strong religious and theological bent to both enterprises—the crusading mentality that William Urban mentions as underpinning the very notion of missionary war. Both Baltic crusader and New World conquistador sought to convert the pagan peoples they encountered. When asked by native leaders why they had come, Bernal Díaz put the following explanation of the mission to the New World in Cortes' mouth: "Our lord and king had sent us so that we might become brothers to them, for he had heard about them and prayed God to give us grace, so that by our hands and through our intercession they might be saved. And we all said Amen."[22]

Both also used the concept of "get the king, get the people" that had worked so well for centuries. Unfortunately, the approach came with the same shortcomings as before. Díaz recorded that the chieftains of Tlascala feared, like barbarian kings in Europe, that their people would depose them if they adopted the new religion: "Even if we old men were to do so in order to please you, would not all our papas and our neighbors, our youths and children throughout the province, rise against us?"[23]

The urge to baptize en masse at the conclusion of military victory did seem to the conquistadors, in fairness, merely to create apostates rather than actual Christians. A friar advised Cortes not to press the natives on baptism as "it would not be right to make them Christians by force" and that the rite should not be applied "until they have some knowledge of our holy faith."[24] But the constant insistence on the adoption of Christian beliefs and practices remained a recurring theme in the New World as in the Baltic. The conquistadors repeatedly demanded the pagans they encountered to venerate the Holy Cross and, like the Teutonic Knights in the Baltic, images of the Virgin Mary. On Palm Sunday following the brutal Battle of Cintla in 1519, Cortes ordered all the defeated chieftains and their people to come "to worship the holy image of Our Lady and the cross."[25]

But a complicating, and contradictory, feature in this version of missionary war was that the Spanish were not convinced, at least initially, of the natives' status as human beings. Bartolomé de las Casas was an active participant in the debate that raged for decades in the Spanish court and culture as to whether or not the pagans of the New World even had souls that may be saved. Díaz apparently assumed that they did as he recorded Cortes on more than one occasion affirming their need for salvation, even to the great Aztec emperor Montezuma.

> The Emperor (Charles V of Spain and the Holy Roman Empire), he said, had sent us to this country to visit him (Montezuma), and to beg them to become Christians, like our Emperor and all of us, so that his soul and those of all his vassals might be saved.[26]

But the brutal mistreatment of the native populations was justified by some on the ground that the subject peoples were not fully human. This was done despite the fact that Pope Paul III (r. 1534–49) had ruled in June 1537 that "we ... consider ... that the Indians are truly men and that they are not only capable of understanding the Catholic faith but, according to our information, they desire exceedingly to receive it" and had gone on to say that the proper way to convert the natives was "by preaching the word of God and by the example of good and holy living."[27] Yet it was only in 1550, after a series of laws promulgated in 1513 and 1542 had proven unpopular and largely unenforceable, that the Spanish dealt with the native Americans' humanity. A debate, which was much more akin to an argument by each side before a high court rather than a give-and-take, face-to-face consideration of the issues, was arranged at Valladolid between Las Casas and the chief theoretician for those who believed the Indians lacked true humanity, Juan Ginés de Sepúlveda.[28] While the "debate" was informative, by then much of the Americas had been subjugated and a different rationalization was needed. This was to be found in the concept of "reduction," or the process of transforming the natives into copies of European Christians by voiding their culture as well as their religious beliefs. This conformed to the division of land among the victorious conquistadors that was known as the *encomienda*, a type of revived feudalism implanted in the Americas and requiring numerous laborers to succeed. Before these rough accommodations were attained, much blood was shed.

At this point another similarity appears between the Baltic Crusades and the Spanish experience in the Americas. Quite apart from the violence, by definition a major factor in any conquest of this period, was the issue of girl-stealing. It is instructive that a commentary on a Teutonic Knights' raid on pagan Kurland in 1263 is described in terms that could have been lifted from Bernal Díaz's description of practices in the Americas: "Then they (the Teutonic Knight crusaders) divided the men, women, children, cattle and horses equally and rode to their dwellings."[29]

That women- and girl-stealing was a regular feature of the Spanish experience in the New World is attested by numerous references in Díaz's account. After the pivotal Battle of Cintla in March 1519, the Spanish took twenty women as spoils of war. Cortes gifted each of his captains with one; the only saving grace, in Díaz's eyes, was that "they were the first women in New Spain to become Christians."[30] There is no mention of whether these women became domestic slaves or wives. Later, the defeated Tlascalan chieftains admitted they feared Cortes and his native allies were coming "in order to steal their women and children."[31] So prevalent was this urge toward girl-stealing that Cortes, giving his men some early rules of engagement as they prepared to attack Montezuma's capital, required that his men should take "neither men nor women prisoners" from their native allies.[32] Apparently the Conquistadores would have to be content with their own hard-won spoils of war. The Aztec commander, Guatemoc, complained bitterly to Cortes about girl- and women- stealing, noting that these victims were the wives and daughters of the leading men of his society. Cortes gave him no comfort, answering only "that it would be difficult to take them from their present masters."[33] In most, if not all, of these instances the only thing separating these behaviors from the Baltic Crusades are the changed names and locations.

What then is the legacy of these "eternal crusades" from more than six centuries ago? The poem ascribed to a Christian Swede rhyming on the encounter with the pagan Finns seems to sum up the general attitude of many:

> And he who was fain to bend the knee
> and go to the font and a Christian be,
> They left him his life and goods to enjoy,
> To live in peace, without annoy,
> But the heathen who still denied Our Lord
> They gave him death for his reward.[34]

And what use is it to become aware of their prehistory, especially as it relates to "missionary war"? Is not "the legacy" more of a post-history rather than a prehistory of the Baltic Crusades? Yet if it is important to trace the sweep of events and practices that led up to the Baltic Crusades in order to have a fuller picture of the subject, the sweep should not end with the last official "act" of the Baltic Crusades. The aftershocks are just as much a part of the story as the antecedents.

If one views crusading in general and the Baltic Crusades in particular as movements that emerged *de novo* and then ran their course, they become episodic, and episodes need not recur. They can safely be put on the oddity shelf of history, as items engendering curiosity and scholarly debate with little or nothing to say to our contemporary situation. But if one takes the *longue dureé*, viewing the Crusades as yet another chapter in an unfolding saga, the implications for the present are apparent. The antiquity of animosity and the conflict that such animus produces are likely to recur, albeit in a different situational form. The best preventative, or at least ameliorating, approach will be based upon a fuller knowledge of all the developmental factors that produced the chapter known as the Baltic Crusades.

There is more uncertainty concerning the idea of "missionary war." There may be widespread unanimity on the need to avoid a rebirth, or even a modern version, of crusading due to the generally negative implementation and outcomes of the Crusades.

"Missionary war," however, was productive of decidedly mixed results. The prosecution of this "war" was unquestionably violent and often quite repellent, but the end result was equally effective. William Urban describes it well:

> Superficially, the crusade was a success. The Christians defeated many of the pagans, brought the coastal lands into the circle of Christendom, ended piracy and made trade routes safe. . . .Yet almost everyone today agrees that the crusade was a moral failure.[35]

Several Baltic peoples were absorbed into the German version of civilization, so much so that one of them, the Prussians, became the generic term for all things German in later centuries. Later independent states such as Latvia and Estonia became functioning parts of Christendom as a whole because of the crude, bloody sorties east of the Elbe begun as early as 1147. In effect, an arc of newly Christianized literate territories replaced Bartlett's descriptive "arc of non-literate polytheism." Many question whether or not the price for this success was too high. Edgar Johnson sums up this sentiment thus:

> The cost of this superior western civilization was so high that the Baltic peoples refused to pay. It had to be imposed on them by conquest, crusade, and German settlement. The Baltic peoples would be made to pay for the new freedom of the Germans with the loss of their own.[36]

Opinions have hardly moved from this condemnation today. Had the Baltic Crusades been thrown back with little or no lasting influence on the local populations, such a clear negative, and dismissive, judgment on their significance would be in order. But the long-term success, bought in blood, raises the philosophical question of whether the ends justify the means. Success is often a poor indicator of rectitude. It is not enough to blame this violent conversion on the need to convert tribal peoples. Ireland became Christian without conquest and, while remaining flagrantly and stubbornly tribal, with all the political chaos that entails, needed no "missionary war" to enter Christendom.

Given the slaughter, beheadings, girl-stealing, forcible baptism, and land-grabbing that comprise the Baltic Crusade, it is easy, perhaps inescapable, for anyone associated with Christianity to recoil and condemn. Yet there are two explanations for the use of force, such as missionary war, that are not mitigating excuses but perhaps worthy of consideration while making a judgment of the crusaders' actions, whether it is condemnatory or rehabilitative. First, the target peoples viewed their culture as a monism and thus a change in religion was tantamount to an abnegation of their identity. While it is true that Christianity by design seeks to transform both the individual believer as well as his or her culture, the Baltic crusaders seem to have missed an important point at the heart of any missionary enterprise, whether violent or peaceful: the careful separation of the timeless Christian values from temporal and culturally conditioned ones. The Baltic people need not become "German" or even "Latin" in every, or perhaps most, cases. In short, they could become Christian and still be Slavs and Balts. Secondly, the newly planted churches that were the result of preaching rather than force of arms were, despite efforts by some to minimize the historical record,[37] subject to repeated and often exterminating attacks.

This second situation follows from the first, that the pagans perceived that Christianity was a threat to their whole culture. This fear of cultural annihilation is bound to provoke a backlash productive of violent attacks and growing lists of martyrs, much like the situation in seventeenth-century Japan that led to the closing of the nation to outside contact for more than two centuries. The legacy of the Baltic Crusades is far more than the mere continuation of certain crusading practices or their eventual success or failure. These have, for the most part, long receded into history. The enduring legacy remains the historical evaluation of these events. That evaluation often turns upon the question of the motivation of the crusaders. The question of whether the crusaders were driven by simple greed for land and power or by religious beliefs that mandated their actions seems to occupy much of the discussion. Both these approaches depend heavily for their results on whether the evaluator sees the Baltic Crusades as driven by land hunger or as a legitimate, if misguided by contemporary standards, religious movement. The divide between the old trope that the Crusades were for "faith and fiefs" lives on. However, our contemporary separation of religion and politics as well as our heritage of religious pluralism inhibits our understanding of cultures, whether crusader or pagan, who saw these elements as one. Monism, the very thing that enabled the attackers and the attacked to relate to each other, is almost invisible to us. We are therefore at a disadvantage when ascribing motivation to and passing judgment on the Baltic Crusades.

Finally, the legacy of the Baltic Crusades in general and the concept of missionary war in particular comes down to an individual judgment call that rests upon two main issues: the level of trust one has in the available sources and the relative weight one ascribes to the adoption of atrocious local practices by the crusading forces. Among those practices are not only battlefield violence and girl-stealing but also territorial expansion and economic exploitation. In these matters Baltic missionary war mimics the larger questions posed by the just war theory. The *ius ad bellum*, or acceptable reasons for going to war, plays into the issue of trust for the sources. If our sources are accurate, rather than fabricated as justification, then the practitioners of Baltic missionary war are correct in launching campaigns in order to protect fledgling Christian communities from attack. If the sources are indeed doctored for effect, then Baltic missionary war is not justified.

The second matter, the adoption of local war-making habits and territorial control, falls under the just war concept of *ius in bello*, or the right prosecution of a justified war. Here it is quite difficult to accept the wholehearted participation by the missionary warriors in the violently repellant behaviors of the Baltic Crusades. There is an almost *joie de combat* in the chortling accounts of violence. It is not enough to excuse these actions on the grounds that the crusaders were simply applying in the Baltic what they did customarily at home.[38] This is only partly true. Certainly medieval warfare in the Christian West seems shockingly violent to our modern sensibilities, but there are many practices used on the Baltic front that were beyond normal Western behavior. The military coinage of this new realm should have been exchanged for that of the crusaders' homeland. This exchange may leave a form of crusading that would shock us still, but not the medieval societies involved. Despite the very real presence of aberrant, individual misconduct by even the best military forces, it is not likely that large-scale adoption of the violent methods on display in the Baltic would reappear among civilized, Western armies. Girl-stealing, decapitations, and the like are still to be seen in international affairs, but as the actions of pariahs.

A more insidious threat is the impulse to allow a justifiable military intervention to slide almost imperceptibly into a larger, aggressive operation. The same *quid pro quo* battlefield calculus that lured Baltic crusaders into embracing pagan war practices exists today, albeit with different technology. Retaliation is a powerful human response that can alter the highest of campaign plans. It is easier to be victorious over an opponent than to be better than him. On a macro-level it can manifest as mission creep, while on a micro-level it informs even squad-level behavior. When one reads the accounts of missionary war in the Baltic the long tradition of just this type of behavior, its prehistory, continues apace. Contemporary governments and their armies, now largely secularized unlike their medieval ancestors, are still susceptible to a similar allure. The legacy of Baltic missionary war is therefore a cautionary one. The study of its causes, implementation, and prehistory may supply the perspective needed to avoid the same pitfalls experienced by those on the *reisens*.

The legacy is a form of post-history of this movement that drew upon centuries of preconditioning and played out along the frigid shores of the northern seas. This post-history amounts to more than the simple formulation of an opinion on the relative rectitude of these missionary wars. Thomas Madden has shown how the study of the post-history of the Crusades has impacted our present world, particularly in the Middle East.[39] The legacy of the Baltic Crusades, its post-history, has great potential impact for today when intervention to protect threatened populations is a major international issue across the globe. Rather than dismissing the Baltic Crusades and their prehistory, it might be essential to look at them from the angle of vision of justified, or unjustified, intervention campaigns. How we view this medieval intervention and its long prehistory may shape how we decide on necessary interventions today. Today's international situation bears much resemblance to the dynamic that pertained in that long ago period. Particular similarities, whether they are hyper-violent, such as beheadings, or ethnocidal, such as girl-stealing, mask the essential congruence between the Baltic Crusades and our present predicament. The essence is one of intervention on behalf of threatened innocents. William L. Urban recognized this when he likened the crusade to a protective intervention and enumerated some of the problems associated with this type of operation: "who is in command, where does the money come from, and who provides the volunteers; (and) lastly, what do you do when you succeed?"[40]

All that is missing from his evaluation is a question about mission creep and the adoption of the opponents' violent customs. We can learn from both the mistakes and successes and avoid unnecessary adventures that lead to further, even more destructive, situations. That the Baltic missionary war was a religious one need not foreclose such an examination. Current issues of intervention are not necessarily religious, but human rights driven.[41] Intervention to save lives and cultures is as laudable for a secular worldview as in a religious one. One can replace theology with human rights concerns and still find the Baltic model useful. The dangers are twofold: the almost irresistible temptation toward mission creep and the seductive adoption of the basest war-making practices. As with those crusaders in the "eternal crusades" the modern warriors may easily elide into an unjust prosecution of a just intervention. The fervor that motivated the crusaders is often matched by our contemporary enthusiasm for human rights and inclusiveness. It is a different heaven that is sought, but an imperative motivating ideal just the same.

Thus the true legacy of the Baltic Crusade use of missionary war may not lie in the realm of practice—for example, in the issue of whether the Spanish used these mechanisms in the New World—but in the realm of applicable theory. If missionary war is seen as a form of intervention to protect innocents, it stands as an instructive, even cautionary, tale. While modern interventions are based on human rights, not on religious doctrine (at least to date), a similar dynamic applies. The slippery slope from defense of the innocents to outright conquest in offensive assault is still a threat. How much, and what kind of military activity is sufficient to assure the defense of the innocent, or the alteration of policies that violate human rights? How far afield should these objectives be chased? The same siren song luring the enterprise from defense to offense plays in the ear of the participants. We would do very well to study this song's origins and its impact on the Baltic Crusades not only for its own sake, but for ours. While the Baltic Crusades and their version of missionary war did incorporate several new nations into Christendom, the conclusion of the crusades was only the beginning, in many ways, of the process. Forcing Christianity via battlefield victory and baptism by treaty does not automatically ensure social change. The imposition of a new system may take generations, if not centuries, to work its way down to the personal level, as Richard Fletcher described so eloquently in his *The Barbarian Conversion*.[42] The stubborn adherence to old ways and customs has much to say that goes beyond the era of the Crusades and the resultant conversions. Modern interventions to impose Western ideals, however laudable, may encounter a similar fate. Absent a continuing pressure, the population may well revert to its previous normal. Just as nature undoes mankind's best efforts after the passage of years, so may the mother culture regain its prominence over an adopted culture. It may require a contemporary version of "eternal crusade" to solidify the initial gains. In either case the undertaking resembles state building. This possibility is yet another cautionary point illuminated better by a glance backward into the prehistory of such projects. The context may change, but the dynamic seems the same.

The fundamental dilemma is "how does a political entity, whether secular government or church, protect those in agreement from hostile neighbors without resort to military conquest or occupation?" The motivating credo may be theological, as in the Baltic, or secular humanitarianism, as today. But the question remains. It is not the purpose of this study to solve such a pressing riddle, but merely to illuminate the fact that this riddle has deep and instructive historical roots. Therefore, this work concludes where it began, with an appeal to open discussion on this part of a neglected chapter in world history. It is a necessary chapter for study because so much of the earlier period is replicating today. We may all await the results.

Questions for discussion

Are the criticisms of the Baltic Crusades as a "lightly baptized land grab" justified? Was this land acquisition a new development, or one with a long history?

Were the Baltic Crusades successful? What constitutes "success" in this context?

What are the differences and what are the similarities between the Baltic Crusades' missionary war and the Spanish experience in the New World?

What lessons might the Baltic experience teach us today? Is anything similar to the Baltic Crusades possible in our modern world? Can there be a modern version of missionary war?

NOTES

Acknowledgments

1   John Murray, ed., *The Autobiographies of Edward Gibbon*, 2nd edn (London: John Murray, 1897), 333–4.

Introduction

1   Christopher Tyerman, *The Invention of the Crusades* (Toronto: University of Toronto Press, 1998), 1.
2   Thomas F. Madden, review of Christopher Tyerman, *God's War: A New History of the Crusades*, *First Things* 168 (December 2006): 44.
3   Giles Constable, *Crusaders and Crusading in the Twelfth Century* (Burlington, VT: Ashgate, 2008), 241.
4   Carl Erdmann, *The Origin of the Idea of Crusade*, trans. Marshall W. Baldwin and Walter Goffart (Princeton: Princeton University Press, 1977). In his original 1935 edition, Erdmann used the term *missionskrieg* to describe warfare fought for conversion.
5   A commendable exception is the recent text by Barbara H. Rosenwein, *A Short History of the Middle Ages*, 2nd edn (Peterborough, ON: Broadview Press, 2004). Although she keeps to her plan of brevity, Professor Rosenwein includes a good synopsis of Baltic crusading that even features a fine map.
6   Simon Winder, *Germania: In Wayward Pursuit of the Germans and Their History* (New York: Picador/Farrar, Strauss and Giroux, 2010), 60.
7   Anatol Rapoport, ed., *Carl von Clausewitz: On War* (Harmondsworth: Penguin Books, 1968), 101.
8   James A. Brundage, trans., *The Chronicle of Henry of Livonia* (New York: Columbia University Press, 2003), 176. The Latin reads: *Quorum negocium sanctum erat, eo quod vocati venerunt*

ad baptizandum paganos vineamque Domini plantandam, quam sanguine suo plantaverunt. MGH, XXIII, 4, 158.

9 Stubbs said: "Scarcely a single movement now visible in the current of modern affairs but can be traced back with some distinctiveness to its origin in the early Middle Ages." In Norman F. Cantor, ed., *William Stubbs on the English Constitution* (New York: Thomas Y. Crowell Company, 1966), 14.

10 Sverre Bagge, *Kings, Politics, and the Right Order of the World in German Historiography, c. 950-1150* (Leiden: Brill, 2002), 20–1.

11 Peter Brown, "A Life of Learning: The Charles Homer Haskins Lecture for 2003" (Philadelphia: The American Council of Learned Societies, Occasional Paper No. 55, 2003), 7–8.

12 Peter Brown, *Augustine of Hippo: A Biography* (Berkeley: University of California Press, 1967).

13 David Hackett Fischer, *Historians' Fallacies: Toward a Logic of Historical Thought* (New York: Harper Torchbook, 1970), 299.

14 Peter Brown used Febvre's term to great effect in analyzing Augustine's views on religious coercion in "St. Augustine's Attitude to Religious Conversion," *The Journal of Roman Studies* 54 (1964): 107. The *outillage moral* that each of us possess, whether wittingly or not, determines to a large degree how we see issues of a morally debatable nature.

15 Lewis Thorpe, trans., *Gregory of Tours: History of the Franks* (Harmondsworth: Penguin Books, 1974), 208–9. Gregory is quoting the great Roman historian Sallust (*Catilina*, 3).

16 Richard Fletcher, *The Barbarian Conversion: From Paganism to Christianity* (New York: Henry Holt and Company, 1997), 522.

Chapter 1

1 David Ganz, *Einhard and Notker the Stammerer: Two Lives of Charlemagne* (London: Penguin Books, 2008). Notker mentioned that Louis "built new oratories of wonderful workmanship at Frankfurt and Regensburg," 99. "The chapel of the Saviour at Frankfurt was consecrated in 852," fn. 26; 129.

2 Perhaps the best summary of the multiple events leading up to the Second Crusade and the Diet at Frankfurt is by Jonathan Phillips, *The Second Crusade: Extending the Frontiers of Christendom* (New Haven, CT: Yale University Press, 2007); also Friedrich Lotter,

"The Crusading Idea and the Conquest of the Region East of the Elbe," in Robert Bartlett and Angus MacKay, eds, *Medieval Frontier Societies* (Oxford: Clarendon Press, 1989), 267–306, is quite helpful in setting the stage for the Frankfurt Diet.

3 Austin Lane Poole, *Henry the Lion: The Lothian Historical Essay for 1912* (Oxford: B.H. Blackwell, 1912), 6.

4 Phillips, *Second Crusade*, xvii–xviii, does a good job in summarizing the event, while Christopher Tyerman, *God's War: A New History of the Crusades* (Cambridge, MA: The Belknap Press of Harvard University Press, 2006), 268–75, gives the event its historical due.

5 Thomas Asbridge, *The First Crusade: A New History* (Oxford: Oxford University Press, 2004), 149–52; and Thomas F. Madden, *The New Concise History of the Crusades* (Lanham, MD: Rowman & Littlefield, 2005), 25–6, give accounts of the seizure of Edessa by Baldwin as does Tyerman, *God's War*, 134, although Madden downplays Baldwin's duplicity in the matter.

6 John France, "Crusading Warfare," in Helen Nicholson, ed., *Palgrave Advances in the Crusades* (London: Palgrave MacMillan, 2005), 58–80, 72; "The most important military problem of the settlers (in the Crusader states) was that they were few." This echoes the earlier view of John Beeler, *Warfare in Feudal Europe, 730-1200* (Ithaca, NY: Cornell University Press, 1971), 123; "The principal weakness of the Christian states was a lack of manpower. . . . It has been estimated that the short-lived County of Edessa never attracted more than 100 European noble and knightly families."

7 Philippe Contamine, *War in the Middle Ages*, trans. Michael Jones (Oxford: Basil Blackwell, 1984), 64, calls *turcopoles* "native troops" and notes that they were able to draw "their Turkish bows without dismounting," 70. Asbridge, *First Crusade*, mentions that the Byzantines used *turcopoles* at the siege of Nicaea in June 1097, and calls them "well-armed mercenaries of half-Greek, half-Turkish stock," 129.

8 Phillips, *Second Crusade*, 280–2, uses Jonathan Riley-Smith's fine translation of the text.

9 Edward Peters, ed., *The First Crusade: The Chronicle of Fulcher of Chartres and Other Source Materials* (Philadelphia: University of Pennsylvania Press, 1998), 27.

10 It is a common practice for new alien peoples to be named after the first tribe or clan encountered. The standard European name for Muslim opponents was "Saracens," which was the name of an

Arabian tribe first met by Western forces during the late Roman period. Since so many Franks were participants in the First Crusade, the Muslim public considered that all crusaders, then and in the future, were "Franks." This became so routine that mention of it has even penetrated the standard textbooks for medieval history courses, for example, R. H. C. Davis, *A History of Medieval Europe: From Constantine to Saint Louis*, 3rd edn (Harlow, UK: Pearson Longman, 2006), 6: "The natives of Syria call modern Europeans '*franji*,' because until the modern age they had known no European colonists since the crusades. Even in Greece Europeans are called Franks, since Greece was conquered by crusaders in the thirteenth century."

11 Phillips, *Second Crusade*, 62–4.
12 Tyerman, *God's War*, 279.
13 Constable, *Crusaders and Crusading*, 293. Monks, no matter how famous, generally were prohibited from preaching without episcopal or, more importantly, papal authorization. Even though Bernard was the former mentor of Pope Eugenius, such authorization would be necessary to validate his preaching efforts.
14 Phillips, *Second Crusade*, 2. Conrad of Staufen, later the king, went to the Holy Land in 1124.
15 Ibid., 129. The young king was crowned on March 30, 1147, and ruled "jointly" with his father until his untimely death at thirteen in 1150. The designation "Henry VI" was used to denote a later Hohenstaufen emperor, Henry VI, who ruled from Frederick Barbarossa's death in 1190 until 1197.
16 The English translation appears in Phillips, *Second Crusade*, 28.
17 Charles Christopher Mierow, trans., *The Deeds of Frederick Barbarossa by Otto of Freising* (New York: W.W. Norton & Company, 1966), 78.
18 Tyerman, *God's War*, 288. He sees the episode as a useful visual illustration of how the physical arm of the state could support the church: "The image of the tall, well-built Conrad rescuing the slight, frail Bernard from an adoring mob during the Diet of Frankfurt in March 1147 by picking him up and carrying him out of the crowd provided a less cosmic but no less potent opportunity for royal association with the great forces of Christendom."
19 Otto of Freising, *Deeds*, 78.
20 Phillips, *Second Crusade*, 129.
21 Lotter, "Crusading Idea," 273–83, gives a succinct account of the rivalry and its impact on Saxon-Slavic relations.

22 Phillips, *Second Crusade*, 134.
23 Francis Joseph Tschan, trans., *The Chronicle of the Slavs by Helmold, Priest of Bosau* (New York: Columbia University Press, 1935), 172.
24 Hans Eberhard Mayer, in *The Crusades*, trans. John Gillingham (Oxford: Oxford University Press, 1972), is a typical proponent of this view: "If the example of the Wendish Crusade were to be followed then the Holy Land might lose much of the support it so desperately needed, for heathens could be fought in many parts of the world, not just in the Holy Land," 102–3.
25 Eric Christiansen, trans. and ed., *The Works of Sven Aggesen: Twelfth-Century Danish Historian* (London: Viking Society for Northern Research, 1992), 50.
26 *Divina dispensatione* II. Here Eugenius explicitly gives the same protection to Wendish crusaders as Urban had done for the crusaders to Jerusalem in 1095. J.-P. Migne, ed., *Patrologiae Latinae*, v. 180, col. 1203: *Quorum nos devotionem attendentes, omnibus illis qui crucem eamdem Hierosolymam non acceperunt, et contra Sclavos ire, et iu ipsa expeditione, sicut statutum est, devotionis intuitu manere decreverunt, illam remissionem peccatorum quam praedecessor noster felicis memoriae papa Urbanus Hierosolymam tranuentibus instituit.*
27 Ibid.
28 Bernhard Walter Scholz with Barbara Rogers, trans., *Carolingian Chronicles: Royal Frankish Annals and Nithard's Histories* (Ann Arbor, MI: The University of Michigan Press, 1970), 76.
29 Robert Bartlett, *The Making of Europe: Conquest, Colonization and Cultural Change, 950-1350* (Princeton: Princeton University Press, 1993), 15. Also, Lotter, "Crusading Idea," 267, gives the clearest geographical positioning of these peoples, at least as far as Livonia. Of course, the nature of boundaries among tribally organized peoples is by definition fluid.
30 Ibid.
31 Bruno Scott James, trans., *The Letters of St. Bernard of Clairvaux* (Chicago: Henry Regnery Company, 1953), 463. In the letter to the duke and people of Bohemia, Bernard claimed that "this time is not like any time that has gone before."
32 Ibid., 462.
33 Ibid., 466–8. This key epistle is numbered as Letter 457 in the standard corpus of Bernard's work.

34 Ibid., 467. See Lotter, "Crusading Idea," 289ff., for an attempt to discern Bernard's true meaning of this explosive phrase. Lotter first enunciated his position in a brief 92-page text that Bernard's vexed *aut ritus ipse aut natio deleatur* passage meant the destruction of pagan social norms, not genocide. See *Die Konzeption des Wendenkreuzzugs: ideengeschichte, kirchenrechtliche und historisch-politische Voraussetzungen der Missionierung von Elb- und Ostseeslawen um die Mitte des 12. Jahrhunderts* (Sigmaringen: Jan Thorbecke, 1977).
35 Ibid.
36 Ibid., 467–8.
37 Helmold, *Chronicle*, 175.
38 Ibid., 177.
39 Eric Christiansen, *The Northern Crusades: The Baltic and the Catholic Frontier, 1100-1525* (Minneapolis: University of Minnesota Press, 1980), 53.
40 Helmold, *Chronicle*, 180.
41 Ane Bysted, Carsten Selch Jensen, Kurt Villads Jensen, and John H. Lind, *Jerusalem in the North: Denmark and the Baltic Crusades, 1100-1522* (Turnhout: Brepols, 2012), 66.
42 Niels-Knud Liebgott, "Pilgrimages and Crusades," in Else Roesdahl and David M. Wilson, eds, *From Viking to Crusader: The Scandinavians and Europe, 800-1200* (New York: Rizzoli International Publications, 1992), 111.
43 William L. Urban, *The Baltic Crusade*, 2nd edn (Chicago: Lithuanian Research and Studies Center, 1994), 51.
44 Ibid., 99.
45 Henry, *Chronicle* XXX, 3; Brundage, 239.
46 Ibid., 240.
47 Jonathan Riley-Smith, *The Crusades: A History*, 2nd edn (New Haven, CT: Yale University Press, 2005), 253.
48 Ibid.
49 Henry, *Chronicle* II, 10; Brundage, 34.
50 Ibid., 60.
51 Urban, "The Sense of Humor among the Teutonic Knights," *Illinois Quarterly* 42 (1979): 45.
52 Henry, author of the *Livonian Chronicle*, candidly acknowledged the union of war and conversion when he observed: "And quite properly theological doctrine followed the wars, since ... after the

above-mentioned wars, the whole of Livonia was converted and baptized." Brundage, *Chronicle*, 65.
53 Concerning the taking of girls and women, the crusaders are shown to participate willingly in this pagan custom in Books XII and XIII of Henry's *Chronicle*, and no less than nine instances are recounted just in Book XV. Brundage, *Chronicle*, 86–122.
54 See Benjamin Z. Kedar, *Crusade and Mission: European Approaches toward the Muslims* (Princeton, NJ: Princeton University Press, 1984).

Chapter 2

1 Marcia L. Colish, *Faith, Fiction & Force in Medieval Baptismal Debates* (Washington, DC: The Catholic University of America Press, 2014), 264.
2 Geoffrey Hindley, *The Crusades: Islam and Christianity in the Struggle for World Supremacy* (New York: Carroll & Graf Publishers, 2003), 75–6. He does venture an opinion that "paradoxically, Pope Eugenius may not have been pleased at the news of German participation. Agitation in Rome against papal rule there had forced him into exile and he seems to have been hoping for German support to restore him," 76. This calls into question Eugenius' willingness to send Bernard on a recruitment tour to Germany.
3 Rodney Stark, *God's Battalions: The Case for the Crusades* (New York: HarperCollins, 2009), 187.
4 Eva Eihmane, "The Baltic Crusades: A Clash of Two Identities," in Alan V. Murray, ed., *The Clash of Cultures on the Medieval Baltic Frontier* (Burlington, VT: Ashgate Publishing Company, 2009), 37–8.
5 Urban, *Baltic Crusade*, i.
6 Helmold, *Chronicle*, 152–8.
7 Henry, *Chronicle* I, 5–6; Brundage, 26.
8 Ibid.
9 Jean Richard, "National Feeling and the Legacy of the Crusades," in Nicholson, *Palgrave Advances*, 206. He mentions that these terms were used by the canonist Hostiensis in the mid-thirteenth century.
10 Jill M. Claster, *Sacred Violence: The European Crusades to the Middle East, 1095-1396* (Toronto: University of Toronto Press, 2009), 267. Despite her title, Professor Claster includes a treatment of the Baltic Crusades, but considers them "within Europe" using the medieval *crux cismarina* geographical interpretation.

11 See the *Patrologia Latinae* 115: 656–7 for Leo IV's use of the term and the *PL* 126: 816 for Pope John VIII's promise of a type of indulgence for those "fighting bravely against pagans or unbelievers."
12 Ibid.
13 Christiansen, *Northern Crusades*, 56.
14 Bysted, *Jerusalem in the North*, 27.
15 Lotter, "Crusading Idea," 290–1.
16 Henry, *Chronicle* XXX, 5–6; Brundage, 245.
17 Ibid.
18 Kedar, *Crusade and Mission*. Kedar notes that "the link between Muslim conversion and anti-Muslim warfare that will become fully articulated by the mid-thirteenth century (will be) harnessed for a novel purpose in the sixteenth," x.
19 Henry, *Chronicle*, 27, 34, and 51.
20 Andris Sne, "The Emergence of Livonia: The Transformations of Social and Political Structures in the Territory of Latvia during the Twelfth and Thirteenth Centuries," in Murray, *Clash of Cultures*, 54.
21 Kurt Villads Jensen, "Sacralization of the Landscape: Converting Trees and Measuring Land in the Danish Crusade against the Wends," in Murray, *Clash of Cultures*, 148. Jensen notes that Bishop Albert of Buxhövden got the Fourth Lateran Council under the direction of Pope Innocent III (r. 1198–1216) to declare Livonia of "no less importance" than Palestine, 148.
22 William Urban, review of Iben Fonnesberg-Schmidt, *The Popes and the Baltic Crusades, 1147-1254*. *Speculum* 83 (January 2008), 195. Urban rightly calls this flexible use of the word *peregrini* "a special problem for scholars." Pope Eugenius III had not used the term *peregrini* for the Baltic crusaders in his *Divina dispensatione II*, preferring to use pronouns rather than descriptors, but the word was used in further accounts of the Baltic enterprise.
23 Erdmann, *Origin*, 105ff.
24 Henry, *Chronicle*, xxvii, and Jerry C. Smith and William L. Urban, trans., The *Livonian Rhymed Chronicle* (Bloomington, IN: Indiana University Press, 1977), xxi.
25 Henry, *Chronicle*, Brundage, xxviii.
26 Thomas Asbridge, *The Crusades: The Authoritative History of the War for the Holy Land* (New York: HarperCollins, 2010), 212.
27 Constable, *Crusaders and Crusading*, 241.
28 Shami Ghosh, "Conquest, Conversion, and Heathen Customs in Henry of Livonia's *Chronicon Livoniae* and the *Livländische Reimchronik*," *Crusades* 11 (2012): 105.

29 Housley, *Contesting*, 110.
30 Christiansen, *Northern Crusades*, 250.
31 Bysted, *Jerusalem in the North*, 81.
32 Iben Fonnesberg-Schmidt, *The Popes and the Baltic Crusades, 1147-1254* (Leiden: Brill, 2007), especially 249–55.
33 Ibid.

Chapter 3

1 France, "Crusading Warfare," 66.
2 Tyerman, *Debate*, 220.
3 Frederick Russell, *Just War in the Middle Ages* (Cambridge: Cambridge University Press, 1975); also see J. Daryl Charles, *Between Pacifism and Jihad: Just War and Christian Tradition* (Downers Grove, IL: InterVarsity Press, 2005).
4 Thomas Madden, "Crusaders and Historians," *First Things* (June 2005): 26.
5 The works of John Pryor, especially his *Commerce, Shipping, and Naval Warfare in the Medieval Mediterranean* (London: Variorum, 1987) and *Geography, Technology and War: Studies in the Maritime History of the Mediterranean, 649-1571* (Cambridge: Cambridge University Press, 1988) are useful as is Ruthy Gertwagen and Elizabeth Jeffreys, eds, *Shipping, Trade and Crusade in the Medieval Mediterranean: Studies in Honour of John Pryor* (Burlington, VT: Ashgate Publishing Company, 2012).
6 John France, *Victory in the East: A Military History of the First Crusade* (Cambridge: Cambridge University Press, 1994), 368. France believes that "without Byzantine help it is difficult to see how the western fleets could have operated so successfully."
7 France, *Western Warfare in the Age of the Crusades, 1000-1300* (Ithaca, NY: Cornell University Press, 1999); and Ronnie Ellenblum, *Crusader Castles and Modern Histories* (Cambridge: Cambridge University Press, 2007). Also see David Nicolle, *Warriors and Their Weapons Around the Time of the Crusades: Relationships Between Byzantium, the West and the Islamic World* (Burlington, VT: Ashgate Publishing Company, 2002).
8 Housley, *Contesting*, 2.
9 Ibid., 166.
10 Tyerman, *Debate*, 225.
11 Constable, *Crusaders*, 23.

12 Tyerman, *The Invention of the Crusades* (Toronto: University of Toronto Press, 1998). Ernst-Dieter Hehl, "Was ist eigentlich ein Kreuzzug?," *Historische Zeitschrift* 259 (1994): 333, warns against seeing crusading as a wholly novel enterprise situated on the edge of medieval society, preferring to view it as something central.
13 John Gilchrist, "The Erdmann Thesis and the Canon Law, 1083-1141," in Peter W. Edbury, ed., *Crusade and Settlement: Papers read at the First Conference of the Society for the Study of the Crusades and the Latin East and presented to R.C. Smail* (Cardiff: University College Cardiff Press, 1985), 38.
14 Edward LeRoy Long, Jr., *War and Conscience in America* (Philadelphia: The Westminster Press, 1968), 33–47.
15 Housley, *Contesting*, 78.
16 Constable, "The Historiography of the Crusades," in Angeliki Laiou and Roy Mottahedeh, eds, *The Crusades from the Perspective of Byzantium and the Muslim World* (Washington, DC: Dumbarton Oaks, 2001), 1–22.
17 Ibid., 18–22.
18 Jonathan Riley-Smith, *The Crusades: A Short History* (New Haven, CT: Yale University Press, 1987), xxviii.
19 Riley-Smith, *The Crusades, Christianity, and Islam* (New York: Columbia University Press, 2008), 9.
20 Housley, *Contesting*, 20.
21 Henri Daniel-Rops, *The Church in the Dark Ages*, v. ii, trans. Audrey Butler (Garden City, NY: Image Books, 1962), 15–17.
22 Alexander F. C. Webster and Darrell Cole, *The Virtue of War: Reclaiming the Classic Christian Traditions East & West* (Salisbury, MD: Regina Orthodox Press, Inc., 2004), 15: "The entire history of Islam has been, to coin a term, one long 'crescade' against unbelievers.... The term is shorthand for crusade for the crescent moon, the perennial symbol of Islam."
23 Tyerman, *Invention*, 4.
24 Chevedden has outlined his position in a series of articles: "The Islamic Interpretation of the Crusades: A New (Old) Paradigm for Understanding the Crusades," *Der Islam* (2006): 90–136; "The Islamic View and the Christian View of the Crusades: A New Synthesis," *History* 93, no. 2 (April 2008): 181–200; and "The View of the Crusades from Rome and Damascus: The Geo-Strategic and Historical Perspectives of Pope Urban II and 'Ali ibn Tahir al-Sulami" *Orient* 39 (2011): 257–329.

25 Paul M. Cobb, *The Race for Paradise: An Islamic History of the Crusades* (Oxford: Oxford University Press, 2014), 8.
26 Charles Homer Haskins, *The Normans in European History* (New York: W.W. Norton and Company, Inc., 1966), 208. Haskins: "We may think of the conquest of Sicily as a sort of crusade before the Crusades."
27 Chevedden, "Islamic View," 183.
28 Chevedden, "View of the Crusades," 262.
29 Ibid.
30 Cobb, *Race*, 7.
31 Chevedden, "View of the Crusades," 263.
32 Ibid., 289.
33 Constable, *Crusaders*, 229–300.
34 Bysted, *Jerusalem in the North*, 9.

Chapter 4

1 Leopold von Ranke, *Weltgeschichte*, v. 8, *Kreuzzug und päpstliche Weltherrschaft* (Leipzig: Duncker & Humblot, 1887), 374. Von Ranke used the term *urgeschichte des Kreuzzüge* or "original history of the Crusades." More recently, when the issue has come up, German scholars favor the use of the word *vorgeschichte*, or "before-history." See Albrecht Noth, *Heiliger Krieg und Heiliger Kampf in Islam und Christentum: Beiträge zur Vorgeschichte und Geschichte der Kreuzzüge*, Bonner Historische Forschungen, Bd. 28 (Bonn: Ludwig Rohrscheid Verlag, 1966).
2 See respectively: Brian Hayden, *Shamans, Sorcerers, and Saints: A Prehistory of Religion* (Washington, DC: Smithsonian Books, 2003); David Armitrage, "Is There a Prehistory of Globalization?," in Deborah Cohen and Maura O'Connor, eds, *Comparison and History: Europe in Cross-National Perspective* (London: Routledge, 2004), 165–76; Rudolf Botha and Chris Knight, eds, *The Prehistory of Language* (Oxford: Oxford University Press, 2009).
3 Bysted, *Jerusalem in the North*, 23.
4 Carl Erdmann, *The Origin of the Idea of Crusade*, trans. Marshall W. Baldwin and Walter Goffart (Princeton, NJ: Princeton University Press, 1977). Originally published as *Die Entstehung des Kreuzzuggedankens* in 1935, the excellent translation of this landmark work did not produce a flurry of Crusade prehistory studies.

5 Joshua Prawer, review of *A History of the Crusades: The First Hundred Years* (1095-1189), Kenneth M. Setton and Marshall W. Baldwin, eds, *Revue belge de philologie et d'histoire* 37 (1959): 167.
6 Tertullian, *De praescriptione haereticorum*, vii, 9: *Quid ergo Athenis et Hierosolymis? Quid academiae et ecclesiae?*
7 James Waltz, review of Benjamin Z. Kedar, *Crusade and Mission: European Approaches toward the Muslims, Speculum* 61, no. 2 (April 1986): 433.
8 Kedar, *Crusade and Mission*, ix and 7 respectively. Also, E. Randolph Daniel, *The Franciscan Concept of Mission in the High Middle Ages* (Lexington, KY: University Press of Kentucky, 1975), connects the delayed appearance of the conversion impetus to the solidifying of the notion of *societas Christiana*: "The attitude of Latin Christians toward non-Christians was a natural corollary of the *societas Christiana*. Anyone who was not a *fidelis* automatically became an alien, and a potential—if not an actual—enemy," 3.
9 Fletcher, *Barbarian Conversion*, 485.
10 Jean Flori, "Ideology and Motivations in the First Crusade," in Nicholson, *Palgrave Advances*, 15.
11 France, *Victory in the East*, 4 and 7.
12 Marcus Bull, "Origins," in Jonathan Riley-Smith, ed., *The Oxford Illustrated History of the Crusades* (Oxford: Oxford University Press, 1997), 17.
13 Ganz, *Two Lives*, 96.
14 Matthew Gabriele, *An Empire of Memory: The Legend of Charlemagne, the Franks, and Jerusalem before the First Crusade* (Oxford: Oxford University Press, 2011), 5.
15 Ibid., 6.
16 Ibid., 97.
17 Helmold, *Chronicle*, 53.
18 Hamilton Gibb, "The Influence of Islamic Culture on Medieval Europe," in Sylvia Thrupp, ed., *Change in Medieval Society: Europe North of the Alps, 1050-1500* (New York: Appleton-Century-Crofts, 1964), 155.
19 Christopher Dawson, *The Making of Europe: An Introduction to the History of European Unity* (New York: Meridian Books, 1956), 17.
20 Matthew Arnold, "Dover Beach," in A. Dwight Culler, ed., *Poetry and Criticism of Matthew Arnold* (Boston: Houghton Mifflin Company, 1961), 161–2.
21 For example, Jacob Burckhardt, *The Civilization of the Renaissance in Italy*, trans. Irene Gordon (New York: New American Library,

1960); Charles Homer Haskins, *The Renaissance of the Twelfth Century* (Cambridge, MA: Harvard University Press, 1927).
22 Erdmann, *Origin*, devoted most of his first chapter to this topic by focusing on banners.
23 Martin Heinzelmann, "Heresy in Books I and II of Gregory of Tours' *Historia*," in Alexander Callander Murray, ed., *After Rome's Fall: Narrators and Sources of Early Medieval History, Essays presented to Walter Goffart* (Toronto: Toronto University Press, 1998), 78.
24 Columbanus, *Epistola* I in G. S. M. Walker, ed., *Sancti Colombani: Opera* (Dublin: The Dublin Institute for Advanced Studies, 1957), 13.
25 Marc Bloch, *Feudal Society*, v. I, trans. L. A. Manyon (Chicago: University of Chicago Press, 1968), 113.
26 Tertullian, "On the Veiling of Virgins," I, in Alexander Roberts and James Donaldson, eds, *Tertullian, Part Fourth; Minucius Felix; Commodian; Origen, Parts First and Second* in Ante-Nicene Fathers, vol. 4 (Peabody, MA: Hendrickson Publishers, Inc., 1994), 27.
27 Psalm 79: 1 and 6; *The New International Version Study Bible*, ed. Kenneth Baker (Grand Rapids, MI: Zondervan, 1995), 863.
28 Erdmann, *Origin*, 92.
29 Scholz and Rogers, *Carolingian Chronicles*, 49.
30 Erdmann, *Origin*, dedication. On the dedicatory flyleaf of his magisterial *Origin*, he wrote: "To the memory of my father who lost a professorship at Dorpat (Tartu) in 1893 for remaining true to his mother tongue."
31 I suggested this in Burnam W. Reynolds, "The Prehistory of the Crusades: Toward a Developmental Taxonomy," *History Compass* 6 (May 2008): 884–97.
32 Charles Julian Bishko, "The Frontier in Medieval History," a paper presented at a medieval history session, Annual Meeting of the American Historical Association (Washington, DC: December 29, 1955).
33 Dawson, *Making of Europe*, 19.
34 Marc Bloch, *The Historian's Craft: Reflections on the Nature and Uses of History and the Techniques and Methods of the Men Who Write It*, trans. Peter Putnam (New York: Vintage Books, 1964), 32.

Chapter 5

1 Henry, *Chronicle*, IX, 12; Brundage, 52; MGH, 31: *Nec tamen hec et hiis similia facientes inimici a predicatione verbi Dei christianorum*

obstruunt voces verum eciam per incrementa fidei conspiciunt eos cottidie tam preliando quam predicando magis ac magis invalescere.

2 Ibid., IX, 14; Brundage, 53; MGH, 32: *quia nimirum per bella plurima que sequuntur convertenda erat gentilitas* MGH, 32.
3 Smith and Urban, *Livonian Rhymed Chronicle*, lines 3407–17, 47.
4 Ibid., lines 3909–49, 52.
5 Ibid., lines 3351–407, 47.
6 Bede, I, 20: "So the innocent British army saw its defeats avenged, and became an inactive spectator of the victory granted to it.... So the bishops (Germanus and Lupus) overcame the enemy without bloodshed, winning a victory by faith and not by force." Leo Sherley-Price, trans., *Bede: A History of the English Church and People* (New York: Dorset Press, 1968), 63.
7 *Livonian Rhymed Chronicle*, lines 7851–995, 97.
8 Colish, *Faith, Fiction & Force*, 264.
9 Francis Dvornik, *The Making of Central and Eastern Europe*, 2nd edn (Gulf Breeze, FL: Academic International Press, 1974), 16.
10 Charles Godfrey Leland, trans., *The Works of Heinrich Heine* (London: William Heinemann, 1892), 207–8.
11 *Translatio S. Liborii* 5, ed. Georg Heinrich Pertz, *MGH Scriptores* (Hannover: Hahn Buchhandlung, 1891), 151: *ut ianuam fides aperiret, ferrea quodammodo lingua praedicavit.*
12 Carl Erdmann, *Die Enstethung des Kreuzzugsgedankens* (Darmstadt: Wissenschaftliche Buchgesellschaft, 1972), 10. Though Erdmann used the term repeatedly in his work, its first appearance was on page ten, where he referenced "*das Prinzip des indireckten Missionskriegs aufgestellt*," referring to the letters of Pope Gregory the Great (r. 590–604) that created the possibility of an indirect missionary war.
13 Ibid., 11–12.
14 A nuanced, and quite scholarly, example of this perspective is Ramsay MacMullen's *Christianity and Paganism in the Fourth to Eighth Centuries* (New Haven, CT: Yale University Press, 1997). A far less effective work is Charles Freeman's *The Closing of the Western Mind: The Rise of Faith and the Fall of Reason* (New York: Alfred A. Knopf, 2003). Both these volumes deal with more than the issue of monotheism producing intolerance and violence, but that view underpins much of their argument.
15 Richard Lim, "Christian Triumph and Controversy," in G. W. Bowersock, Peter Brown, and Oleg Grabar, eds, *Interpreting Late Antiquity* (Cambridge, MA: The Belknap Press of Harvard University, 2001), 196.

16 Przemyslaw Urbanczyk, "The Politics of Conversion in North Central Europe," in Martin Carver, ed., *The Cross Goes North: Processes of Conversion in Northern Europe, AD300–1300* (Woodbridge: The Boydell Press, 2005), 22–3.
17 Brent D. Shaw, *Sacred Violence: African Christians and Sectarian Hatred in the Age of Augustine* (Cambridge: Cambridge University Press, 2011), 771–2.
18 Ibid.
19 H. A. Drake, "Monotheism and Violence," *Journal of Late Antiquity* 6, no. 2 (Fall 2013): 256.
20 Shaw, *Sacred Violence*, 793.
21 Matthew 28:19: "Therefore go and make disciples of all nations, baptizing them in the name of the Father and of the Son and of the Holy Spirit, and teaching them to obey everything I have commanded you." *NIV*, 1487.
22 Henry, *Chronicle* I, 13; Brundage, 30; MGH, 7: *non eos deserendoscensuit . . . Remissionem quipped omnium peccatorum indulsit omnibus, qui ad resuscitandum illam primitivam ecclesiam accepta cruce transeant.*
23 Henry, *Chronicle* I, 11; Brundage, 28; MGH, 5: *Unde Lyvonum astucia christianorum timet et suspicatur super se venturm exercitum.*
24 Ibid., 31–2.
25 Kurt Villads Jensen, "Sacralization of the Landscape," in Murray, *Clash of Cultures*, 141.
26 Ibid., 149.
27 II Corinthians 10:3-4, *NIV*, 1774.
28 Louis J. Swift has produced a thoughtful summary of early church writers on war and pacifism in his *The Early Fathers on War and Military Service* (Wilmington, DE: Michael Glazier, 1983). Also see John Helgeland, Robert J. Daly, and J. Patout Burns, *Christians and the Military: The Early Experience* (Philadelphia: Fortress Press, 1985).
29 Long, *War and Conscience*, 22.
30 Helgeland, et al., *Christians and the Military*, 65–6.
31 Swift, *Early Fathers*, 27.
32 Ibid.
33 For a survey of just war thought in the medieval period see Russell, *Just War in the Middle Ages*, and Charles, *Between Pacifism and Jihad*.
34 R. A. Markus, "Saint Augustine's Views on the 'Just War'," in W. J. Shiels, ed., *The Church and War* (Oxford: Basil Blackwell, 1983), 2.
35 Ibid., 13.

36 LeRoy Walters, "The Just War and the Crusade: Antitheses or Analogies?," *Monist* 57 (October 1973): 584.
37 Christopher Tyerman, "Accounting for the Crusades: Faith, Facts and Figures," a plenary address delivered at the Third International Symposium on Crusade Studies (St. Louis, MO: March 1, 2014); also see his *How to Plan a Crusade: Reason and Religious War in the High Middle Ages* (St. Ives: Allen Lane/Penguin Random House, 2015), especially chapter 6, 150–65.
38 Henry, *Chronicle* VII, 1; Brundage, 41.
39 Ibid., XI, 1; Brundage, 68 and XXIII, 1; Brundage, 173.
40 Even though many have noted this, it is presented in a straightforward manner in Henrik Syse, "Augustine and Just War," in Henrik Syse and Gregory M. Reichberg, eds, *Ethics, Nationalism, and Just War: Medieval and Contemporary Perspectives* (Washington, DC: The Catholic University of America Press, 2007), 37.
41 Augustine, *Contra Faustum Manichaeum* libri XXIII, 74; Migne, *PL* 47: 447. *Quid enim culpatur in bello? An quia moriuntur quandoque morituri ut domentur in pace victuri? Hoc reprehendere timidorum est, non religiosorum animus, feritas rebellandi, libido dominandi, et si quia similia haec sunt quae in bellis jure culpantur; quae plerumque ut etiam jure legitimo imperio jubente, gerenda ipsa bella suscipiuntur at bonis, cum in eos vel jubere tale aliquid, vel in talibus obedire juste ordo ipse constringit.*
42 Gregory of Tours, *Historia*, III, 7; Thorpe, 168; Buchner, I, 152.
43 Ibid. *Ecce! Verbum directum habemus: Eamus cum Dei adiuturio contra eos!*
44 Ibid., II, 30; Thorpe, 143.
45 Bede II, 9; Sherley-Price, 114.
46 Ibid., 116.
47 Ibid.
48 J. N. Hillgarth, ed., *The Conversion of Western Europe, 350-750* (Englewood Cliffs, NJ: Prentice-Hall, Inc., 1969), 76. After urging Clovis to bring the faith to these pagan peoples, Avitus also alludes to military control: "So that other pagan peoples, at first being subject to your empire for the sake of religion" A more recent, and thorough, translation and commentary on this letter is that of Danuta Shanzer and Ian Wood, eds, *Avitus of Vienne: Letters and Selected Prose* (Liverpool: Liverpool University Press, 2002). They note that Epistle 46 "is exceptional in urging, at so early a date, the christianisation of barbarian peoples outside what had once been

the Roman Empire" (368) and also cite Avitus' statement that Clovis should "have no fear . . . from now on the very softness of that clothing (baptismal robes) will cause the hardness of your armor to be all the more effective." (372)

49 Gregory, *Historia* II, 40–2; Thorpe, 155–8. Clovis paid assassins with fake gold and suborned rival kings' sons against their fathers. As a type of coup-de-grace, Gregory depicted him as bemoaning his status as a self-made orphan merely to draw out any remaining relatives to kill.

50 Ibid., 253. Buchner, I, 276–7: *Utinam et vos O Regis, in his proelia, in quibus parentes vestri desudaverunt, exercimini, ut gentes, vestra pace conterritae, vestris viribus praemirentur! Recordamini, quid capud victuriarum vestrarum Chlodovechus fecerit, qui adversos reges interficet, noxias gentes elisit, patrias subiugavit, quarum regnum vobis integrum inlesumque reliquit!*

51 Ibid., 156. Buchner I, 136: *Posternebat enim cotidiae Deus hostes eius sub manu ipsius et augebat regnum eius, eo quod ambularet recto corde coram eo et facerit quae placita errant in oculis eius.*

52 Syse, "Augustine," 48.

53 James C. Russell, *The Germanization of Early Medieval Christianity: A Sociohistorical Approach to Religious Transformation* (Oxford: Oxford University Press, 1994), 4.

54 Walter Goffart, *Barbarians and Romans, AD418-584: The Techniques of Accommodation* (Princeton, NJ: Princeton University Press, 1980), contends that the barbarians merely took over the Roman military tax system called *hospitalitas*. Bernard S. Bachrach, *Merovingian Military Organization* (Minneapolis, MN: University of Minnesota Press, 1972), shows that the early medieval Frankish armies were inclusive of Roman elements and practices.

55 J. M. Wallace-Hadrill, *Early Medieval History* (Oxford: Basil Blackwell, 1975), 29.

56 G. Ronald Murphy, trans., *The Heliand: The Saxon Gospel* (Oxford: Oxford University Press, 1992).

57 Ibid., 15, 155, and 158; Songs 5, 55, and 58 respectively.

58 Ibid., 160.

59 Murphy, *The Saxon Savior: The Germanic Transformation of the Gospel in the Ninth-Century Heliand* (Oxford: Oxford University Press, 1989), vii–viii.

60 Bernard S. Bachrach and David S. Bachrach, trans., *Widukind of Corvey: Deeds of the Saxons* (Washington, DC: The Catholic University of America Press, 2014), II, 1, 63.

61 John Howard Yoder, *Nevertheless: The Varieties and Shortcomings of Religious Pacifism* (Scottdale, PA: Herald Press, 1992).
62 See Charles, *Between Pacifism and Jihad*, 67–70 and 169–72.
63 Helmold, *Chronicle*, 59.
64 Bysted, *Jerusalem in the North*, 27.
65 William L. Urban, "Victims of the Baltic Crusade," *Journal of Baltic Studies* 29 (1998): 9.
66 Ibid., 3.
67 Brian Tierney, *The Crisis of Church and State, 1050-1300* (Englewood Cliffs, NJ: Prentice-Hall, Inc., 1964), 31.
68 Anne Julie Semb, "U.N. Authorized Interventions: A Slippery Slope of Forcible Interference," in Syse and Reichberg, *Ethics, Nationalism, and Just War*, 219. Semb writes: "One reason for resisting a softening of the principle of non-intervention is that once one allows for interventions for some normatively defensible purposes, it may prove difficult to establish barriers against a further softening of this principle."
69 Kedar, *Crusade and Mission*, 160.
70 Ibid., 161.
71 *Epistola* VII, 22: His statement was, "We are preserved under God for so many years among swords." James Barmby, trans., *The Book of Pastoral Rule and Selected Epistles of Gregory the Great*, in Philip Schaff and Henry Wace, eds, *Nicene and Post-Nicene Fathers*, vol. I (Peabody, MA: Hendrickson Publishers, 1995), 238.
72 R. A. Markus, *Gregory the Great and His World* (Cambridge: Cambridge University Press, 1997), 100.
73 S. J. Allen and Emilie Amt, eds, *The Crusades: A Reader* (Peterborough, Ontario: Broadview Press, 2003), 19.
74 Migne, *PL*, Tomus CXV: 655–7; Tomus CXXVI: 816.
75 Janet Nelson, "The Church's Military Service in the Ninth Century: A Contemporary Comparative View," in Shiels, ed., *Church and War*, 15.
76 Ibid., 22.
77 *Anglo-Saxon Chronicle, sub anno* 823, 825, 845, 848: The principal bishop for King Egbert, Ealhstan, is cited as leading "a great force" that "drove King Baldred north over the Thames" in 825 (60). Ealhstan had quit the military career, as he reappears in the *Chronicle* under the entry for the year 848, fighting against the Vikings and "made a great slaughter there and won the victory" (64). In 871, Ealhstan's successor, Heahmund, was killed in combat with the Danes at the Battle of Meretun (72).

78 The listings are in multiple annals, but Donnchadh O'Corrain, *Ireland Before the Normans* (Dublin: Gill and MacMillan, 1972), 86–7, and Kathleen Hughes, *The Church in Early Irish Society* (Ithaca, NY: Cornell University Press, 1966), 170 and 190, provide useful synopses.
79 O'Corrain, *Ireland Before*, 87.
80 Lisa Bitel, *Isle of the Saints: Monastic Settlement and Christian Community in Early Ireland* (Ithaca, NY: Cornell University Press, 1993), 117ff. Also see T. M. Charles-Edwards, *Early Christian Ireland* (Cambridge: Cambridge University Press, 2000) for these settlements as monastic cities, 118.
81 Nelson, "Military Service," 23.
82 Boniface, *Epistola* 10 in C. H. Talbot, *The Anglo-Saxon Missionaries in Germany* (New York: Sheed and Ward, 1954), 75.
83 Ibid., *Epistola* 26, 97.
84 Ibid., 58. The passage is from Willibald's *Life of St. Boniface*.
85 Ibid., 232.
86 D. C. Munro, trans., *Translations and Reprints from the Original Sources of European History*, vol. VI, no.5 (Philadelphia: University of Pennsylvania Press, 1900), 11–12.
87 Nelson, "Military Service," 29.
88 A good survey of these movements is Thomas Head and Richard Landes, eds, *The Peace of God: Social Violence and Religious Response in France around the Year 1000* (Ithaca, NY: Cornell University Press, 1992).
89 Thomas Head, "The Judgment of God: Andrew of Fleury's Account of the Peace League of Bourges," in Head and Landes, eds, *Peace of God*, 224.
90 Tyerman, *God's War*, 44.
91 Mayer, *Crusades*, 20–1.
92 Asbridge, *First Crusade*, 28.
93 Malcolm Barber, *The New Knighthood: A History of the Order of the Temple* (Cambridge: Cambridge University Press, 1994) still shines amid the plethora of popular histories of the Templars. See 44–50 for Barber's view on the possible contours of Bernard's thought relative to *De laude novae militiae*.
94 Conrad Greenia, trans., *The Works of Bernard of Clairvaux*, vol. VII, Treatises, 3 (Kalamazoo, MI: Cistercian Fathers Series, 1977). Bernard echoes in large part the view of Augustine on the acceptability of war as phrased in *Contra Faustum Manichaeum* (see fn. 41 *supra*).

Chapter 6

1. H. G. J. Beck, *The Pastoral Care of Souls in South-East France During the Sixth Century. Analecta Gregoriana*, vol. 51 (Rome: Universitatis Gregorianae, 1950).
2. Acts 8:26-40, *NIV*, 1662.
3. Peter Cramer, *Baptism and Change in the Early Middle Ages, c. 200-c.1150* (Cambridge: Cambridge University Press, 1993), 187ff.
4. Henry, *Chronicle* I, 9; Brundage, 27; *MGH*, 4: *baptismum, quem in aqua susceperant, in Duna se lavando removere putant, remittendo in Theuthoniam.*
5. Ibid., II, 8; Brundage, 34.
6. Ibid., IX, 8; Brundage, 51; *MGH*, 29: *et hanc in Duna se lavantes delere sepe dicebant.*
7. Ibid., XXVI, 8; Brundage, 210; *MGH*, 191: *et domos suas et castra lavantes aquis et scopis purgantes, taliter baptismi sacramenta de finibus suis omnio delere conabantur.*
8. Tiina Kala, "Rural Society and Religious Innovation: Acceptance and Rejection of Catholicism among the Native Inhabitants of Medieval Livonia," in Murray, *Clash of Cultures*, 177.
9. Henry, *Chronicle* XXVI, 6; Brundage, 209.
10. Ibid., XI, 6; Brundage, 74.
11. Ibid., XIX, 4; Brundage, 147.
12. Ibid. Baptism by treaty was apparently so well known that some sought it out as a preventative for imminent attack.
13. Ibid., XII, 6; *MGH*, 64: *Sed neque inter christianos et paganos unum cor et una anima neque forma pacis firma esse potent, nisi recepto nobiscum eodem iugo christianitatis et pacis perpetue unum Deum colatis.*
14. Widukind of Corvey, *Deeds*, I, 15; Bachrach and Bachrach, 26.
15. Peter Brown, *The Rise of Western Christendom: Triumph and Diversity, A.D. 200–1000*, 2nd edn (Oxford: Blackwell, 2003), 432.
16. Rasa Mazeika, "Bargaining for Baptism: Lithuanian Negotiations for Conversion, 1250-358," in James Muldoon, ed., *Varieties of Religious Conversion in the Middle Ages* (Gainesville, FL: University Press of Florida, 1997), 131–45.
17. Rapoport, *Clausewitz*, 24.
18. Stark, *God's Battalions*, 29–30. Stark uses the term to describe Muslim conquest, the age of *futuh*, but incorrectly so in that Muslim

conquerors did not immediately initiate their conquered peoples into Islam.
19 Henry, *Chronicle* X, 13; Brundage, 65.
20 A typical example is the recent work of Marina Caffiero, *Forced Baptism: Histories of Jews, Christians, and Converts in Papal Rome*, trans. Lydia G. Cochrane (Berkeley: University of California Press, 2013).
21 Henry, *Chronicle* XV, 1; Brundage, 106–7; *MGH*, 85: *Cognoscimus Deum vestrum maiorem diis nostris, qui nos superando animum nostrum as ipsius culturam inclinavit. Unde rogamus, ut parcendo nobis iugum christianitatis, sicut et Lyvonibus et Lettis, ita et nobis misericorditer imponatis.*
22 Ibid., 107.
23 A good recent account of this with a fresh take on *futuh*, the Arab conquest of vast tracts of territory during the period 632–750, is by Robert G. Hoyland, *In God's Path: The Arab Conquests and the Creation of an Islamic Empire* (Oxford: Oxford University Press, 2015).
24 Fletcher, *The Cross and the Crescent: Christianity and Islam from Muhammad to the Reformation* (New York: Viking, 2003), 30.
25 Hoyland, *In God's Path*, 158 and 164.
26 Ibid., see especially 158–69; Bernard Lewis, *The Arabs in History* (Oxford: Oxford University Press, 1993), 58. The failure of Muslim forces to quickly Islamicize their troops forms the basis for Roger Collins' thesis on why the Muslim empire broke apart in the mid to late eighth century. See Roger Collins, *The Arab Conquest of Spain, 710-797* (Oxford: Basil Blackwell, 1989), 97–9.
27 Thomas F. Glick, *Islamic and Christian Spain in the Early Middle Ages* (Princeton, NJ: Princeton University Press, 1979), 178, comments on the use of this model for Muslim-conquered Spain: "The usual method of dealing with the assimilation of ethnic minorities was to accord the neophyte the status of client (*mawla*), whereby new converts (often entire tribal groups) would attach themselves to a powerful Arab family or tribe, adopting its lineage and social status."
28 The classic treatment is by W. H. C. Frend, *The Donatist Church: A Movement of Protest in Roman North Africa* (Oxford: Oxford University Press, 1985).
29 Garry Wills, *Font of Life: Ambrose, Augustine and the Mystery of Baptism* (Oxford: Oxford University Press, 2012), 137–9.

30 Ibid., 143.
31 In 407, Pope Innocent I (r. 401–17) ruled that infant baptism was the best option given the existence of original sin.
32 Bryan D. Spinks, *Early and Medieval Rituals and Theologies of Baptism: From the New Testament to the Council of Trent* (Burlington, VT: Ashgate Publishing Company, 2006), 63–7.
33 Wills, *Font*, 142–3; also see the position of Pope Gregory II (r. 715–31) who called it "the ancient custom of the Church" that one not be baptized again. The pope went on to say, in true Augustinian fashion, that the baptized had "received the grace not in the name of the minister but in the name of the Trinity." *Letters of Boniface*, 14 in Talbot, *Anglo-Saxon Missionaries*, 82.
34 Frend, *Donatist Church*, 137.
35 See Ephesians 4:5 for a scriptural justification of this position. *NIV*, 1797.
36 León Arsenal, *Godos de Hispania* (Madrid: EDAF, 2013), 202: *Esa situación de irreversibilidad llevó a un Nuevo problema, el de los falsos converses.*
37 E. A. Thompson, *The Goths in Spain* (Oxford: At the Clarendon Press, 1969), 39; also José Orlandis, *Historia del Reino Visigodo Español* (Madrid: Ediciones RIALP, S.A., 2003), deals with the Council in a typical way, mentioning the baptism question especially concerning Jews, but focusing most of his attention on the establishment of an elective monarchy in the wake of the violent and illegal seizure of power of the new king Sisenand, 100–3.
38 Jaroslav Pelikan, *The Growth of Medieval Theology (600-1300)*, vol. 3 in *The Christian Tradition: A History of the Development of Doctrine* (Chicago: The University of Chicago Press, 1978), 37.
39 Isidore of Seville, *History of the Kings of the Goths*, 60, in Kenneth Baxter Wolf, trans., *Conquerors and Chroniclers of Early Medieval Spain* (Liverpool: Liverpool University Press, 1990), 106.
40 Pelikan, *Growth*, 36; Isidore, *Sententiarum Libri Tres*, 2.2.4: "*A quibus autem exigitur violentur, perseverae in eis non potest.*" *PL*, 83.
41 Colish, *Faith, Fiction*, 250.
42 Ibid., 252.
43 Glenn C. J. Byer, *Charlemagne and Baptism: A Study of Responses to the Circular Letter of 811/812* (New York: International Scholars Publications, 1999), 23–9.
44 S. A. Keefe, "Carolingian Baptismal Expositions: A Handlist of Tracts and Manuscripts," in Ute-Renate Blumenthal, ed., *Carolingian Essays:*

Andrew W. Mellon Lectures in Early Christian Studies (Washington, DC: The Catholic University of America Press, 1983), 171.
45 J. M. Wallace-Hadrill, *The Frankish Church* (Oxford: The Clarendon Press, 1983), 183.
46 Yitzhak Hen, "Charlemagne's Jihad," *Viator* (2006): 33–51.
47 Ibid., 47. The temptation to see a mirror image between jihad and crusade is strong. Albrecht Noth, *Heiliger und Kreig*, sees parallels between Muslim and Christian practices of holy war, comparing the "crusade propaganda" of Bernard of Clairvaux to passages in the Quran, and seeing a type of Muslim *ribat* in Christian Tarragona, 141. But he acknowledges that parallels may not intersect when he notes that there is no direct evidence of Muslim influence on the "before-history" of the Crusades, n. 6, 147–8.
48 The topic is lightly treated, but an excellent work on the situation in the Holy Land is Kedar, *Crusade and Mission*.
49 See James Turner Johnson and John Kelsay, eds, *Cross, Crescent, and Sword: The Justification and Limitation of War in Western and Islamic Tradition* (New York: Greenwood Press, 1990).
50 *Capitulatio de partibus Saxoniae*, 8 and 4 respectively, in D. C. Munro, trans., *Translations and Reprints from the Original Sources of European History*, v. VI, no. 5 "Laws of Charles the Great" (Philadelphia: University of Pennsylvania Press, 1900), 2.
51 Richard Winston, *Charlemagne: From the Hammer to the Cross* (New York: Vintage Books, 1954), 78. Winston cites the treatment of the Abodrites and the Frisians, among others, who were not forced into baptism, 119.
52 *Royal Frankish Annals* in Bernhard Scholz and Barbara Rogers, trans., *Carolingian Chronicles* (Ann Arbor, MI: University of Michigan Press, 1970), 74–5.
53 Ibid.
54 Anders Winroth, *The Conversion of Scandinavia: Vikings, Merchants, and Missionaries in the Remaking of Northern Europe* (New Haven, CT: Yale University Press, 2012), 53.
55 Peter Fisher, trans. and Hilda Ellis Davidson, ed., *Saxo Grammaticus: The History of the Danes*, vol. 1 (Cambridge: D.S. Brewer, 1979), 291.
56 *The Anglo-Saxon Chronicle*, *sub anno* 878, gives the account: "The army (the Danes) gave him (Alfred) hostages with many oaths, that they would go out of his kingdom. They told him also, that their king would receive baptism. And they acted accordingly; for in the course of three weeks after, King Guthrum, attended by some thirty of the

worthiest men that were in the army, came to him at Aller, which is near Athelney and there the king (Alfred) became his sponsor in baptism, and his chrism-loosing was at Wedmore." James Ingram, trans., *The Anglo-Saxon Chronicle* (London: J. M. Dent & Sons, 1949), 67.
57 Ibid.
58 Widukind, *Deeds*, Bachrach and Bachrach, 58.
59 A. H. M. Jones, *The Decline of the Ancient World* (New York: Holt, Rinehart and Winston, Inc., 1966), 42.
60 Augustine, *Epistola* 189 in James Houston Baxter, trans., *St. Augustine, Select Letters. The Loeb Classical Library*. (London: William Heinemann, Ltd., 1930), 323–9. Augustine counseled Boniface, the commander of Roman forces in North Africa, on the acceptability of warfare in defense of the innocents by saying, "Do not think that it is impossible for anyone to please God while engaged in military service," 327.
61 Gregory, *Historia* II, 37; Thorpe, 151.
62 Russell, *Germanization*, 14.
63 Wallace-Hadrill, *Early Germanic Kingship in England and on the Continent* (Oxford: Oxford University Press, 1971), 8.
64 Bede, II, 13; Sherley-Price, 128.
65 Ibid.
66 Dvornik, *Slavs: Early History*, 46; Gimbutas, *The Slavs*, 151.
67 Gimbutas, *The Balts*, 183–4.
68 Francis Oakley, *Kingship: The Politics of Enchantment* (Oxford: Blackwell Publishers, 2006), 33.
69 Dvornik, *Slavs: Early History*, 57.
70 Gimbutas, *The Slavs*, 141.
71 Torben K. Nielsen, "Mission and Submission: Societal Change in the Baltic in the Thirteenth Century," in Tuomas M. S. Lehtonen and Kurt Villads Jensen with Janne Malkki and Katja Ritari, eds, *Medieval History Writing and Crusading Ideology. Studia Fennica Historica 9* (Helsinki: Finnish Literature Society, 2005), 218.
72 See my biography of the Irish monastic provocateur: *Columbanus: Light on the Early Middle Ages* (New York: Longman/Pearson, 2011).
73 Gregory, *Historia* II, 31; Thorpe, 144.
74 Bede I, 25; Sherley-Price, 69–70.
75 Santiago Castellanos, *Los Godos y La Cruz: Recaredo y La Unidad de Spania* (Madrid: Alianza Editorial, 2007), 212–13.
76 Hillgarth, *Conversion of Western Europe*, 89.

77 Gregory, *Historia* II, 31; Thorpe, 144.
78 Bede I, 26; Sherley-Price, 71.
79 Gregory, *Historia* II, 34; Thorpe, 149.
80 Ibid.
81 Bysted, *Jerusalem in the North*, 69–71. This is the account given by Saxo Grammaticus.
82 Bede II, 5 and 6; Sherley-Price, 108–11.
83 Ibid., II, 9 and 10; Sherley-Price, 116–20.
84 Lotter, 289.
85 Henry, *Chronicle* XXIV, 5; Brundage, 194; *MGH*, 175: *Donec eciam in illis finibus consummato baptismate paganorum ritus abolevent.*
86 Nielsen, "Mission and Submission," 219.
87 Lee M. Hollander, trans., *Heimskringla: History of the Kings of Norway by Snorri Sturluson* (Austin, TX: University of Texas Press, 1964), 166–7.
88 Winroth, 115.
89 Hollander, *Heimskringla*, 195.
90 Ibid., 199.
91 Brigit and Peter Sawyer, *Medieval Scandinavia: From Conversion to Reformation, circa 800-1500* (Minneapolis, MN: University of Minnesota Press, 1993), 103–4.
92 Hollander, *Heimskringla*, 309.
93 Winroth, 138.
94 Ibid., 161.
95 Dvornik, *The Slavs*, 207–10.
96 Bysted, *Jerusalem in the North*, 66; Helmold, *Chronicle*, 370–82.
97 *Livonian Rhymed Chronicle*, lines 83–113, 2.

Chapter 7

1 Henry, *Chronicle* XXIII, 7; Brundage, 179; *MGH*, 161–2: *Dumque iam eum in sacro linire deberemus oleo, factus est clamor magnus et concursus exercitus nostri per omnes plateas, et currebant omnes ad arma, clamantes magnam paganorum malewam contra nos venientem. Unde nos confestim proiecto sacrosancto crismate ceterisque sacramentis ad clypeorum gladiorumque ministeria cucurrimus.*
2 Ibid., XXVII, 1; Brundage, 213–14. Hans-Dieter Kahl, *Slawen und Deutsche in der Brandenburgischen Geschichte des Zwölfen*

Jahrhunderts (Köln: Böhlau Verlag, 1964), cites Slavic apostasy (*"slawische Apostasie"*) as the justification for the Wendish Crusade, 186.

3   Ibid., II, 5; Brundage, 32; *MGH*, 9: *Respondet episcopus causam, quod tamquam canes ad vomitum, sic a fide sepius ad paganismum redierint.*

4   The word "apostasy" apparently derives from two Greek words: *apostasia*, or "falling away" and *aphistemi*, "departing," as used in I Timothy 4:1. In both cases the meaning is clear: the apostate, as a professing Christian, has chosen to fall away or depart from the faith. See Stephen G. Wilson, *Leaving the Fold: Apostates and Defections in Antiquity* (Minneapolis, MN: Fortress Press, 2004).

5   Johan Huizinga, *Homo Ludens: A Study of the Play Element in Culture* (Boston: Beacon Press, 1955), 12. Huizinga wrote: "In the world of high seriousness, too, the cheat and the hypocrite have always had an easier time of it than the spoil sports, here called apostates, heretics."

6   Philip W. Gray, "Just War, Schism, and Peace in St. Augustine," in Syse and Reichberg, *Ethics, Nationalism and Just War*, 52.

7   Roland H. Bainton gave a good general summary of the origin and application of this in his *Christendom: A Short History of Christianity and Its Impact on Western Civilization* (New York: Harper Torchbook, 1966), 81–3.

8   Jones, *Decline of the Ancient World*, 42. The question of Licinius' conversion and later apostasy has intrigued scholars for years. Adolf von Harnack, *Militia Christi: Die Christliche Religion und der Soldatenstand in den Ersten Drei Jahrhunderten* (Darmstadt: Wissenschaftliche Buchgesellschaft, 1963), believed that Licinius only allied with Constantine because his rival Maximinus Daza had positioned the conflict as one between Christianity and paganism (*zwischen Christentum und Heiden*), 89–90.

9   David G. Bromley, *The Politics of Religious Apostasy: The Role of Apostates in the Transformation of Religious Movements* (London: Praeger, 1998), 118.

10 Fonnesberg-Schmidt, *Popes and the Baltic*, 118.

11 Henry, *Chronicle* XVI, 4; Brundage, 127; *MGH*, 108: *Confortamini, Lyvones, et pugnate, ne serviatis Theuthonicis.*

12 Ibid., 129; *MGH*, 109–10: *Pro eo, quod fidei sacramenta reiecistis et . . . dominos vestros, bello inquietastis et totam Lyvonaim ad ydolatriam retrahere voluistis et maxime in contemptu Dei altissimi*

et ad nostram et omnium christianorum illusionem hircos et cetera animalia dis paganorum immolantes in faciem nostram et tocius exercitus proiecistis, ideo modicam summam argenti, ab omni provincia vestra requirimus.
13 *Livonian Rhymed Chronicle*, lines 11233–317, 134–5.
14 Fletcher, *Barbarian Conversion*, 520.
15 Hamilton Gibb, "The Influence of Islamic Culture," 157.
16 Ibid.
17 Long, *War and Conscience*, 37.
18 Widukind, *Deeds*; Bachrach and Bachrach, 134.
19 Ibid., 135.
20 Ibid.
21 Henry, *Chronicle*, XI, 7; Brundage, 75.
22 *Livonian Rhymed Chronicle*, lines 7209–45, 89.
23 Henry, *Chronicle*; Brundage, xxxiv.
24 Bede I, 30; Sherley-Price, 87.
25 *Livonian Rhymed Chronicle*, lines 2429–50, 34.
26 Henry, *Chronicle* IX, 1; Brundage, 47; *MGH*, 26: *Sed si partes, ad quas tendimus, vicerimus, homnibus captis et occisis villa ipsorum evertemus. Vix enim pulvis civitatis illius pugillo nostri sufficiet.*
27 Ibid., IX, 4; Brundage, 49; *MGH*, 28: *Hunc Semgallorum quidem palpitare videntes, caput eius abscidunt et vehiculus suis imponentes, que solis capitibus Lethonum oneraverant.*
28 Ibid., XIV, 5; Brundage, 98, and XIV, 8; Brundage, 102.
29 Ibid., XIX, 3; Brundage, 144–6; *MGH*, 124–5: *Unde iterum ponentes eum ad ignem tamquam piscem assaverunt . . . et viros omnes, quos comprehendere potuerant, vivus in ultionem Thalibaldi, cremaverunt.*
30 Ibid., XXI, 3; Brundage, 162; *MGH*, 143: *. . . et ceteri caput eius amputantes detulerunt secum in Lyvoniam.*
31 *Livonian Rhymed Chronicle*, lines 4877–935, 63.
32 Henry, *Chronicle* XXIII, 9; Brundage, 184; *MGH*, 166: *et cadebant ex eis ex omni parte tamquam fenum, quod eoram metente se cadit in terram.*
33 Ibid., XXVI, 13; Brundage, 212; *MGH*, 193: *et viros omnes, quos captives duxerunt, capite truncaverunt, ut fieret vindicta de prevaricatoribus et infidelibus illis nationibus.*
34 Ibid., XXIX, 1; Brundage, 229; *MGH*, 207: *timentes, ne sibi similia facerunt, sicut Tarbatensibus intolerant.*
35 Ibid., XXVIII, 6; Brundage, 226; *MGH*, 205: *Ex omnibus itaque viris, qui in castro errant, remansit unus vivus tantum.*

36 *Livonian Rhymed Chronicle*, 11.
37 Nielsen, "Mission and Submission," 222.
38 Urban, "Victims of the Baltic Crusade," 9.
39 Paul the Deacon, *Historia* IV, 37; Foulke, 180–4. One married the king of the Alamanni, another prince of the Bavarians.
40 Gregory, *Historia* III, 7; Thorpe, 168: "When the time came to return home Lothar took with him as his share of the booty Radegund, the daughter of King Berthar."
41 Henry, *Chronicle* XXX, 1; Brundage, 238; *MGH*, 216: *Qui multas et nequicias cum captives et mulierculis et virginibus exercere solebant omni tempore, illudentes eas et copulantes alias sibi in uxores, tres unusquisque vel duas vel plures.*
42 Ibid. *MGH: licitantes sibi illicita, cum non sit coniuncta conveniens Christi cum Belial nec pagani copula congrua cum Christiana.*
43 *Livonian Rhymed Chronicle*, 147.
44 Ibid., lines 3018–55, 42. Later, when the Christians beat the Kurs at Lasen, "the army then filled its hands with booty and herded away the women and children," following this notation with the statement that "glory had been rendered unto God in the manner just mentioned."
45 Urban, *Baltic Crusade*, 27–8.
46 *Livonian Rhymed Chronicle*, 73.
47 Shaw, "War and Violence," in Bowersock, et al., 159.
48 Ibid., 160.
49 Shami Ghosh, "Conquest, Conversion, and Heathen Customs in Henry of Livonia's *Chronicon Livoniae* and the *Livlandische Reimchronik*," *Crusades* 11 (2012): 94.
50 Fonnesberg-Schmidt, *Popes and the Baltic*, 117–18.
51 Ibid., 118–21; also Bede I, 30; Sherley-Price, 87.
52 *Letters of Boniface*, 14, in Talbot, *Anglo-Saxon Missionaries*, 81.
53 Urban, *Baltic Crusade*, 53.
54 Ghosh, "Conquest, Conversion," 95.
55 Widukind, *Deeds* I, 36; Bachrach and Bachrach, 53.
56 Henry, *Chronicle* XX, 3; Brundage, 156–7.
57 Ibid., XIX, 3; Brundage, 145.
58 Deuteronomy 20:13-14; *NIV*, 625.
59 Both Henry's *Livonian Chronicle* and the *Livonian Rhymed Chronicle* feature heavy emphasis on Mary. Although Henry was an active participant in the action he described, he credited Mary a bit

less than the anonymous rhyming chronicler, who was writing almost exclusively from the perspective of the Mary-oriented Teutonic Knights.
60 Henry, *Chronicle* XXVII, 1, and XXIX, 1.
61 Ibid., XXV, 2; Brundage, 198–9.
62 Ibid., 199.
63 Ibid.
64 *Livonian Rhymed Chronicle*, 142.
65 Ibid., 103.
66 Ibid., 99.
67 An excellent introduction to the topic is Peter Brown, *The Cult of the Saints: Its Rise and Function in Latin Christianity* (Chicago: University of Chicago Press, 1981).
68 Ibid., 124. Brown was more concerned with the efficacy of the saint's power at the shrine rather than his or her projection of authority over expanding territories: "It (the saint's power) lay around the shrines of the saints like pools of water on a drying surface. For only in certain places ... could the *praesentia* and the *potentia* of the saints echo with satisfying congruence the deepest wishes of the Christian communities."
69 P. G. Walsh, trans., *The Poems of St. Paulinus of Nola. Ancient Christian Writers*, no. 40 (New York: Newman Press, 1975), 286.
70 Gregory, *Historia* II, 37; Thorpe, 151–2. Clovis is made to exclaim: *Et ubi spes victuriam erunt, si offendimus beato Martino?*
71 Urban, *Baltic Crusade*, 21–2.
72 Julia M. H. Smith, "Review Article: Early Medieval Hagiography in the Late Twentieth Century," *Early Medieval Europe* I (1992): 72.
73 Gabriel LeBras, "The Sociology of the Church in the Early Middle Ages," in Sylvia L. Thrupp, ed., *Early Medieval Society* (New York: Appleton-Century-Crofts, 1967), 47–57.
74 Brown, *Cult of the Saints*, 63: "The role of replication in late antiquity was subtly different: it enabled the Christian communities, by projecting a structure of clearly defined relationships onto the unseen world, to ask questions about the quality of relationships in their own society. The cult of the saints in late antiquity, therefore, did more than dress the ancient dead in contemporary upper-class costume."
75 Christopher Kelly, "Empire Building," in Bowersock et al., *Interpreting Late Antiquity*, 181–2.
76 LeBras, "Sociology," 57.

77 Ibid., 52.
78 Henry, *Chronicle* XXIX, 9; Brundage, 237; *MGH*, 213: *una cum filio suo, eodem domino nostro Iesu Christo, omnes terre iste noviter converse sun asscripte.*
79 Arthur Darby Nock, *Conversion: The Old and the New in Religion from Alexander the Great to Augustine of Hippo* (Oxford: The Clarendon Press, 1933), 5.

Chapter 8

1 Urban, review of *The Popes and the Baltic Crusades, 1147-1254* by Iben Fonnesberg-Schmidt, *Speculum* 83 (January 2008): 195.
2 Diana Webb, *Medieval European Pilgrimage, c.700-c.1500* (New York: Palgrave, 2002), 19–20.
3 John M. Headley, "The Universalizing Principle and Process: On the West's Intrinsic Commitment to a Global Context," *Journal of World History* 13 (Fall 2002): 291–321.
4 *Divina dispensatione II*, in J.-P. Migne, ed., *Eugenii III (Romani Pontificus) Epistolae et Privilegia. Patrologia Latinae, Tomus* 180 (Turnhout: Brepols): col. 1203–4.
5 Henry, *Chronicle*, xxvii. Professor Brundage believes it was completed shortly after the end of the papal legate William of Modena's mission to the contested lands, placing its terminus at 1227 or 1228.
6 Ibid., III, 2; Brundage, 36; *MGH*, 12: (The bishop asked) ... *si bona in Lyvoniam peregrinancium sub tuicione pape ponantur, sicut corum, qui Ierosolimam vadunt?* The royal reply highlighted the *peregrinacionem Lyvoniae*, or "Livonian pilgrimage."
7 Ibid., IV, 6; Brundage, 38.
8 *Livonian Rhymed Chronicle*, 6–7.
9 Brown, *Rise of Western Christendom*, 101–6.
10 Asbridge, *First Crusade*, 37.
11 Jonathan Sumption, *Pilgrimage: An Image of Mediaeval Religion* (London: Faber & Faber, 1975), 129.
12 Linda Kay Davidson and Maryjane Dunn-Wood, *Pilgrimage in the Middle Ages: A Research Guide* (New York: Garland Publishing, Inc., 1993), 13.
13 Giles Constable, *Religious Life and Thought (11th-12th centuries)* (London: Variorum Reprints, 1979), 146.

14 Dee Dyas, *Pilgrimage in Medieval English Literature, 700-1500* (Cambridge: D.S. Brewer, 2001), 3–5.
15 The Synod of Soissons in 744 and the Council of Arles in 813.
16 A useful description of the varieties of Irish martyrdom is found in Clare Stancliffe, "Red, White, and Blue Martyrdom," in Dorothy Whitelock, Rosamond McKitterick, and David Dumville, eds, *Ireland in Early Medieval Europe: Studies in Memory of Kathleen Hughes* (Cambridge: Cambridge University Press, 1982), 21–46.
17 The account of this remarkable man's journey through life is found in Dana Carleton Munro, trans., *The Life of St. Columban by the Monk Jonas*, Translations and Reprints from the Original Sources of European History, vol. II, no. 7 (Philadelphia: University of Pennsylvania Press, 1895).
18 G. S. M. Walker, ed., *Sancti Columbani Opera* (Dublin: The Dublin Institute for Advanced Studies, 1957), 87ff.
19 Ibid.
20 Timothy Fry, ed., *The Rule of Saint Benedict* (New York: Vintage Books, 1998), 8.
21 Cramer, *Baptism and Change*, 185.
22 Constable, *Religious Life and Thought*, 129.
23 John 14:6, *NIV*, 1621.
24 Henry, *Chronicle* VII, 3; Brundage, 43; *MGH*, 20: *Post hec frater Theodericus cum peregrinis, qui per annum illum in Lyvonia sub cruce sua Deo militaverunt, in Theuthoniam abiens quendam Lyvonem.*
25 John M. Howe, "The Conversion of the Physical World: The Creation of a Christian Landscape," in James Muldoon, ed., *Varieties of Religious Conversion in the Middle Ages* (Gainesville, FL: University Press of Florida, 1997), 63–78.
26 Carsten Selch Jensen, "How to Convert a Landscape: Henry of Livonia and the Chronicon Livoniae," in Murray, *Clash of Cultures*, 164.
27 Linda Kaljundi, "Waiting for the Barbarians: The Imagery, Dynamics and Functions of the Other in Northern German Missionary Chronicles, 11th-Early 13th Centuries," Master's Thesis, University of Tartu, 2005, 50.
28 Housley, *Contesting*, 87.
29 Gabriele, *Empire of Memory*, 74–5.
30 Guy Strousma, "Mystical Jerusalem," in Lee I. Levine, ed., *Jerusalem: Its Sanctity and Centrality to Judaism, Christianity, and Islam* (London: Continuum International Publishing Group, 1999), 355–6.

31. Gabriele, *Empire of Memory*, 80.
32. Anu Mand, "Saints' Cults in Medieval Livonia," in Murray, *Clash of Cultures*: 211.
33. Constable, *Crusaders and Crusading*, 197–214.
34. Henry, *Chronicle* III, 2–5; Brundage, 35–6.
35. Ibid.
36. Bysted et al., 148.
37. Howe, "Conversion of the Physical World," 66 and 71.
38. Nicholas Edward Morton, *The Teutonic Knights in the Holy Land, 1190-1291* (Woodbridge: The Boydell Press, 2009), 125.
39. Bede I, 30; Sherley-Price, 86–7.
40. Carsten Selch Jensen, "How to Convert a Landscape," 157.
41. See Roger Collins, *Early Medieval Spain: Unity in Diversity, 400-1000* (New York: St. Martin's Press, 1983).
42. Bernard of Clairvaux, *In Praise of the New Knighthood*; Greenia, *Works*.
43. Brown, *Cult of the Saints*, 4.

Chapter 9

1. Henry, *Chronicle* XXIX, 6; Brundage, 234; *MGH*, 212: *Vironie Danos expellebant, dicentes terram ipsam primitus a Lyvonensibus vexillo beate Virginis ad fidem christianam suiugatem.*
2. Ibid., XXX, 2; Brundage, 239; *MGH*, 214: *Sed post triduum miserti eorum, eo quod christiani essent dimiserunt eos.*
3. Ibid.
4. Ibid.
5. Ibid., XX, 4; Brundage, 157.
6. *Livonian Rhymed Chronicle*, lines 2065–99, 29.
7. Ibid.
8. Ibid., lines 2281–99, 32.
9. Henry, *Chronicle* I, 3; Brundage, 26.
10. Ibid., III, 2; Brundage, 35.
11. Ibid., X, 13; Brundage, 64.
12. Urban, *Baltic Crusade*, 109. Urban cites the tension between a "pro-German faction among the Novgorod merchants and (a) Russia-first" party.
13. Henry, *Chronicle* X, 1; Brundage, 54; *MGH*, 32: *volens domnus Woldemari Regis de Ploceke quam antecessori suo Meynardo exhibuerat episcopo.*

14 Ibid., XVI, 2; Brundage, 122.
15 Jonathan Harris, "The 'Schism' of 1054 and the First Crusade," *Crusades* 13 (2014): 6.
16 Bryan Spinks, *Early and Medieval Rituals and Theologies of Baptism*, 94–5.
17 Henry, *Chronicle* XXIV, 1, 2; Brundage, 188–9.
18 Ibid., XXIV, 5; Brundage, 193.
19 Ibid., XXIV, 2; Brundage, 189.
20 Ibid., XXV, 1; Brundage, 197.
21 Ibid., XVI, 3–4; Brundage, 123–31.
22 Ibid., XI, 3; Brundage, 69.
23 Ibid., XXVIII, 1 and 2; Brundage, 220–1.
24 John 14:6; *NIV*, 1621.
25 James M. Powell, trans., *The Deeds of Pope Innocent III by an Anonymous Author* (Washington, DC: The Catholic University of America Press, 2004), 77–228.
26 Ibid., 77.
27 Tyerman, *God's War*, 568–605. The issue with the heretical Cathars of southern France was made the topic of a best-selling historical work by Emmanuel LeRoy Ladurie, *Montaillou: The Promised Land of Error*, trans. Barbara Bray (New York: Vintage Books, 1979).
28 Ibid., 569.
29 Fletcher, *Barbarian Conversion*, 230; also see Kedar, *Crusade and Mission*.
30 Margaret Jubb, "The Crusaders' Perceptions of their Opponents," in Nicholson, *Palgrave Advances*, 229. Jubb observes that the term pagan was used routinely for Muslim opponents in the Holy Land: "In the epics and in many of the crusading chronicles, the opponents of the Christians are described as 'pagans,' and they are endowed with the polytheistic and idolatrous traits of ancient paganism." Also see the papal decrees of Leo IV, Nicholas I, and John VIII.
31 *Livonian Rhymed Chronicle*, lines 6315–587 and 7121–209, 88–9.
32 See Rasa Mazeika, "Bargaining for Baptism," in Muldoon, *Varieties of Religious Conversion*, 131–45.
33 *Livonian Rhymed Chronicle*, 8, fn. 19.
34 Colish, *Faith, Fiction & Force*, 266–7, and 272. Also see Edgar Johnson, "The German Crusade on the Baltic," in Setton, *History of the Crusades*, 549. He focuses on "the cost of western civilization" that the Baltic peoples would "be made to pay."
35 Henry, *Chronicle* XXIX, 4; Brundage, 233. See also 231 and 234.

36 Fletcher, *Barbarian Conversion*, 439.
37 Ibid., 440.
38 Erdmann, *Origin*, 11: "The ecclesiastical unity of the West was restored (following the resolution of the Arian question) and stood unshaken until a new sort of sectarianism made its appearance in the second millennium."
39 A. B. E. Hood, trans., *St. Patrick: His Writings and Muirchu's Life* (Totowa, NJ: Rowman and Littlefield, 1978), 55.
40 Helmold, *Chronicle*, 180ff.
41 Brian Tierney and Joan Scott, eds, *Western Societies: A Documentary History*, vol. I (New York: Alfred A. Knopf, 1984), 254.
42 Allen and Amt, *Crusades: A Reader*, 44.
43 Ibid., 41.
44 Gregory, *Historia* V, *Praefatio*; Thorpe, 253.
45 Ibid., 254.
46 J. M. Wallace-Hadrill, *The Frankish Church* (Oxford: At the Clarendon Press, 1983), 143.
47 Vincent's position, sometimes called "The Vincentian Canon," sought to use tradition as a corrective to incorrect practice and as an aid to understanding Scripture. Tradition was "that which has been believed everywhere, always, and by all."
48 Gray, "Just War, Schism, and Peace," in Syse and Reichberg, 52.
49 A pioneer in this was C. J. Bishko. His work, "The Frontier in Medieval History," addressed the utility of Frederick Jackson Turner's frontier thesis for the Middle Ages. For a more contemporary view, see Nora Berend, "Frontiers," in Nicholson, *Palgrave Advances*, 148–71.
50 Ian Wood, "Missionaries and the Christian Frontier," in Pohl, et al., *The Transformation of Frontiers*, 216.
51 Walter Pohl, "Conclusion," in *Transformation*, 247. Pohl is citing the etymology of Isidore of Seville.
52 *Epistola* 394 in James, *Letters of St. Bernard*, 467.
53 Helmold, *Chronicle*, 180.
54 Gregory, *Historia* II, 32; Thorpe, 146–7.
55 Lisa Woolverton, trans., *Cosmas of Prague: The Chronicle of the Czechs* (Washington, DC: The Catholic University of America Press, 2009), 128–9.
56 Helmold, *Chronicle*, 180.
57 Ibid.
58 Henry, *Chronicle* X, 9; Brundage, 60.

59 Peter Brown, *The Ransom of the Soul: Afterlife and Wealth in Early Western Christianity* (Cambridge, MA: Harvard University Press, 2015). So fervid was the desire to aid the poor that "those who attempted to appropriate church lands . . . were regularly denounced as *necatores pauperum*—as 'murderers of the poor,'" 172.
60 Fletcher, *Barbarian Conversion*, 460-1.
61 Beck, *Pastoral Care*, 330-1.
62 Hillgarth, *Conversion*, 95.
63 Eddius Stephanus, "Life of Wilfrid," in J. F. Webb and D. H. Farmer, trans., *The Age of Bede* (London: Penguin Books, 2004), 120.
64 Hillgarth, *Conversion*, 96.
65 Robert M. Latouche, *Caesar to Charlemagne: The Beginnings of France*, trans. Jennifer Nicholson (London: J.M. Dent & Sons, Ltd., 1968), 290.
66 Paul the Deacon, *Historia* IV, 41; Foulke, 192-3. Referring to Columbanus' founding of Bobbio in northern Italy, Paul wrote: "In this place also many possessions were bestowed by particular princes and Langobards."
67 See Reynolds, *Columbanus*, 56-67; especially 65-6.
68 Fletcher, *Barbarian Conversion*, 178.
69 *Life of Wilfrid*, in *Age of Bede*, 121.
70 Ibid.

Chapter 10

1 Christiansen, *Northern Crusades*, 220.
2 Ibid.
3 The most notable was the Thirteen Years' War (1453–66), that featured the Teutonic Knights losing to Poland and relinquishing control of the region around the Vistula River.
4 Histories of the Council focus generally on the reforms engendered there; for example, Philip H. Stump, *The Reforms of the Council of Constance (1414-1418)* (Leiden: E.J. Brill, 1994), or the handling of the Czech controversy surrounding the trial and execution of Jan Hus.
5 Christiansen, *Northern Crusades*, 223-32. Frank Welsh, *The Battle for Christendom: The Council of Constance, 1415, and the Struggle to Unite Against Islam* (London: Constable & Robinson, Ltd., 2008), barely mentions Tannenberg (95) while treating the peace between the Polish-Lithuanians and the Teutonic Knights as a mere sideline

to the overall problem of unity in the face of the growing Muslim Turkish menace to the southeast. It seems crusading along the Baltic and the survival of a military order were no longer pressing geopolitical needs, 156 and 195.

6   Christiansen, *Northern Crusades*, 226.
7   Riley-Smith, *Crusades, Christianity, Islam*, 14.
8   See Charles, *Between Pacifism and Jihad*, 67–70, and 169–72.
9   Christiansen, *Northern Crusades*, 225.
10 Ibid.
11 Ibid., 229.
12 Urban, *Baltic Crusade*, i.
13 Lewis Hanke, *The Spanish Struggle for Justice in the Conquest of America* (Philadelphia: University of Pennsylvania Press, 1949), 139–45.
14 Ibid., 145.
15 The often cited quote from Bernal Díaz is: "We came here to serve God and His Majesty, and also to grow rich." Hanke, *Struggle*, 7.
16 Nigel Griffin, trans., *Bartolomé de Las Casas: A Short Account of the Destruction of the Indies* (New York: Penguin Books, 1992).
17 William Urban describes the similarities between the black legend and a Baltic version: "Like the Spanish churchmen in the New World three centuries later, in their effort to reform behavior and protect the native peoples, German churchmen would provide contemporaries and later generations alike with the stories of misconduct and cruelty that molded the stereotype of the evil crusade. . . . The Spanish Legenda Negra [sic] is paralleled by a Baltic counterpart," *Baltic Crusade*, 39.
18 Las Casas, *Short Account*, 7.
19 Bagge, *Kings, Politics and Right Order*, 2.
20 Ibid., 6.
21 Bysted, *Jerusalem in the North*, 27, believes the pagan god was a syncretistic product of the cult of St. Vitus and notes that "Svantevit, as the Slavic name for St. Vitus was preserved in Latin sources." The various spellings for the god's name include Saxo Grammaticus' "Suantovitus" and Helmold's "Zuantevit," both connecting back to St. Vitus. Ibid., 66.
22 J. M. Cohen, trans., *Bernal Díaz: The Conquest of New Spain* (Harmondsworth: Penguin Books, 1963), 181.
23 Ibid., 177.
24 Ibid., 178.

25 Ibid., 83; also 62, 81, and 82.
26 Ibid., 220.
27 Hanke, *Struggle*, 73.
28 Las Casas, *Short Account*; Griffin, xxv–xxx.
29 *Livonian Rhymed Chronicle*, lines 7349–91, 90.
30 Díaz, *Conquest*, 82.
31 Ibid., 164.
32 Ibid., 354.
33 Ibid., 408.
34 Quoted in Christiansen, *Northern Crusades*, 114.
35 Urban, *Baltic Crusade*, 324.
36 Johnson, "German Crusade on the Baltic," 549.
37 Some discount the need for defense of newly converted fellowships in favor of a simple rejection of the sources. Marcia Colish accuses the author of the *Livonian Rhymed Chronicle* of inventing the need for defensive war: "The author thus rewrites the Baltic Crusades as defensive wars, not as wars of justified aggression." *Faith, Fiction, and Force*, 270.
38 Barbara Tuchman, *A Distant Mirror: The Calamitous Fourteenth Century* (New York: Ballantine Books, 1978), includes several poems that celebrate war as the ultimate defining activity, for example: "Lords, mortgage your lands, but never give up war!" (16).
39 Madden, *New Concise History*, 217–22.
40 Urban, *Victims of the Baltic Crusades*, 3.
41 Syse and Reichberg, *Ethics, Nationalism and Just War*, especially 218–45 and 323–51.
42 Fletcher, *Barbarian Conversion*, chapter 15: "Slouching Toward Bethlehem," 508–24.

GLOSSARY OF PEOPLE AND TERMS

Abodrites. Sometimes spelled "Obodrites," or "Obotrites," they were a Slavic tribe situated to the east of the neck of the Jutland Peninsula in the territory still known as Mecklenburg. During Charlemagne's time they served as a defensive buffer to Danish depredations, eventually becoming the target for Christianization by the Dukes of Saxony. One of their princes, Gottschalk, became a Christian and was murdered in the Slavic uprising of 1066. A twelfth-century prince, Niclot, played a major role in the inception of the Baltic Crusades as a sometime ally of Count Adolf II of Holstein.

Adelskirche. Literally "church of the nobility," this is a term devised by German church historians to describe the tendency of early medieval churchmen to focus on the conversion of the kings and nobility. The premise was that gaining the leadership for the faith would facilitate the conversion of the rest of their society.

Adolf II of Schauenberg, Count of Holstein (1128–64). Becoming Count of Holstein at the age of two, Adolf was shepherded through his childhood by the regency of his mother Hildewa. Coming of age at fourteen, he founded Lübeck, destined to become one of the most important trading cities in Germany, and for a year served as regent to Henry the Lion, although the latter was only one year his junior. He was a Welf supporter in the Wendish Crusade, although he was once on friendly terms with Niclot of the Abodrites.

Albert "The Bear" Margrave of Brandenburg (1100–70). For a time the Duke of Saxony (1138–42), Albert later expanded the old Nordmark into something bigger and became the margrave of Brandenburg. This began a noble line that would eventually evolve into the Kingdom of Prussia. He was a Hohenstaufen partisan and an enthusiastic participant in the Wendish Crusade.

Albert von Buxhövden (c. 1165–1229). Named bishop of Livonia in 1201, Albert founded Riga (in modern Latvia) as a trade/defensive compound to protect the newly Christianizing Livs from Lithuanian raids. He is noted for founding the "Swordbrothers," a military crusade order that participated in much of the conquest and Christianization of the eastern Baltic littoral.

Anomie, literally "without rule," is the sense of rootlessness that grips a people or society in great cultural change. The introduction of Christianity to the Baltic peoples and the concomitant destruction of their cultural practices may have produced just such a sensation.

Anselm of Havelberg (c.1100–58). Bishop of Havelberg in Albert the Bear's territory of the Nordmark, Anselm was appointed as papal legate for the Wendish Crusade by Pope Eugenius III. In that role, he participated as a military commander as well as an ecclesiastical representative.

Apostasy, the deliberate rejection of the faith by a Christian. From the Greek *apostasies* meaning "standing away," it can refer to an individual or a group renouncing their Christian status. Those tribal peoples who, once baptized, then repudiate their faith are subject to punishment as apostates.

St. Augustine (354–430). Bishop of Hippo Regius near Carthage, Augustine is considered to be one of the foremost Church Fathers. For our study, he is an early formulator of the just war theory, holding that for a war to be just it must satisfy several key criteria: just cause, right authority, proper personnel, just behavior on the battlefield, and the correct attitude.

Bartolomé de Las Casas (1484–1576) participated in the conquest of Cuba as a very young man and then became a member of the Dominican order. Las Casas was sickened by what he witnessed in the Americas and became the principal proponent of Indian rights during the sixteenth century, comparing the accomplishments of the central American civilizations to those of the ancient Greeks. His most sensational work, *A Short Account of the Destruction of the Indies*, published in 1542, was followed by numerous writings including a general history of the Americas. His accounts of Spanish behavior formed the basis for the *leyenda negra*, or "black legend," denouncing the conquests and their subsequent governance.

Bede, "The Venerable" (673–735). A learned monk in the north of Anglo-Saxon England, Bede wrote the *History of the English Church and People*, leaving one of the few accounts of the development of early medieval England. In this fundamentally historical work, he included many descriptions of the spread of Christianity among the Anglo-Saxons and the early development of missionary war.

Bernal Díaz del Castillo (1492–c.1580). A participant in the conquest of Mexico, Díaz composed a recollection of the enterprise in about 1568, when he was seventy-six: *A History of the Conquest of New Spain*. His approach is largely approving of the Spanish mission and behavior, making him the one pole of a very polarized view on the conquest.

Bernard of Clairvaux (1090–1153). Entering the monastic community at Cîteaux in his early twenties, Bernard rapidly became a leading voice in Western Christendom. He is perhaps most notable for his role in the inception of the Knights Templars and his enthusiastic preaching of the Second Crusade.

Capitulatio de partibus Saxoniae, a decree issued by Charlemagne, probably in the 790s, outlining harsh measures for Saxons who refused or renounced Christianization. This capitulary is part of the heritage of German encroachment on eastern lands during the Middle Ages and stands as a model for much of the rationale in the missionary war of the Baltic Crusades.

Catechumen, those under Christian instruction in preparation for baptism. From the Greek for "one being taught by word of mouth" (*katechein*), in the early church it consisted of a rather long period of instruction. For the Baltic Crusade era, the catechumenate was either very brief or nonexistent.

Charlemagne (742–814), second Carolingian king of the Franks (768–814) and first Holy Roman Emperor (800–14). Among his many accomplishments, he fought a 33-year war with the pagan Saxons, thereby setting the precedent for the much later Baltic Crusades. Charlemagne became the prototypical medieval monarch and his policies, although frequently subject to mythologizing, were often held up as models for later actions.

Columbanus (543–615), Irish monk and missionary who popularized the notion of white martyrdom during his more than twenty-year sojourn on the Continent in both Gaul and Lombardy. Most notable for triggering more than ninety monastic foundations, Columbanus was responsible for offering an alternative pilgrimage vision to the accepted one of place pilgrimage.

Conrad III (1093–1152). From the Swabian House of Hohenstaufen, Conrad was the grandson of the Emperor Henry IV (r. 1056–1106) and thus claimed the imperial throne upon the death of Henry V in 1125. By 1127, the situation had deteriorated into civil war with the Welf supporters of the new emperor Lothair. Upon Lothair's death, Conrad was able to become king, reigning from 1138–52, but was never crowned as emperor. The first four years of his reign were marked by yet another civil war with the Welfs, until a peace was brokered in 1142. This dynastic turmoil served as the backdrop to the calling of the Wendish Crusade at Frankfurt in 1147 and would linger as a political backdrop throughout the bulk of the Baltic Crusade era.

Conrad "the Great" of Wettin, Margrave of Meissen (c. 1097–1157). When Conrad was given Meissen by Lothair in 1124, the Empeor Henry V was unable to counter the appointment. He was a Welf supporter and, despite his advancing years, a participant in the

Wendish Crusade of 1147. He actually retired from his position one year before his death.

Conrad of Zähringen (1088/90–1152). Duke of Zähringen from 1122, he is sometimes referred to as "Duke of Burgundy" but the reference is to a part of the Schwarzwald and some of the Switzerland rather than the French territory commonly called "Burgundy." Conrad was present at Frankfurt as a Welf supporter and was reported to have pushed for the Wendish Crusade on the grounds that it was closer and thus more possible than one to the Holy Land.

***Divina dispensatione*, I and II,** Papal *bullae* of Eugenius III clarifying the crusade call of 1145/46. The first, issued on October 1, 1146 was designed to recruit northern Italian crusaders. The second, issued on April 11, 1147, *after* the Diet of Frankfurt, expanded the crusade call to include action against the Wends as well as ongoing reconquest efforts in the Iberian Peninsula. This second *Divina dispensatione*, more than any other document, is the birth certificate of the Baltic Crusades.

Donatism. Named after their leader, Donatus, the Donatists were a Christian sect that emerged in the wake of the last great persecution of Christians under Diocletian in the early fourth century AD. During these trying times, many churchmen renounced their Christianity only to return to the faith when the persecutions ceased. The Donatists believed that baptisms performed by these apostate clerics were invalid. The church eventually solved the schism with force and with the theological decision that baptism, even if performed by an unworthy priest, was valid. This focus on the exterior sacrament rather than the interior purity of the officiant became a key early piece in what would later become baptism by treaty.

Edessa, capital of Armenia, traditionally the first kingdom to convert to Christianity in the early fourth century. This Christian city was taken treacherously by Baldwin of Flanders during the First Crusade and became one of the four Crusader states of the eleventh century. Zengi's conquest of the city sparked the Second Crusade, and by extension, the Wendish Crusade as well.

Elbe River. Emptying into the North Sea just west of the Jutland Peninsula, the Elbe River served as the old Roman *limes*, or border, and became the demarcation between the Christianized Saxon territories and the Slavic peoples by the commencement of the Wendish Crusade in 1147.

Elision, the ignoring of differences in order to make two things that are different the same. Perhaps the Baltic crusaders ignored the fundamental differences between defensive war and offensive war and made missionary war a conquest-oriented enterprise rather than a simple defense of vulnerable enclaves of new Christians.

Encomienda, landed estates granted to the Spanish conquerors of the New World that operated much like feudal holdings. These estates were worked largely by native conscripts giving the *encomenderos*, or the holders of the land, revenue and power. This system mimicked much of the land division scheme used in the Baltic Crusades.

Eugenius III (r. 1145–53). Born in Pisa sometime around 1090, Bernardo Paganelli, after meeting St. Bernard, left a promising career in the church to join the monastery at Clairvaux. Under Bernard's tutelage he became an abbot of another Cistercian house and was the surprise selection as pope in February 1145. He issued the crusade bull *Quantum predecessors* (in two forms), as well as the clarifying bulls *Divina dispensatione* I and II. His pontificate was with opposition and he died on July 8, 1153, some forty-three days before his mentor, St. Bernard.

Fath. Sometimes transliterated as *fatah*, with a plural of *futuh*, it means "opening" and signifies the Muslim view of conquest as a way of opening up other lands to Islam. The great age of *futuh*, which spawned a genre of literature by the same name, was from the death of Muhammad in 632 AD to the defeat of the Muslim forces at the Battle of Tours/Poitiers in central France in 733 AD.

Frankfurt. City on the Main River, originally a Roman settlement and later called *Francovorud* or "the Frank Ford (on the river)," it was the site of a great theological debate over the question of adoptionism in 794. It was also the site of the calling of the Wendish Crusade, the first of the Baltic Crusades, and later, particularly after Emperor Charles IV's "Golden Bull" of 1356, became the election spot for Holy Roman Emperors.

Gregory of Tours (538–94). The nineteenth bishop of Tours in central France from 573–94, Gregory wrote a key history of the sixth century: *Libri Historiarum Decem*, or "Ten Books of History." Although Gregory paid much attention to Gallo-Roman issues as well as church matters, as he wrote during the era of Frankish dominance, his work is frequently called "The History of the Franks."

Helmold of Bosau (c. 1120–77). Priest of the German town of Bosau, Helmold is the author of a key source for the period just before and during the opening years of the Baltic Crusades: his *Chronicon Slavorum*, or Chronicle of the Slavs.

Henry Berengar (c. 1137–50). Young son of Conrad III, Henry Berengar was proclaimed king at the Frankfurt Diet on March 13, 1147 and crowned in Aachen at mid-Lent on March 30. Dying before his father, Henry was not officially "Henry V" of the empire. That designation was taken later by the successor of Frederick Barbarossa, the "official" Henry V (r. 1190–97).

Henry "The Lion," Duke of Saxony (1129–95). A Welf partisan, Henry's father had been deprived of his duchy upon the accession of Conrad

III in 1138. When Henry's father died the next year, Albert the Bear attempted to rule Saxony and the young Henry, under the capable guardianship of his mother, Gertrude, and grandmother, Richenza, was able to hold onto the duchy. At Frankfurt, Henry the Lion posed the greatest threat to Conrad's plan for crusade. But, Henry became one of the major leaders in the Wendish Crusade.

Henry "of Livonia," chronicler and participant in the Baltic Crusades during the first decades of the 1200s. He is often called "of Livonia" since his *Livonian Chronicle* is one of the best sources for these crusades, even though he was actually a German from the monastery of Segeberg.

Hohenstaufen. One of the two major noble factions that developed around the imperial succession claims in twelfth-century Germany, the Hohenstaufens were represented by the Dukes of Swabia and most notably produced the monarchs King Conrad III and the Holy Roman Emperor Frederick "Barbarossa" (r. 1152–90).

***Ius ad Bellum*:** A major subset of the just war theory, *ius ad bellum* deals with the proper reasons for declaring war. These generally include self-defense, restoration of illegally seized property, and the elastically controversial permission to prevent greater injuries.

***Ius in Bello*.** Another subset within just war theory, *ius in bello* deals with the proper conduct of a just war. A force may retain or lose justness according to its performance in the treatment of noncombatants, honoring treaties, and the like.

Just War. A system of belief that holds that, while peace is preferable, some wars may be necessary if they comply with certain strict qualifications. First appearing in inchoate form in the pagan cultures of China, India, Greece, and Rome, the just war received its first Christian form at the hands of Bishop Ambrose of Milan (340–397 AD). Ambrose's pupil, Augustine of Hippo (354–430 AD) expanded and clarified the concept and by the twelfth century the components of just war theory had been included in standard church writings such as those of Gratian and Peter Lombard. In the last half of the thirteenth century, Thomas Aquinas gave the theory its most systematic form in his *Summa Theologica*. The just war remains a point of analysis for anyone examining the underlying principles of crusading.

Livonia. An elastic geographical term that varied depending on the vagaries of war and conquest but usually encompassing the lands inhabited by the Latvians, the Livs, and the Estonians. The term was generally applied after the German conquest and Christianization of these tribally fragmented regions.

Louis VII, King of France (1120–80). Upon becoming king in 1137, Louis married Eleanor of Aquitaine and thereby gained much land and power for the still developing Kingdom of France. Louis was the first monarch to respond to crusading and has been blamed for much of the ultimate failure of the Second Crusade.

"Missionary War." A term invented by Carl Erdmann in 1935 as *missionskrieg*, it became a useful tag for a war waged to accomplish the extension of a particular religion. The major debate about the term usually revolves around whether simple conquest, or conquest accompanied by conversion/baptism accomplishes the deed.

Niklot (?–1160). The prince of the Abodrites, one of the target peoples of the Wendish Crusade, Niklot was a skillful manipulator of the Christian princes of northern Germany, alternately effecting alliances with Adolf II and others, and attacking when it suited his policies. He was ultimately killed in combat in 1160.

Otto of Freising (c. 1111/14–1158). Bishop of Freising and half-brother to Conrad III, Otto was one of the finest historians of the twelfth century. A Cistercian, like Bernard, Otto did not confine his active life to church affairs, but was deeply involved in the politics of Germany and even went on the Second Crusade with Conrad's forces. Upon his return he wrote an account of the first five years of the reign of Frederick I "Barbarossa," his nephew.

Pacifism. Derived from the Vulgate translation of the Sermon on the Mount, "beati pacifici" or "blessed are the peacemakers," pacifism is understood generally to be the complete rejection of war, whether in direct participation or support of the enterprise.

St. Patrick (c. 396–461). A British lad taken as a slave by pagan Irish raiders, Patrick grew up to become the principal missionary to Ireland. While much of his life is encrusted by legend, we know from his surviving writings that he rebuked, in the strongest possible terms, the violent attacks by a Christian British king on his new converts, describing an early example of Christian on Christian violence.

Peregrinus. "Pilgrim" in Latin, Peregrinus was the standard designation of crusaders during the age of the Crusades. The use of the term in the Baltic context raises questions about the nature of their pilgrimage since there were no sacred pilgrimage sites for these "pilgrims" to visit in these pagan lands.

Pope Gregory I "The Great" (c. 540–604). Pope from 590, Gregory was a key player in missions outreach, especially to the Anglo-Saxons, as well as in the development of the acceptability of war for Christians. The joining of these two will set the stage for the concept of missionary war. He is considered one of the greatest medieval popes, often signing himself modestly as *servus servorum Dei*, or "servant of the servants of God."

Pope Innocent III (1161–1216). Originally Lothario di Segni, Innocent ruled as pope from 1198 until his death in 1216. Innocent is noted for calling the Fourth Lateran Council in 1215, where, among other significant decisions, the crusading territory along the Baltic was deemed to be the property of the Virgin Mary. Innocent also broke new ground by authorizing crusades within Europe against heretics and apostates, thus further reinforcing the crusading efforts in the Baltic.

Quantum praedecessores. Pope Eugenius III's papal bull calling for the Second Crusade, it was issued in two versions, one on December 1, 1145, and the second on March 1, 1146. The documents played heavily on the notion that the present generation of would-be crusaders must honor the memories of the First Crusade generation by reclaiming Edessa and extending the borders of Christian territory in the Holy Land.

Reduction. A policy developed during the Spanish conquest of the Americas that sought to Christianize the native population by emptying them of their pagan culture. This led to the destruction of worship sites, any literature (such as the Mayan writings) pertaining to their past, and the suppression of their pre-Christian customs.

Reisen. Term used in the Baltic Crusades for the act of taking up arms to fight against the pagans. Originally, it meant the yearly crusading journey eastward, but later was subdivided into two seasonal *reisens*: the *sommer-reysa*, a main crusading offensive each summer designed to take and hold territory from the pagan peoples along the Baltic, and the *winter-reysa*, or a smaller expedition during the winter when the frozen streams and inlets allowed for access to places previously accessible by boat. The *winter-reysa* was designed to keep the pagans from rebuilding their forces during the off season rather than as a campaign to gain new territory.

"Res precedes *verbum*," "The thing precedes the word." A theory of the British scholar John Headley that holds that actions and institutions exist before their actual naming. This has importance for the prehistory of the Crusades in that some elements of crusading appear to have existed long before they were designated as such.

Speyer. A city on the Rhine River and originally a Roman border town, by the twelfth century it had become a key city in German politics. Here, at Christmastide in 1146, Conrad III took the cross for the Second Crusade.

Svantovit. Pagan god of several Slavic tribes along the Baltic, Svantovit had his main cult center on the island of Rügen. He was depicted in wooden form as a being with four faces and is thought to be a corruption of some half-understood Christian teaching from earlier missionary efforts. His base was conquered and destroyed by the crusading Danish king Vlademar "the Great" in 1168.

Swordbrothers. Officially the *Fratres militiae Christi Livoniae* (in German *Schwertbruderorden*), this military order was founded by

Bishop Albert of Livonia in 1202 to defend the newly Christianized Livs from outside attack, principally by the Lithuanians. They played a major role in conquering lands in the eastern Baltic until their defeat in 1236. The surviving Swordbrothers were absorbed into the Teutonic Knights although they remained a distinct subset of that order.

Sympathetic Magic, a belief common among primitive peoples that "like begats like." In this perspective one would utilize a tangible item to obtain a desired ability. This has been used to explain head-hunting: the taking of a valorous opponent's head would also give the possessor his attribute of bravery. In our Baltic context, baptismal water and the status it conferred might be reversed by washing it off with other water.

Syncretism, the union of opposing views. It is often used to describe the adoption of local custom or pagan practices at odds with orthodox behavior by Christian groups. In the Baltic Crusades, it meant the inclusion of certain tribal war techniques that violated the principles of Christian just war theory.

Syntality, a sociological term to describe the collective personality of a group. As such it would encompass the sum total of the cultural traits of the subject group.

Teutonic Knights. A military order begun at the siege of Acre in the Holy Land in 1190, these crusaders eventually moved their operations to Northern Europe, first to Hungary and then to respond to the request of Conrad of Mazovia. After the Swordbrothers were decimated by defeat at the Battle of the Saule in 1236, the Teutonic Knights absorbed their remnants and became the leading force in the Baltic Crusades until their defeat at Tannenberg in 1410. The Knights created a type of state along the Baltic which later was absorbed into the emergence of Prussia.

Theodwin (?–1151). Cardinal Bishop of Santa Rufina, Theodwin was the leading German churchman of his age and was formerly abbot of the famed Cluniac house at Gorze in the low countries. Theodwin had crowned Conrad III at Aachen on March 13, 1138, and was thus summoned to appear at the Diet of Frankfurt for the March 13 ceremony that elected Conrad's son, Henry Berengar, as successor that began the Wendish Crusade.

Valdemar I, King of Denmark (1131–82). Surviving a three-way civil war in 1157, Valdemar "the Great" was able to defeat and kill the Abodrite Prince Niklot in 1160 and conquer the Wends by 1168. His capture of their stronghold at Arkona provided one of the most dramatic scenes in the Baltic Crusade era when their shrine to the god Svantovit was destroyed.

Vézelay, city in Burgundy that was the site of Louis VII's taking of the crusade cross at Eastertide 1146. This action is generally regarded as the inception of the Second Crusade.

Welfs, one of the two major noble factions involved in the intermittent civil wars concerning royal succession in twelfth- and thirteenth-century Germany. The Welf side managed to get Lothair of Supplinburg elected as Emperor in 1125, but lost control of the monarchy upon his death in 1137. Their banner was carried by Henry "the Lion" during the period of the Wendish Crusade.

Wends, an umbrella term for the Slavic peoples living east of the Elbe River and along the Baltic littoral. Although tribal designations are often difficult to assign, the Wends are generally thought to have comprised five tribes: the Abodrites, Pomeranians, Liutizians, Rugians, and Wagrians. These tribes had been struggling against German pressures eastward for several centuries when the Wendish Crusade began what would be the opening of the multi-century Baltic Crusades (c. 1147–1410).

White Martyrdom. A form of life pilgrimage begun in Ireland by Columba and carried to the Continent by Columbanus in the late sixth century, it consisted of the pilgrim going wherever God led for the duration of life. White Martyrdom was ultimately superseded by place pilgrimage, but offered an early model of an alternate type of pilgrimage that may have affected the Baltic crusaders' interpretation of pilgrimage.

Zengi, real name and title: Emir Imad ad-Din Zengi (1085–1146). As *atabeg* (or "ruler") of Mosul, Zengi was able to gather enough Muslim support to take the crusader city of Edessa in December/January 1144/45. This event triggered the Second Crusade. Zengi's murder in 1146 did not end the Muslim resurgence as his successor, Nur ad-Din, continued the pressure on the remaining Crusader states.

BIBLIOGRAPHY

Primary Sources

Arbusow, Leonid and Albert Bauer, eds. *Heinrichs Livlandische Chronik*, *MGH Scriptores Rerum Germanicarum*, 31. Hannover: Hahnsche Buchhandlung, 1955.

Bachrach, Bernard S., trans. and ed. *Liber Historiae Francorum*. Lawrence, KS: Coronado Press, 1973.

Bachrach, Bernard S. and David S. Bachrach, trans. *Widukind of Corvey: Deeds of the Saxons*. Washington, DC: The Catholic University of America Press, 2014.

Barmby, James, trans. "The Book of Pastoral Rule and Selected Epistles of Gregory the Great," in Philip Schaff and Henry Wace, eds, *Nicene and Post-Nicene Fathers*, vol. 1, 73–243. Peabody, MA: Hendrickson Publishers, 1995.

Baxter, James Houston, trans. *St. Augustine: Select Letters*. London: William Heinemann Ltd, 1930.

Brundage, James A., trans. *The Chronicle of Henry of Livonia*. Madison, WI: University of Wisconsin Press, 1961.

Buchner, Rudolf, ed. *Gregor von Tours: Zehn Bucher Geschichten*, 2 vol. Berlin: Rütten & Loening, 1955–56.

Christiansen, Eric, trans. and ed. *The Works of Sven Aggesen: Twelfth Century Danish Historian*. London: Viking Society for Northern Research, 1992.

Cohen, J. M., trans. *Bernal Díaz: The Conquest of New Spain*. Harmondsworth, UK: Penguin Books, Ltd., 1963.

Culler, A. Dwight, ed. *Poetry and Criticism of Matthew Arnold*. Boston: Houghton Mifflin Company, 1961.

Fisher, Peter, trans. and Hilda Ellis Davidson, ed. *Saxo Grammaticus: The History of the Danes*, vol. I. Cambridge: D.S. Brewer, 1979.

Foulke, William Dudley, trans. and Edward Peters, ed. *Paul the Deacon: History of the Lombards*. Philadelphia: The University of Pennsylvania Press, 1974.

Fry, Timothy, ed. *The Rule of Saint Benedict*. New York: Vintage Books, 1998.
Ganz, David, trans. *Einhard and Notker the Stammerer: Two Lives of Charlemagne*. London: Penguin Books Ltd., 2008.
Garmonsway, G. N., trans. *The Anglo-Saxon Chronicle*. London: J. M. Dent and Sons, 1975.
Greenia, Conrad, trans. *The Works of Bernard of Clairvaux*, vol. VII, *Treatises*. Kalamazoo, MI: Cistercian Fathers Series, 1977.
Griffin, Nigel, trans. *Bartolomé de las Casas: A Short Account of the Destruction of the Indies*, London: Penguin Books Ltd., 1992.
Hollander, Lee M., trans. *Heimskringla: History of the Kings of Norway by Snorri Sturluson*. Austin, TX: University of Texas Press, 1964.
Hood, A. B. E., trans. *St. Patrick: His Writings and Muirchu's Life*. Totowa, NJ: Rowman and Littlefield, 1978.
Ingram, James, trans. *The Anglo-Saxon Chronicle*. London: J. M. Dent & Sons, 1949.
James, Bruno Scott, trans. *The Letters of St. Bernard of Clairvaux*. Chicago: Henry Regnery Company, 1953.
Leland, Charles Godfrey, trans. *The Works of Heinrich Heine*. London: William Heinemann, 1892.
McClure, Judith and Roger Collins, eds. *Bede: The Ecclesiastical History of the English People, The Greater Chronicle, Bede's Letter to Egbert*. Oxford: Oxford University Press, 1999.
Mierow, Charles C., trans. *The Deeds of Frederick Barbarossa by Otto of Freising*. New York: W.W. Norton, 1966.
Migne, Jacques-Paul, ed. *Patrologiae Latinae Cursus Completus*, 221 vols. Paris: Migne, 1844–57.
Munro, Dana Carleton, trans. *The Laws of Charles the Great*. Translations and Reprints from the Original Sources of European History, vol. VII, no. 5. Philadelphia: University of Pennsylvania Press, 1900.
Munro, Dana Carleton, trans. *The Life of St. Columban by the Monk Jonas*. Translations and Reprints from the Original Sources of European History, vol. II, no. 7, Philadelphia: University of Pennsylvania Press, 1895.
Murphy, G. Ronald, trans. *The Heliand: The Saxon Gospel*. Oxford: Oxford University Press, 1992.
Murray, John, ed. *The Autobiographies of Edward Gibbon*, 2nd edn. London: John Murray, 1897.
Pertz, Georg Heinrich, ed. *Translatio S. Liborii* in *MGH Scriptores* 4. Hannover: Hahn Buchhandlung, 1891.
Peters, Edward, ed. *The First Crusade: The Chronicle of Fulcher of Chartres and Other Source Materials*. Philadelphia: University of Pennsylvania Press, 1998.

Powell, James M., trans. *The Deeds of Pope Innocent III by an Anonymous Author*. Washington, DC: The Catholic University of America Press, 2004.

Rapoport, Anatol, ed. *Carl von Clausewitz: On War*. Harmondsworth, UK: Penguin Books, 1968.

Roberts, Alexander and James Donaldson, eds. *Tertullian, Part Fourth; Minucius Felix; Commodian; Origen, Parts First and Second* in *Ante-Nicene Fathers*, vol. 4. Peabody, MA: Hendrickson Publishers, Inc., 1994.

Schaff, Philip, ed. *Agustin: On the Holy Trinity, Doctrinal Treatises, Moral Treatises, A Select Library of the Christian Church*, vol. 3. Peabody, MA: Hendrickson Publishers, Inc., 1995.

Scholz, Bernhard Walter with Barbara Rogers, trans. *Carolingian Chronicles: Royal Frankish Annals and Nithard's Histories*. Ann Arbor, MI: The University of Michigan Press, 1970.

Shanzer, Danuta and Ian Wood, eds. *Avitus of Vienne: Letters and Selected Prose*. Liverpool: Liverpool University Press, 2002.

Sharpe, Richard, trans. *Adomnan of Iona: Life of St. Columba*. London: Penguin Books, 1995.

Sherley-Price, Leo, trans. *Bede: A History of the English Church and People*. New York: Dorset Press, 1985.

Smith, Jerry C. and William L. Urban, trans. *The Livonian Rhymed Chronicle*. Bloomington, IN: The University of Indiana Press, 1977.

Talbot, C. H., trans. and ed. *The Anglo-Saxon Missionaries in Germany: Being the Lives of SS. Willibrord, Boniface, Sturm, Leoba, and Lebuin, together with the Hodoeporicon of St. Willibald and a selection from the correspondence of St. Boniface*. New York: Sheed and Ward, 1954.

Thorpe, Lewis, trans. *Gregory of Tours: History of the Franks*. Harmondsworth: Penguin Books, 1974.

Tschan, Francis Joseph, trans. *Adam of Bremen: History of the Archbishops of Hamburg-Bremen*. New York: Columbia University Press, 1959.

Tschan, Francis Joseph, trans. *The Chronicle of the Slavs by Helmold, the Priest of Bosau*. New York: Columbia University Press, 1935.

Walker, G. S. M., ed. *Sancti Columbani Opera*. Dublin: Dublin Institute for Advanced Studies, 1957.

Walsh, P. G., trans. *The Poems of St. Paulinus of Nola*. Ancient Christian Writers, no. 40. New York: Newman Press, 1975.

Webb, J. F. and D. H. Farmer, trans. *The Age of Bede*. London: Penguin Books, 2004.

Wolf, Kenneth Baxter, trans. *Conquerors and Chroniclers of Early Medieval Spain*. Liverpool: Liverpool University Press, 1990.

Woolverton, Lisa, trans. *Cosmas of Prague: The Chronicle of the Czechs*. Washington, DC: The Catholic University of America Press, 2009.

Secondary Sources

Allen, S. J. and Emilie Amt, eds. *The Crusades: A Reader*. Peterborough, Ontario: Broadview Press, Ltd., 2003.
Armitage, David. "Is There a Prehistory of Globalization?" in Deborah Cohen and Maura O'Connor, eds. *Comparison and History: Europe in Cross-National Perspective*, 165–76. London: Routledge, 2004.
Armstrong, Guyda and Ian N. Wood, eds. *Christianizing Peoples and Converting Individuals*. International Medieval Research, vol. 7. Turnhout: Brepols Publishers, 2000.
Arsenal, León. *Godos de Hispania*. Madrid: EDAF, 2013.
Asbridge, Thomas. *The Crusades: The Authoritative History of the War for the Holy Land*. New York: HarperCollins, 2010.
Asbridge, Thomas. *The First Crusade: A New History*. Oxford: Oxford University Press, 2004.
Bachrach, Bernard S. *Merovingian Military Organization, 481-751*. Minneapolis, MN: University of Minnesota Press, 1972.
Bachrach, David S. *Religion and the Conduct of War, c. 300-1215*. Woodbridge: The Boydell Press, 2003.
Bagge, Sverre. *Kings, Politics and the Right Order of the World in German Historiography, c. 950–1150*. Leiden: Brill, 2002.
Bainton, Roland H. *Christendom: A Short History of Christianity and Its Impact on Western Civilization*, 2 vols. New York: Harper Torchbooks, 1966.
Barber, Malcolm. *The New Knighthood: A History of the Order of the Temple*. Cambridge: Cambridge University Press, 1994.
Barraclough, Geoffrey. *The Origins of Modern Germany*. New York: Capricorn Books, 1963.
Bartlett, Robert. "The Conversion of a Pagan Society in the Middle Ages." *History* 70 (1985): 185–201.
Bartlett, Robert. *The Making of Europe: Conquest, Colonization and Cultural Change, 950-1350*. Princeton, NJ: Princeton University Press, 1993.
Bartlett, Robert and Angus MacKay, eds. *Medieval Frontier Societies*. Oxford: Clarendon Press, 1989.
Beck, H. G. J. *The Pastoral Care of Souls in Southeastern France in the Sixth Century*. Rome: Universitas Gregoriana, 1950.
Beeler, John. *Warfare in Feudal Europe, 730-1200*. Ithaca, NY: Cornell University Press, 1971.
Berend, Nora. "Frontiers," in Helen Nicholson, ed. *Palgrave Advances in the Crusades*, 148–71. London: Palgrave MacMillan, 2005.
Berry, Virginia G. "The Second Crusade," in Kenneth M. Setton, ed. *A History of the Crusades*, vol. I, 463–512. Madison, WI: University of Wisconsin Press, 1969.

Beumann, Helmut, ed. *Heidenmission und Kreuzzugsgedanke in der deutschen Ostpolitik des Mittelalters*, Wege der Forschung 7. Darmstadt: Wissenschaftliche Buchgesellschaft, 1963.

Bishko, Charles Julian. "The Frontier in Medieval History." Presented at the Annual Meeting of the American Historical Association. Washington, DC: December 29, 1955.

Bitel, Lisa M. *Isle of the Saints: Monastic Settlement and Christian Community in Early Ireland*. Ithaca, NY: Cornell University Press, 1993.

Blake, E. O. "The Formation of the 'Crusade Idea'." *Journal of Ecclesiastical History* 21 (1970): 11–31.

Bliese, John R. E. "The Just War Concept and Motive in the Central Middle Ages." *Medievalia et Humanistica* n.s. 17 (1991): 1–26.

Bloch, Marc. *Feudal Society*. 2 vols. Trans. L. A. Manyon. Chicago: University of Chicago Press, 1968.

Bloch, Marc. *The Historian's Craft: Reflections on the Nature and Uses of History and the Techniques and Methods of the Men Who Write It*. Trans. Peter Putnam. New York: Vintage Books, 1964.

Bonner, Michael. *Jihad in Islamic History: Doctrine and Practice*. Princeton, NJ: Princeton University Press, 2006.

Botha, Rudolf and Christ Knight, eds. *The Prehistory of Language*. Oxford: Oxford University Press, 2009.

Bowersock, G. W., Peter Brown, and Oleg Grabar, eds. *Interpreting Late Antiquity: Essays on the Postclassical World*. Cambridge, MA: The Belknap Press of Harvard University, 2001.

Bromley, David C., ed. *The Politics of Religious Apostasy: The Role of Apostates in the Transformation of Religious Movements*. London: Praeger, 1998.

Brown, Peter. "A Life of Learning: The Charles Homer Haskins Lecture for 2003." Philadelphia: The American Council of Learned Societies, Occasional Paper No. 55, 2003.

Brown, Peter. *Augustine of Hippo: A Biography*. Berkeley: University of California Press, 1967.

Brown, Peter. "St. Augustine's Attitude to Religious Conversion." *The Journal of Roman Studies* 54 (1964): 107–116.

Brown, Peter. *The Cult of the Saints: Its Rise and Function in Latin Christianity*. Chicago: University of Chicago Press, 1981.

Brown, Peter. *The Ransom of the Soul: Afterlife and Wealth in Early Western Christianity*. Cambridge, MA: Harvard University Press, 2015.

Brown, Peter. *The Rise of Western Christendom: Triumph and Diversity, A.D. 200-1000*. 2nd edn. Oxford: Blackwell Publishing, 2003.

Brundage, James A. *Medieval Canon Law and the Crusader*. Madison, WI: University of Wisconsin Press, 1969.

Bull, Marcus. "Origins," in Jonathan Riley-Smith, ed. *The Oxford Illustrated History of the Crusades*, 13–33. Oxford: Oxford University Press, 1997.

Bull, Marcus. Review of Matthew Gabriele, *An Empire of Memory: The Legend of Charlemagne, the Franks, and Jerusalem before the First Crusade*. *Crusades* 11 (2012): 256–7.
Burckhardt, Jacob. *The Civilization of the Renaissance in Italy*. Trans. Irene Gordon. New York: New American Library, 1960.
Byer, Glenn C. J. *Charlemagne and Baptism: A Study of Responses to the Circular Letter of 811/812*. New York: International Scholars Publications, 1999.
Bysted, Ane, Carsten Selch Jensen, Kurt Villads Jensen, and John H. Lind, eds. *Jerusalem in the North: Denmark and the Baltic Crusades, 1100-1522*. Turnhout: Brepols Publishers, 2012.
Caffiero, Marina. *Forced Baptism: Histories of the Jews, Christians, and Converts in Papal Rome*. Trans. Lydia G. Cochrane. Berkeley: University of California Press, 2012.
Cantor, Norman F. *William Stubbs on the English Constitution*. New York: Thomas Y. Crowell Company, 1966.
Carroll, Christopher. "The bishoprics of Saxony in the first century after Christianization." *Early Medieval Europe* 8 (1999): 219–45.
Carver, Martin, ed. *The Cross Goes North: Processes of Conversion in Northern Europe, AD 300-1300*. Woodbridge: The Boydell Press, 2003.
Castellanos, Santiago. *Los Godos y La Cruz: Recaredo y La Unidad de Spania*. Madrid: Alianza Editorial, 2007.
Charles, J. Daryl. *Between Pacifism and Jihad: Just War and Christian Tradition*. Downers Grove, IL: InterVarsity Press, 2005.
Charles-Edwards, T. M. *Early Christian Ireland*. Cambridge: Cambridge University Press, 2000.
Chevedden, Paul. "The Islamic Interpretation of the Crusade: A New (Old) Paradigm for Understanding the Crusades." *Der Islam* Bd.83 (2006): 90–136.
Chevedden, Paul. "The Islamic View and the Christian View of the Crusades: A New Synthesis." *History* 93 (April 2008): 181–200.
Chevedden, Paul. "The View of the Crusades from Rome and Damascus: The Geo-Strategic and Historical Perspectives of Pope Urban II and 'Ali ibn Tahir al-Sulami." *Oriens* 39 (2011): 257–329.
Christiansen, Eric. *The Northern Crusades: The Baltic and the Catholic Frontier, 1100-1525*. Minneapolis, MN: University of Minnesota Press, 1980.
Claster, Jill N. *Sacred Violence: The European Crusades to the Middle East, 1095-1396*. Toronto: University of Toronto Press, 2009.
Cobb, Paul M. *The Race for Paradise: An Islamic History of the Crusades*. Oxford: Oxford University Press, 2014.
Colish, Marcia L. *Faith, Fiction & Force in Medieval Baptismal Debates*. Washington, DC: The Catholic University of America Press, 2014.

Collins, Roger. *Early Medieval Spain: Unity in Diversity, 400-1000.* New York: St. Martin's Press, 1983.
Collins, Roger. *The Arab Conquest of Spain, 710-797.* Oxford: Basil Blackwell, 1989.
Constable, Giles. *Crusaders and Crusading in the Twelfth Century.* Burlington, VT: Ashgate Publishing Company, 2008.
Contamine, Philippe. *War in the Middle Ages.* Trans. Michael Jones. Oxford: Basil Blackwell, Ltd., 1984.
Cowdrey, H. E. J., "The Genesis of the Crusades: The Springs of Western Ideas of Holy War," in Thomas Patrick Murphy, ed. *The Holy War*, 9–32. Columbus, OH: The Ohio State University Press, 1976.
Craig, Gordon V. *The Germans.* New York: New American Library, 1982.
Cramer, Peter. *Baptism and Change in the Early Middle Ages, c. 200-c. 1150.* Cambridge: Cambridge University Press, 1993.
Cutler, A. "The First Crusade and the Idea of 'Conversion'." *The Muslim World* 58 (1968): 57–71.
Damgaard-Sorensen, Tinna. "Danes and Wends: a study of the Danish attitude towards the Wends," in Ian Wood and Neils Lund, eds. *People and Places in Northern Europe, 500-1600: Essays in Honour of Peter Hayes Sawyer*, 171–86. Woodbridge: The Boydell Press, 1991.
Daniel, E. Randolph. *The Franciscan Concept of Mission in the High Middle Ages.* Lexington, KY: The University Press of Kentucky, 1975.
Daniel-Rops, Henri. *The Church in the Dark Ages*, vol. II. Trans. Audrey Butler. Garden City, NY: Image Books, 1962.
Davidson, Linda Kay and Maryjane Dunn-Wood. *Pilgrimage in the Middle Ages: A Research Guide.* New York: Garland Publishing, Inc., 1993.
Davis, R. H. C. *A History of Medieval Europe: From Constantine to Saint Louis*, 3rd edn. Harlow, UK: Pearson Longman, 2006.
Dawson, Christopher. *The Making of Europe: An Introduction to the History of European Unity.* New York: Meridian Books, 1966.
Drake, H. A. "Monotheism and Violence." *Journal of Late Antiquity* 6 (2) (Fall 2013): 251–63.
Duggan, Lawrence G. "'For Force Is Not of God?' Compulsion and Conversion from Yahweh to Charlemagne," in James Muldoon, ed. *Varieties of Religious Conversion in the Middle Ages*, 49–62. Gainesville, FL: University Press of Florida, 1997.
Dutton, Paul Edward. *Carolingian Civilization: A Reader.* Peterborough, Ontario: Broadview Press, 1993.
Dvornik, Francis. *The Making of Central and Eastern Europe.* 2nd edn. Gulf Breeze, FL: Academic International Press, 1974.
Dvornik, Francis. *The Slavs: Their Early History and Civilization.* Boston: American Academy of Arts and Sciences, 1956.
Dyas, Dee. *Pilgrimage in Medieval English Literature, 700-1500.* Cambridge: D. S. Brewer, 2001.

Edbury, Peter W., ed. *Crusade and Settlement: Papers read at the First Conference of the Society for the Study of the Crusades and the Latin East and presented to R. C. Smail*. Cardiff: University College Cardiff Press, 1985.

Eihmane, Eva. "The Baltic Crusades: A Clash of Two Identities," in Alan V. Murray, ed. *The Clash of Cultures on the Medieval Baltic Frontier*, 37–51. Burlington, VT: Ashgate Publishing Company, 2009.

Ekdahl, Sven. "Crusades and Colonization in the Baltic," in Helen Nicholson, ed. *Palgrave Advances in the Crusades*, 172–203. London: Palgrave MacMillan, 2005.

Ellenblum, Ronnie. *Crusader Castles and Modern Histories*. Cambridge: Cambridge University Press, 2007.

Erdmann, Carl. *Die Entstehung des Kreuzzugsgedankens*. Darmstadt: Wissenschaftliche Buchgesellschaft, 1972.

Erdmann, Carl. *The Origin of the Idea of Crusade*. Trans. Marshall Baldwin and Walter Goffart. Princeton, NJ: Princeton University Press, 1977.

Favreau-Lilie, Marie-Louise, "Mission to the Heathen in Prussia and Livonia: The Attitudes of the Religious Military Orders Toward Christianization," in Guyda Armstrong and Ian N. Wood, eds. *Christianizing Peoples and Converting Individuals*, 147–54. Turnhout: Brepols Publishers, 2000.

Fischer, David Hackett. *Historians' Fallacies: Toward a Logic of Historical Thought*. New York: Harper Torchbook, 1970.

Fletcher, Richard. *The Barbarian Conversion: From Paganism to Christianity*. New York: Henry Holt and Company, 1997.

Fletcher, Richard. *The Cross and the Crescent: Christianity and Islam from Muhammad to the Reformation*. New York: Viking, 2003.

Flori, Jean. "Ideology and Motivations in the First Crusade," in Helen Nicholson, ed. *Palgrave Advances in the Crusades*, 15–30. London: Palgrave Macmillan, 2005.

Fonnesberg-Schmidt, Iben. "Pope Honorius III and Mission and Crusades in the Baltic Region," in Alan V. Murray, ed. *The Clash of Cultures on the Medieval Baltic Frontier*, 103–22. Burlington, VT: Ashgate Publishing Company, 2009.

Fonnesberg-Schmidt, Iben. *The Popes and the Baltic Crusades, 1147-1254*. Leiden: Brill, 2007.

France, John. "Crusading Warfare," in Helen Nicholson, ed. *Palgrave Advances in the Crusades*, 58–80. London: Palgrave MacMillan, 2005.

France, John. *Victory in the East: A military history of the First Crusade*. Cambridge: Cambridge University Press, 1994.

France, John. *Western Warfare in the Age of the Crusades*. Ithaca, NY: Cornell University Press, 1999.

Freeman, Charles. *The Closing of the Western Mind: The Rise of Faith and the Fall of Reason*. New York: Alfred A. Knopf, 2003.

Frend, W. H. C. *The Donatist Church: A Movement of Protest in Roman North Africa*. Oxford: Oxford University Press, 1985.
Gabriele, Matthew. *An Empire of Memory: The Legend of Charlemagne, the Franks, and Jerusalem before the First Crusade*. Oxford: Oxford University Press, 2011.
Gabriele, Matthew and Jace Stuckey, eds. *The Legend of Charlemagne in the Middle Ages: Power, Faith, and Crusade*. New York: Palgrave MacMillan, 2008.
Gaddis, Michael. *There is No Crime for Those Who Have Christ: religious violence in the Christian Roman Empire*. Berkeley: University of California Press, 2005.
Ganshof, F. L. *The Carolingians and the Frankish Monarchy: Studies in Carolingian History*. Trans Janet Sondheimer. London: Longman Group Limited, 1971.
Geary, Patrick J. *Before France and Germany: the creation and transformation of the Merovingian World*. New York: Oxford University Press, 1988.
Geary, Patrick J. *The Myth of Nations: The Medieval Origins of Europe*. Princeton, NJ: Princeton University Press, 2002.
Gertwagen, Ruthy and Elizabeth Jeffreys, eds. *Shipping, Trade and Crusade in the Medieval Mediterranean: Studies in Honour of John Pryor*. Burlington, VT: Ashgate Publishing Company, 2012.
Ghosh, Shami. "Conquest, Conversion, and Heathen Customs in Henry of Livonia's *Chronicon Livoniae* and the *Livlandische Reimchronik*." *Crusades* 11 (2012): 87–108.
Gibb, Hamilton. "The Influence of Islamic Culture on Medieval Europe," in Sylvia L. Thrupp, ed. *Change in Medieval Society: Europe North of the Alps, 1050-1500*, 155–67. New York: Appleton-Century-Crofts, 1964.
Gilchrist, John. "The Erdmann Thesis and the Canon Law, 1083-1141," in Peter Edbury, ed. *Crusade and Settlement*, 37–45. Cardiff: University College Cardiff Press, 1985.
Gilchrist, John. "The Papacy and War against the 'Saracens,' 795-1216." *The International History Review* 10 (May 1988): 174–97.
Gimbutas, Marija. *The Balts*. New York: Praeger, 1963.
Gimbutas, Marija. *The Slavs*. New York: Praeger, 1971.
Glick, Thomas F. *Islamic and Christian Spain in the Early Middle Ages*. Princeton, NJ: Princeton University Press, 1979.
Goetz, Hans-Werner, "Concepts of Realm and Frontiers from Late Antiquity to the Early Middle Ages," in Walter Pohl, Ian Wood, and Herbert Reimitz, eds. *The Transformation of Frontiers: From Antiquity to the Carolingians*, 73–82. Leiden: Brill, 2001.
Goffart, Walter. *Barbarians and Romans, AD418–584: The Techniques of Accommodation*. Princeton, NJ: Princeton University Press, 1980.

Gray, Phillip W., "Just War, Schism, and Peace in St. Augustine," in Henrik Syse and Gregory M. Reichberg, eds. *Ethics, Nationalism, and Just War: Medieval and Contemporary Perspectives*, 51–71. Washington, DC: The Catholic Univesity of America Press, 2007.
Halsall, Guy, ed. *Violence and Society in the Early Medieval West*. Woodbridge: The Boydell Press, 1998.
Hanke, Lewis. *The Spanish Struggle for Justice in the Conquest of America*. Philadelphia: University of Pennsylvania Press, 1949.
Harnack, Adolf von. *Militia Christi: Die Christliche Religion und der Soldatenstand in den Ersten Drei Jahrhunderten*. Darmstadt: Wissenschaftliche Buchgesellschaft, 1963.
Harnack, Adolf von. *Militia Christi: The Christian Religion and the Military in the First Three Centuries*. Trans. David McInnes Gracie. Philadelphia: Fortress Press, 1981.
Harper-Bill, Christopher, Christopher J. Holdsworth, and Janet L. Nelson, eds. *Studies in Medieval History presented to R. Allen Brown*. Woodbridge: The Boydell Press, 1989.
Harris, Jonathan. "The 'Schism' of 1054 and the First Crusade." *Crusades* 13 (2014): 1–20.
Haskins, Charles Homer. *The Normans in European History*. New York: W.W. Norton and Company, Inc., 1966.
Haskins, Charles Homer. *The Renaissance of the Twelfth Century*. Cambridge, MA: Harvard University Press, 1927.
Hayden, Brian. *Shamans, Sorcerers, and Saints: A Prehistory of Religion*. Washington, DC: Smithsonian Books, 2003.
Head, Thomas and Richard Landes, eds. *The Peace of God: Social Violence and Religious Response in France around the Year 1000*. Ithaca, NY: Cornell University Press, 1992.
Headley, John M., "The Universalizing Principle and Process: On the West's Intrinsic Commitment to a Global Context." *Journal of World History* 13 (Fall 2002): 291–321.
Hedeager, Lotte. *Iron Age Societies: From Tribe to State in Northern Europe, 500BC to AD700*. Trans. John Hines. Oxford: Basil Blackwell, 1992.
Hehl, Ernst-Dieter. *Kirche und Krieg im 12. Jahrhundert: Studien zu kanonischem Recht und politischer Wirklichkeit*. Monographien zur Geschichte des Mittelalters, 19. Stuttgart: A. Hiersemann, 1980.
Hehl, Ernst-Dieter. "Was ist eigentlich ein Kreuzzug?" *Historische Zeitschrift* 259 (1994): 297–336.
Heinzelmann, Martin. "Heresy in Books I and II of Gregory of Tours' Historia," in Alexander Callander Murray, ed. *After Rome's Fall: Narrators and Sources of Early Medieval History*, 78. Buffalo, NY: University of Toronto Press, 1998.
Helgeland, John, Robert J. Daly, and J. Patout Burns. *Christians and the Military: The Early Experience*. Philadelphia: Fortress Press, 1985.

Hen, Yitzhak. "Charlemagne's Jihad." *Viator* 37 (2006): 33–51.
Herrmann, Joachim, "The West Slav Lands and the North," in Else Roesdahl and David M. Wilson, eds. *From Viking to Crusader: The Scandinavians and Europe 800-1200*, 84–7. New York: Rizzoli International Publications, 1992.
Hillgarth, J. N., ed. *The Conversion of Western Europe 350-750*. Englewood Cliffs, NJ: Prentice-Hall, Inc., 1969.
Hindley, Geoffrey. *The Crusades: Islam and Christianity in the Struggle for World Supremacy*. New York: Carroll & Graf Publishers, 2003.
Hodgkin, Thomas. *Charles the Great*. London: MacMillan and Co., Ltd., 1897.
Holdsworth, Christopher J. "Ideas and Reality: Some Attempts to Control and Defuse War in the Twelfth Century," in W. J. Sheils, ed. *The Church and War*, 59–78. Oxford: Basil Blackwell, 1983.
Housley, Norman. *Contesting the Crusades*. Oxford: Blackwell, 2006.
Howe, John. *Church Reform and Social Change in Eleventh-Century Italy*. Philadelphia: University of Pennsylvania Press, 1997.
Howe, John. "The Conversion of the Physical World: The Creation of a Christian Landscape," in James Muldoon, ed. *Varieties of Religious Conversion in the Middle Ages*, 63–78. Gainesville, FL: University Press of Florida, 1997.
Hoyland, Robert G. *In God's Path: The Arab Conquests and the Creation of an Islamic Empire*. Oxford: Oxford University Press, 2015.
Hughes, Kathleen. *The Church in Early Irish Society*. Ithaca, NY: Cornell University Press, 1966.
Huizinga, Johan. *Homo Ludens: A Study of the Play Element in Culture*. Boston: Beacon Press, 1955.
Jensen, Carsten Selch. "How to Convert a Landscape: Henry of Livonia and the *Chronicon Livoniae*," in Alan V. Murray, ed. *The Clash of Cultures on the Medieval Baltic Frontier*, 151–68. Burlington, VT: Ashgate Publishing Company, 2009.
Jensen, Carsten Selch. "Urban Life and the Crusaders in North Germany and the Baltic Lands in the Early Thirteenth Century," in Alan V. Murray, ed. *Crusade and Conversion on the Baltic Frontier, 1100-1500*, 75–94. Burlington, VT: Ashgate Publishers, 2001.
Jensen, Janus Moller. Review of *The Clash of Cultures on the Medieval Baltic Frontier*. Alan V. Murray, ed. *Crusades* 10 (2011): 198–199.
Jensen, Kurt Villads. "Introduction," in Alan V. Murray, ed. *Crusade and Conversion on the Baltic Frontier, 1100-1500*, xx–xxii. Burlington, VT: Ashgate Publishers, 2001.
Jensen, Kurt Villads. "Sacralization of the Landscape: Converting Trees and Measuring Land in the Danish Crusades against the Wends," in Alan V. Murray, ed. *The Clash of Cultures on the Medieval Baltic Frontier*, 141–50. Burlington, VT: Ashgate Publishing Company, 2009.

Johnson, Edgar N. "The German Crusade on the Baltic," in Kenneth M. Setton, ed. *A History of the Crusades*, vol. III, 545–85. Madison, WI: University of Wisconsin Press, 1975.
Johnson, James Turner and John Kelsay, eds. *Cross, Crescent, and Sword: The Justification and Limitation of War in Western and Islamic Tradition*. New York: Greenwood Press, 1990.
Jones, A. H. M. *Constantine and the Conversion of Europe*. New York: Collier Books, 1962.
Jones, A. H. M. *The Decline of the Ancient World*. New York: Holt, Rinehart and Winston, Inc., 1966.
Jubb, Margaret. "The Crusaders' Perceptions of Their Opponents," in Helen Nicholson, ed. *Palgrave Advances in the Crusades*, 225–44. London: Palgrave Macmillan, 2005.
Kahl, Hans-Dietrich. *Slawen und Deutsche in der Brandenburgischen Geschichte des Zwölften Jahrhunderts*, 2v. Köln: Böhlau Verlag, 1964.
Kala, Tiina. "Rural Society and Religious Innovation: Acceptance and Rejection of Catholicism among the Native Inhabitants of Medieval Livonia," in Alan V. Murray, ed. *The Clash of Cultures on the Medieval Baltic Frontier*, 169–90. Burlington, VT: Ashgate Publishing Company, 2009.
Kala, Tiina. "The Incorporation of the Northern Baltic Lands into the Western Christian World," in Alan V. Murray, ed. *Crusade and Conversion on the Baltic Frontier, 1100-1500*, 3–20. Burlington, VT: Ashgate Publishers, 2001.
Kaljundi, Linda. "Waiting for the Barbarians: The Imagery, Dynamics and Functions of the Other in Northern German Missionary Chronicles, 11th-Early 13th Centuries." Master's Thesis, University of Tartu, 2005.
Karras, Ruth Mazo. "Pagan Survivals and Syncretism in the Conversion of Saxony." *The Catholic Historical Review* 72 (October 1986): 553–72.
Kedar, Benjamin Z. *Crusade and Mission: European Approaches toward the Muslims*. Princeton, NJ: Princeton University Press, 1984.
Keefe, S. A. "Carolingian Baptismal Expositions: A Handlist of Tracts and Manuscripts," in Ute-Renate Blumenthal, ed. *Carolingian Essays: Andrew W. Mellon Lectures in Early Christian Studies*, 169–273. Washington, DC: The Catholic University of America Press, 1983.
Kelly, Christopher. "Empire Building," in G. W. Bowersock, Peter Brown, and Oleg Grabar, eds. *Interpreting Late Antiquity*, 170–95. Cambridge, MA: The Belknap Press of Harvard University Press, 2001.
Laiou, Angeliki and Roy Mottahedeh, eds. *The Crusades from the Perspective of Byzantium and the Muslim World*. Washington, DC: Dumbarton Oaks, 2001.

Latouche, Robert M. *Caesar to Charlemagne: The Beginnings of France.* Trans. Jennifer Nicholson. London: J. M. Dent & Sons, Ltd., 1968.
LeBras, Gabriel. "The Sociology of the Church in the Early Middle Ages," in Sylvia L. Thrupp, ed. *Early Medieval Society*, 47–57. New York: Appleton-Century-Crofts, 1967.
Lehtonen, Tuomas M. S. and Kurt Villads Jensen with Janne Malkki and Katja Ritari, eds. *Medieval History Writing and Crusading Ideology.* Studia Fennica, Historica 9. Helsinki: Finnish Literature Society, 2005.
Lewis, Bernard. *The Arabs in History.* Oxford: Oxford University Press, 1993.
Leyser, Karl J. *Rule and Conflict in an Early Medieval Society: Ottonian Saxony.* Bloomington, IN: Indiana University Press, 1979.
Liebgott, Niels-Knud. "Pilgrimages and Crusades," in Else Roesdahl and David M. Wilson, eds. *From Viking to Crusader: The Scandinavians and Europe 800-1200*, 110–11. New York: Rizzoli International Publications, 1992.
Lim, Richard. "Christian Triumph and Controversy," in G. W. Bowersock, Peter Brown, and Oleg Grabar, eds. *Interpreting Late Antiquity: Essays on the Postclassical World*, 196–218. Cambridge, MA: The Belknap Press of Harvard University, 2001.
Long, Edward LeRoy, Jr. *War and Conscience in America.* Philadelphia: The Westminster Press, 1968.
Lotter, Friedrich. *Die Konzeption des Wendenkreuzzugs: ideengeschichte, kirchen-rechtliche und historisch-politischen Voraussetzungen der Missionierung von Elb- und Ostseeslawen um die Mitte des 12. Jahrhunderts.* Sigmaringen: Jan Thorbecke, 1977.
Lotter, Friedrich. "The Crusading Idea and the Conquest of the Region East of the Elbe," in Robert Bartlett and Angus McKay, eds. *Medieval Frontier Societies*, 267–306. Oxford: Clarendon Press, 1989.
Loud, G. A. "The Church, Warfare and Military Obligation in Norman Italy," in W. J. Sheils, ed. *The Church and War*, 31–45. Oxford: Basil Blackwell, 1983.
MacEvitt, Christopher. *The Crusades and the Christian World of the East: Rough Tolerance.* Philadelphia: University of Pennsylvania Press, 2008.
MacMullen, Ramsay. *Christianity and Paganism in the Fourth to Eighth Centuries.* New Haven: Yale University Press, 1997.
Madden, Thomas F. "Crusaders and Historians." *First Things* 154 (June 2005): 26–31.
Madden, Thomas F. "Inventing the Crusades." *First Things* 194 (June 2009): 41–4.
Madden, Thomas F. Review of Christopher Tyerman, *God's War: A New History of the Crusades. First Things* 168 (December 2006): 44–6.

Madden, Thomas F. *The New Concise History of the Crusades: Updated Edition.* Lanham, MD: Rowman & Littlefield, 2005.
Mänd, Anu. "Saints' Cults in Medieval Livonia," in Alan V. Murray, ed. *The Clash of Cultures on the Medieval Baltic Frontier*, 191–223. Burlington, VT: Ashgate Publishing Company, 2009.
Markus, R. A. *Gregory the Great and His World.* Cambridge: Cambridge University Press, 1997.
Markus, R. A. "Saint Augustine's Views on the 'Just War'," in W. J. Sheils, ed. *The Church and War*, 1–13. Oxford: Basil Blackwell, 1983.
Mayer, Hans Eberhard. *The Crusades.* Trans. John Gillingham. Oxford: Oxford University Press, 1972.
Mazeika, Rasa. "Bargaining for Baptism: Lithuanian Negotiations for Conversion, 1250-1358," in James Muldoon, ed. *Varieties of Religious Conversion in the Middle Ages*, 131–45. Gainesville, FL: University Press of Florida, 1997.
Mazeika, Rasa. "Violent Victims? Surprising Aspects of the Just War Theory in the Chronicle of Peter von Dusburg," in Alan V. Murray, ed. *The Clash of Cultures on the Medieval Baltic Frontier*, 123–37. Burlington, VT: Ashgate Publishing Company, 2009.
McCormack, Michael. "The Liturgy of War in the Early Middle Ages: Crisis, Litanies, and the Carolingian Monarchy." *Viator* 15 (1984): 1–23.
McKitterick, Rosamond. *The Frankish Kingdoms Under the Carolingians, 751-987.* London: Longman, 1983.
Morton, Nicholas. *The Teutonic Knights in the Holy Land, 1190-1291.* Woodbridge: Boydell Press, 2009.
Muldoon, James. *Popes, Lawyers, and Infidels: The Church and the Non-Christian World, 1250-1550.* Philadelphia: University of Pennsylvania Press, 1979.
Muldoon, James, ed. *Varieties of Religious Conversion in the Middle Ages.* Gainesville, FL: University Press of Florida, 1997.
Murphy, G. Ronald. *The Saxon Savior: The Germanic Transformation of the Gospel in the Ninth-Century Heliand.* Oxford: Oxford University Press, 1989.
Murray, Alan V., ed. *Crusade and Conversion on the Baltic Frontier, 1150-1500.* Burlington, VT: Ashgate Publishing Company, 2001.
Murray, Alan V., ed. *The Clash of Cultures on the Medieval Baltic Frontier.* Burlington, VT: Ashgate Publishing Company, 2009.
Murray, Alexander Callander, ed. *After Rome's Fall: Narrators and Sources of Early Medieval History.* Buffalo, NY: University of Toronto Press, 1998.
Nelson, Janet L. "Ninth century Knighthood: the Evidence of Nithard," in Christopher Harper-Brill, Christopher J. Holdsworth, and Janet

Nelson, eds. *Studies in Medieval History presented to R. Allen Brown*, 255–66. Woodbridge: The Boydell Press, 1989.

Nelson, Janet L. "The Church's Military Service in the Ninth Century: A Contemporary Comparative View?," in W. J. Sheils, ed. *The Church and War*, 15–30. Oxford: Basil Blackwell, 1983.

Nelson, Janet L. "Violence in the Carolingian World and the ritualization of ninth-century warfare," in Guy Halsall, ed. *Violence and Society in the Early Medieval West*, 90–107. Woodbridge: The Boydell Press, 1998.

Nicholson, Helen, ed. *Palgrave Advances in the Crusades*. London: Palgrave MacMillan, 2005.

Nicolle, David. *Warriors and Their Weapons Around the Time of the Crusades: Relationships Between Byzantium, the West and the Islamic World*. Burlington, VT: Ashgate Publishing Company, 2002.

Nielsen, Torben K. "Mission and Submission: Societal Change in the Baltic in the Thirteenth Century," in Tuomas M. S. Lehtonen and Kurt Villads Jensen with Janne Malkki and Katja Ritari, eds. *Medieval History Writing and Crusading Ideology*, 216–31. Studia Fennica, Historica 9. Helsinki: Finnish Literature Society, 2005.

Nock, Arthur Darby. *Conversion: the Old and the New in Religion from Alexander the Great to Augustine of Hippo*. Oxford: Clarendon Press, 1933.

Noth, Albrecht. *Heiliger Krieg und Heiliger Kampf in Islam und Christentum: Beiträge zur Vorgeschichte und Geschichte der Kreuzzüge*. Bonner Historische Forschungen, Bd. 28. Bonn: Ludwig Rohrscheid Verlag, 1966.

Oakley, Francis. *Kingship: The Politics of Enchantment*. Oxford: Blackwell Publishers, 2006.

O'Corrain, Donnchadh. *Ireland Before the Normans*. Dublin: Gill and MacMillan, 1972.

Orlandis, José. *Historia del Reino Visigodo Español: Los acontecimientos, las instituciones, la sociedad, los protagonistas*. Madrid: Ediciones RIALP, S.A., 2003.

Painter, Sidney. "Western Europe on the Eve of the Crusades," in Kenneth M. Setton, ed. *A History of the Crusades*, vol. I, 3–29. Madison, WI: University of Wisconsin Press, 1969.

Pelikan, Jaroslav. *The Growth of Medieval Theology (600-1300)*. Vol. 3 in *The Christian Tradition: A History of the Development of Doctrine*. Chicago: The University of Chicago Press, 1978.

Phillips, Jonathan. *The Second Crusade: Extending the Frontiers of Christendom*. New Haven, Connecticut: Yale University Press, 2007.

Pohl, Walter, Ian Wood, and Helmut Reimitz, eds. *The Transformation of Frontiers: From Antiquity to the Carolingians*. Leiden: Brill, 2001.

Poole, Austin Lane. *Henry the Lion: The Lothian Historical Essay for 1912*. Oxford: B. H. Blackwell, 1912.
Prawer, Joshua. Review of *A History of the Crusades: The First Hundred Years*. Kenneth M. Setton and Marshall W. Baldwin, eds. *Revue belge de philologie et d'histoire* 37 (1959): 167–70.
Pryor, John H. *Commerce, Shipping, and Naval Warfare in the Medieval Mediterranean*. London: Variorum, 1987.
Pryor, John H. *Geography, Technology and War: Studies in the Maritime History of the Mediterranean, 649-1571*. Cambridge: Cambridge University Press, 1988.
Reynolds, Burnam W. *Columbanus: Light on the Early Middle Ages*. New York: Longman, 2011.
Reynolds, Burnam W. "The Prehistory of the Crusades: Toward a Developmental Taxonomy." *History Compass* 6 (May 2008): 884–97.
Richard, Jean. "National Feeling and the Legacy of the Crusades," in Helen Nicholson, ed. Palgrave *Advances in the Crusades*, 204–22. London: Palgrave MacMillan, 2005.
Riley-Smith, Jonathan. *The Crusades: A History*. 2nd edn. New Haven, CT: Yale University Press, 2005.
Riley-Smith, Jonathan. *The Crusades: A Short History*. New Haven, CT: Yale University Press, 1987.
Riley-Smith, Jonathan. *The Crusades, Christianity, and Islam*. New York: Columbia University Press, 2008.
Riley-Smith, Jonathan. "The First Crusade and the Persecution of Jews," in W. J. Sheils, ed., *Persecution and Toleration*, 51–72. Oxford: Basil Blackwell, 1984.
Riley-Smith, Jonathan, ed. *The Oxford Illustrated History of the Crusades*. Oxford: Oxford University Press, 1997.
Robinson, I. S., "Gregory VII and the Soldiers of Christ." *History* 58 (1973): 169–92.
Roesdahl, Else and David M. Wilson, eds. *From Viking to Crusader: The Scandinavians and Europe 800–1200*. New York: Rizzoli International Publications, 1992.
Rosenwein, Barbara H. *A Short History of the Middle Ages*. 2nd edn. Peterborough, Ontario: Broadview Press, 2004.
Russell, Frederick H. *The Just War in the Middle Ages*. Cambridge: Cambridge University Press, 1975.
Russell, James C. *The Germanization of Early Medieval Christianity: A Sociological Approach to Religious Transformation*. Oxford: Oxford University Press, 1994.
Sawyer, Birgit and Peter Sawyer. *Medieval Scandinavia: From Conversion to Reformation, circa 800-1500*. Minneapolis, MN: University of Minnesota Press, 1993.

Semb, Anne Julie, "U.N. Authorized Interventions: A Slippery Slope of Forcible Interference?" in Henrik Syse and Gregory M. Reichberg, eds. *Ethics, Nationalism, and Just War: Medieval and Contemporary Perspectives*, 218–45. Washington, DC: The Catholic University of America Press, 2007.

Setton, Kenneth M., ed. *A History of the Crusades*, 6 vols. Madison, WI: University of Wisconsin Press, 1969–89.

Shaw, Brent D. *Sacred Violence: African Christians and Sectarian Hatred in the Age of Augustine*. Cambridge: Cambridge University Press, 2011.

Shaw, Brent D. "War and Violence," in G. W. Bowersock, Peter Brown, and Oleg Grabar, eds. *Interpreting Late Antiquity: Essays on the Postclassical World*, 130–69. Cambridge, MA: The Belknap Press of Harvard University, 2001.

Sheils, W. J., ed. *Persecution and Toleration*. Vol. 21 of *Studies in Church History*. Oxford: Basil Blackwell, 1984.

Sheils, W. J., ed. *The Church and War*. Vol. 20 of *Studies in Church History*. Oxford: Basil Blackwell, 1983.

Siberry, Elizabeth. "Missionaries and Crusaders, 1095-1274: Opponents or Allies?" in W. J. Sheils, ed. *The Church and War*, 103–10. Oxford: Basil Blackwell, 1983.

Smith, Julia M. H. "Review Article: Early Medieval Hagiography in the Late Twentieth Century." *Early Medieval Europe* 1, no. 1 (1992): 69–76.

Sne, Andris. "The Emergence of Livonia: The Transformations of Social and Political Structures in the Territory of Latvia during the Twelfth and Thirteenth Centuries," in Alan V. Murray, ed. *The Clash of Cultures on the Medieval Baltic Frontier*, 53–71. Burlington, VT: Ashgate Publishing Company, 2009.

Spinks, Bryan D. *Early and Medieval Rituals and Theologies of Baptism: From the New Testament to the Council of Trent*. Burlington, VT: Ashgate Publishing, 2006.

Stancliffe, Clare. "Red, White, and Blue Martyrdom," in Dorothy Whitelock, Rosamond McKitterick, and David Dumville, eds. *Ireland in Early Medieval Europe: Studies in Memory of Kathleen Hughes*, 21–46. Cambridge: Cambridge University Press, 1982.

Stark, Rodney. *God's Battalions: The Case for the Crusades*. New York: HarperCollins, 2009.

Strousma, Guy. "Mystical Jerusalem," in Lee I. Levine, ed. *Jerusalem: Its Sanctity and Centrality to Judaism, Christianity, and Islam*. London: Continuum International Publishing Group, 1999.

Sullivan, Richard E. "Carolingian Missionary Theories." *The Catholic Historical Review* 42, no. 3 (1956): 273–95.

Sullivan, Richard E. "Early Medieval Missionary Activity: A Comparative Study of Eastern and Western Methods." *Church History* 23 (1954): 17–35.
Sullivan, Richard E. "The Carolingian Missionary and the Pagan." *Speculum* 28 (1953): 705–40.
Sullivan, Richard E. "The Medieval Monk as Frontiersman," in William W. Savage, Jr. and Stephen I. Thompson, eds. *The Frontier: Comparative Studies*, vol. 2., 25–49. Norman, OK: University of Oklahoma Press, 1979.
Sumption, Jonathan. *Pilgrimage: An Image of Mediaeval Religion.* London: Faber & Faber, 1975.
Swift, Louis J. *The Early Fathers on War and Military Service.* Wilmington, DE: Michael Glazier, 1983.
Syse, Henrik. "Augustine and Just War," in Henrik Syse and Gregory M. Reichberg, eds. *Ethics, Nationalism, and Just War: Medieval and Contemporary Perspectives*, 36–50. Washington, DC: The Catholic University of America, 2007.
Syse, Henrik and Gregory M. Reichberg, eds. *Ethics, Nationalism, and Just War: Medieval and Contemporary Perspectives.* Washington, DC: The Catholic University of America Press, 2007.
Thompson, E. A. *The Goths in Spain.* Oxford: At the Clarendon Press, 1969.
Thompson, James Westfall. *Feudal Germany.* Chicago: University of Chicago Press, 1928.
Thrupp, Sylvia L., ed. *Change in Medieval Society: Europe North of the Alps, 1050-1500.* New York: Appleton-Century-Crofts, 1964.
Thrupp, Sylvia L., ed. *Early Medieval Society.* New York: Appleton-Century-Crofts, 1967.
Tierney, Brian. *The Crisis of Church and State, 1050-1300.* Englewood Cliffs, NJ: Prentice-Hall, Inc., 1964.
Tierney, Brian and Joan Scott, eds. *Western Societies: A Documentary History*, vol. 1. New York: Alfred A. Knopf, 1984.
Tuchman, Barbara. *A Distant Mirror: The Calamitous Fourteenth Century.* New York: Ballantine Books, 1978.
Tveito, Olav. "St. Olaf—Missionary with an Iron Tongue." *Historisk Tidsskrift* 3 (2003): 355–83.
Tyerman, Christopher. "Accounting for the Crusades: Faith, Facts and Figures." Plenary address delivered at the Third International Symposium on Crusade Studies. St. Louis, MO: Saint Louis University, March 1, 2014.
Tyerman, Christopher. *God's War: A New History of the Crusades.* Cambridge, MA: The Belknap Press of Harvard University Press, 2006.

Tyerman, Christopher. *How to Plan a Crusade: Reason and Religious War in the High Middle Ages*. St. Ives, UK: Allen Lane/Penguin Random House, 2015.
Tyerman, Christopher. *The Debate on the Crusades*. Manchester: Manchester University Press, 2011.
Tyerman, Christopher. *The Invention of the Crusades*. Toronto: University of Toronto Press, 1998.
Ullmann, Walter. *The Carolingian Renaissance & the Idea of Kingship: The Birkbeck Lectures, 1968-9*. London: Methuen & Co., Ltd., 1969.
Urban, William. "Rethinking the Crusades." *AHA Perspectives* 36 (October 1998): 1–5.
Urban, William. Review of Iben Fonnesberg-Schmidt, *The Popes and the Baltic Crusades, 1147-1254*. *Speculum* 83 (January 2008): 195–6.
Urban, William. *The Baltic Crusade*. 2nd edn. Chicago: Lithuanian Research and Studies Center, 1994.
Urban, William. "The Frontier Thesis and the Baltic Crusade," in Alan V. Murray, ed. *Crusade and Conversion on the Baltic Frontier, 1100-1500*, 35–71. Burlington, VT: Ashgate Publishers, 2001.
Urban, William. *The Livonian Crusade*. 2nd edn. Chicago: Lithuanian Research and Studies Center, 2004.
Urban, William. *The Samogitian Crusade*. 2nd edn. Chicago: Lithuanian Research and Studies Center, 2006.
Urban, William. "The Sense of Humor among the Teutonic Knights." *Illinois Quarterly* 42 (1979): 45.
Urban, William. "Victims of the Baltic Crusade." *Journal of Baltic Studies* 29, no. 3 (1998): 195–212.
Urbanczyk, Przemyslaw. "The Politics of Conversion in North Central Europe," in Martin Carver, ed. *The Cross Goes North*, 15–27. Woodbridge: The Boydell Press, 2005.
Vetlesen, Arne Johan. "Genocide: A Case for the Responsibility of the Bystander," in Henrik Syse and Gregory M. Reichberg, eds. *Ethics, Nationalism, and Just War*, 352–71. Washington, DC: The Catholic University of America Press, 2007.
Von Ranke, Leopold. *Weltgeschichte*, vol. 8, *Kreuzzuge und papstliche Weltherrschaft*. Leipzig: Duncker & Humblot, 1887.
Wallace-Hadrill, J. M. *Early Germanic Kingship in England and on the Continent*. Oxford: At the Clarendon Press, 1971.
Wallace-Hadrill, J. M. *Early Medieval History*. New York: Harper & Row, 1976.
Wallace-Hadrill, J. M., trans. *The Fourth Book of the Chronicle of Fredegar and its Continuations*. London: Thomas Nelson, 1960.
Wallace-Hadrill, J. M. *The Frankish Chuch*. Oxford: Clarendon Press, 1983.

Walters, LeRoy, "The Just War and the Crusade: Antitheses or Analogies?" *Monist* 57 (October 1973): 584–94.
Waltz, James. Review of Benjamin Z. Kedar, *Crusade and Mission: European Approaches toward the Muslims*. *Speculum* 61 (April 1986): 431–3.
Webb, Diana. *Medieval European Pilgrimage, c. 700-c. 1500*. New York: Palgrave, 2002.
Webster, Alexander F. C. and Darrell Cole. *The Virtue of War: Reclaiming the Classic Christian Traditions East and West*. Salisbury, MA: Regina Orthodox Press, 2004.
Weinfurter, Stefan. *The Salian Century: Main Currents in an Age of Transition*. Trans. Barbara M. Bowlus. Philadelphia: University of Pennsylvania Press, 1999.
Wills, Garry. *Font of Life: Ambrose, Augustine & The Mystery of Baptism*. Oxford: Oxford University Press, 2012.
Wilson, Derek. *Charlemagne*. New York: Vintage Books, 2007.
Wilson, Stephen G. *Leaving the Fold: Apostates and Defections in Antiquity*. Minneapolis: Fortress Press, 2004.
Winder, Simon. *Germania: In Wayward Pursuit of the Germans and Their History*. New York: Picador/Farrar, Straus and Giroux, 2010.
Winroth, Anders. *The Conversion of Scandinavia: Vikings, Merchants, and Missionaries in the Remaking of Northern Europe*. New Haven, CT: Yale University Press, 2012.
Winston, Richard. *Charlemagne: From the Hammer to the Cross*. New York: Vintage Books, 1954.
Wood, Ian. "Missionaries and the Christian Frontier," in Walter Pohl, Ian Wood, and Helmut Reimitz, eds. *The Transformation of Frontiers: From Antiquity to the Carolingians*, 209–18. Leiden: Brill, 2001.
Wood, Ian and Neils Lund, eds. *People and Places in Northern Europe, 500-1600: Essays in Honour of Peter Hayes Sawyer*. Woodbridge: The Boydell Press, 1991.
Yoder, John Howard. *Nevertheless: The Varieties and Shortcomings of Religious Pacifism*. Scottdale, PA: Herald Press, 1992.

INDEX

Abbot of Corbie 90
Abodrites 20, 22, 30
Adam of Bremen 59
adelskirche ("church of the
   nobility") 113, 163
"adhesion" 161
Adolf II of Holstein 16
Adolf of Holstein 19, 22, 30
Aelia Capitolina 151
Aethelbehrt 114, 115
Aethelred 117
Aggessen, Sven 19
Aimon of Bourges 94
Alabrand 126
Alamanni 81–2
Albert of Anhalt 80
Albert of Ballenstedt
   ("The Bear") 16, 19, 23–4
Albert of Buxhövden 133, 143,
   151, 159–60, 164, 174
Albert of Riga 25, 30, 33, 36
Alboin 130
Alcuin 101
Alfred the Great 110
"Alleluia Victory" 70
Al-Manzor 153
Anabaptists 106
Anglo-Saxons 90, 110, 133,
   147–8, 153
Anselm II of Lucca 95
Anselm of Havelberg 16, 22
apostasy 121–3, 183
apostates 121–3, 128, 166, 172
Arctic Circle 20

Arian Christians 106, 111
Arianism 114, 169–70
Arian-Trinitarian conflicts 170
Aridius 175
Arnold, Matthew 59
Arnold of Meiendorf 79
Arsenal, León 106
Arthurian legend 146
Articuli contra cruciferos
   ("The Articles Against the
   Crusaders") 181
Asbridge, Thomas 37, 95, 144
aspersio 116
Atabeg of Mosul 11
auctoritas 78
audiente ("hearer") 97
authorization 78, 80, 89
Avars 109, 130
Avitus of Vienne 82, 114, 171

Bagge, Sverre 184
Baldric of Dol 171
Baldwin of Boulogne 12
ballistarii (missile warriors) 176
Baltic Sea 1, 24, 32, 62, 72–3,
   127, 140
"baptism by treaty" 97–119, 123
The Barbarian Conversion
   (Fletcher) 57, 193
Bartlett, Robert 20, 189
Battle of Cintla 186
Battle of Cooldrevny 146
Battle of Poitiers 91
Battle of Tannenberg 179, 182

Battle of the River
 Saule 131, 179
Battle of Vouillé 111
Becket, Thomas á 153
Bede 82, 112
Belial 131
belliolum ("little war") 90
bellorum civilium 83
bellum (war) 90
Berengar, Henry 14, 18
Bernard of Seehausen 79
Berthold 72, 98, 101, 121
"big bang theory" 50–1, 54
Bishko, C. J. 64
Bishop of Hippo 80
Bismarck, Otto von 70
Blessed Virgin 158
Bloch, Marc 64
blot 112
Boniface 91–2, 111, 147
Bonizio of Sutri 95
Bretislav 175
Brief Account of the Destruction of the Indies (Casas) 184
Brown, Peter 137, 139, 156
Brundage, James 127
Bull, Marcus 58
Burckhardt, Jacob 59
Buxhövden, Albert von 24, 79
Bysted, Ane 51, 87
Byzantine civil war 118
Byzantine-Serb treaty 161

campus stellae ("field of stars") 153
Canterbury Cathedral 153
The Canterbury Tales 153
Capitulatio de partibus Saxoniae 108
Casas, Bartolomé de las 184, 186–7
casati ("housed ones") 90, 94
Castillo, Bernal Díaz del 184–5, 187
casus belli 72, 167, 169
Cathar heresy 169

Celestine II, Pope 72
Celtic church 146
Celtic life pilgrimage 146
Charlemagne 13, 20, 58, 60, 62–3, 74, 84–5, 87, 91–3, 100–1, 107–10, 115
Chaucer, Geoffrey 153
Chevedden, Paul 49–51, 54, 57
Children's Crusade 47
Chlotar I 130
Christian conflicts 158–78
Christian Count of Edessa 11
Christian on Christian violence 158–78
Christian Saxony 19
Christiansen, Eric 32, 38, 181
Christian warfare participation 75
Christian West 12, 49, 53, 107, 110, 153, 191
Chronicle of the Slavs (Helmold) 58
Church Council of Constance 180, 182
Church of the Holy Sepulchre 144, 150–1, 156
Cianachta of Louth 90
The City of God (Augustine) 78
Clausewitz, Carl von 3, 101
Clovis 81–3, 91, 111, 113, 115, 138, 171, 175
Cnut the Great 30
Cobb, Paul M. 49–50
Coifi 112
Colish, Marcia L. 28, 107, 167
Columba 146
Columbanus 113, 146–7, 155, 177
comitatus (retinue) 177
Commonitorium (Vincent of Lerins) 172
condita (founding) 156
conquistadores 183, 187
Conrad III 11, 14, 16, 29
Conrad of Zähringen 16

Conrad the Great 17–19
"consequential baptism" 102
Constable, Giles 37, 46–7, 51, 64, 145
Constantia 122
Constantine 59–60, 75–6, 81, 110–11, 122, 144, 151
Constantinian revolution 59, 91
Continental church 147
contra apostatas ("against apostates") 121
Contra Faustum 80
Convent of the Holy Cross 177
convivencia 72
Corinthians II 75
Coroticus 170
Cortes, Hernan 184–7
Cosmas of Prague 175
Council of Clermont 13, 49–50, 53–4, 61, 148
Council of Orléans 176
Council of Troyes 95, 155
Count of Flanders 61
Count of Pyrmont 80
County of Edessa 12
Cramer, Peter 148
crucesignati (those signed with the cross) 142
Crusade and Mission (Kedar) 56
"crusade era" 49
crusade revolution 43–5
Crusader states 12, 14
crusading ethos 46
"crusading king" 159
crux cismarina ("crusading on this side of the sea") 31
crux transmarina ("overseas crusading") 31–2

Danes 88, 109–10, 135, 158–60, 163, 165, 171
Daniel of Lennewarden 176
Daniel-Rops, Henri 48
Danish baptism 162–3
Danish-Rigan dispute 163

Dar-al-Islam 103
Dark Ages 59
Daugava 128
Daugava River 34, 98
Davidson, Linda Kay 145
Dawson, Christopher 59, 64
Decretum 89
De Ecclesiis et Capellis (Hincmar of Rheims) 90
The Deeds of Pope Innocent III 165
De laude novae militiae (Bernard) 95, 155
Deus ultor (vengeful God) 136
dhimmi 103
dhimmitude 103
Diet of Frankfurt 21
Diets 11, 14, 17, 20
dilatatio Christianitas 30–1, 155, 163
Diocletian 75, 104
Divina dispensatione 20–1
Divina dispensatione II 34, 143, 174
Dnieper River 118
Donatists 104–6
Dorotheus 140
Dorpat 129
Drake, H. A. 72
Duchy of Saxony 19
Duke of Saxony 80
Dunn-Wood, Maryjane 145
Dvornik, Francis 70, 112
Dyas, Dee 146

Eadbald 115
Easter 97
Edgar 88
"edge crusade" 149
Edwin 81–2, 91, 112, 115
Eihmane, Eva 29
Elbe River 18–19
elision 87
encomienda 187
Episcopal system 176–7
Erdmann, Carl 35, 38, 55–6, 62–3, 71, 111, 169

Esths 21
"eternal crusades" 24–5, 32, 184, 188, 193
"ethnocide" 132
ethno-political approach 101
Eugenius III, Pope 12–13, 15, 19, 32, 34, 49, 143, 174
Euphrates River 11
exterius (exogenic crusading) 31

"faith and fiefs" 174, 190
Fall of Rome 78
fath (opening) 71, 102–3, 108–9
Ferns 90
fidelitas 95
Finns 188
First Crusade 1, 11–13, 18, 48–50, 57, 74, 142, 145, 148, 170
Fischer, David Hackett 5
Fletcher, Richard 7, 57, 124, 166, 168, 177, 193
Flori, Jean 57
forced baptism 102
Fourth Council of Toledo 106–7
Fourth Crusade 166
Fourth Lateran Council 151
France, John 43, 57
The Frankish Annals 62
Franks (*Franji*) 13, 20, 58, 60, 82–3, 90–1, 93, 107, 111, 171
Fratres militiae Christi Livoniae (Swordbrothers) 25
Frederick of Swabia 17
Frend, W. H. C. 106
Frisian county of Rüstringen 109
Fulcher of Chartres 170–1
Fulrad 93

Gabriele, Matthew 58
Garden of Gethsemane 85
generalists 47
Germanization 84, 85
Gesta Innocentii III 165
Ghosh, Shami 38, 132

Gibb, Hamilton 59, 125
Gideon/Joshua scenario 70
Gimbutas, Marija 112
goldwine ("gold friend") 117
Gospel of John 85, 165
Gottschalk 80
Grammaticus, Saxo 109, 168
Gray, Phillip W. 121, 172
Great Commission 72
Great Schism 180
Gregory I, Pope 89, 127, 133, 153
Gregory II, Pope 133
Gregory VII, Pope 49, 63, 94–5
Gregory of Tours 81–3, 111, 114, 170–1
Gregory XII, Pope 180
Grifo 91
Guatemoc 187
Gundobad 114–15, 175
Guthrum 110
gyrovagi 147

Hadrian 151
Hakon, Earl 117
Harald Bluetooth 116
Harris, Jonathan 161
Haskins, Charles Homer 50, 59
Headley, John 143
Hebbus 99
Heine, Heinrich 70
Heinzelmann, Martin 61
Helena, Augusta 144–5, 151
The Heliand 85
Helmold of Bosau 19, 23, 58, 87, 168, 175
Hen, Yitzhak 108
Henry II 153
Henry III 175
Henry of Mainz 18
Henry "the Fowler" 110, 134
Henry "the Lion" 16, 19
Henry V 17, 161
Henry VI (Henry Berengar) 18
Heraclius 48

Hermanfrid   80
Hermann I   17
Hildebert of Mainz   86
Hincmar of Rheims   90
Hindley, Geoffrey   29
Hippo Regius   104
Histories (Gregory of Tours)   83
A History of the Crusades   55
History of the Lombards (Paul the Deacon)   177
Hohenstaufen   14, 16–17, 19
Holy Cross   186
Holy Land   1–3, 12, 14, 16–20, 25–6, 28–32, 34–5, 37, 44–5, 47–51, 58, 65, 79, 142, 144, 149–53, 155, 174, 183
Holy Roman Emperor   91, 143
Holy Roman Empire   21
Honorius III   34
"housed ones" *(casati)*   90, 94
Housley, Norman   38, 45, 48, 150
Howe, John   149, 151
Hoyland, Robert   103
Huizinga, Johan   121

Iberian Peninsula   31, 183
immersio   116
indulgentia   89
Innocent III, Pope   24, 38, 49, 133, 135, 143, 165, 169
Innocent IV, Pope   89
interius (endogenic crusading)   31
Iona   146
isapostle ("new apostle")   76
Isidore of Seville   106–7
Italian Renaissance   59
ius ad bellum (causative sense)   44–5, 86, 182, 191
ius in bello   44, 191

Jagiello   180
Jarimar   115
Jensen, Carsten Selch   149
Jensen, Kurt Villads   74

Jerusalem   12, 143–5, 148, 150–2, 155–6, 163
Jerusalem in the North   151
Jogaila   166
John, Master   158
John VIII, Pope   89
John of Falkenberg   180
Johnson, Edgar   189
joie de combat   191
Jordan River   144
Joshua/Gideon scenario   70
just war theory   33, 36, 44, 74, 76–80, 83–4, 86–7, 91, 128, 130, 136, 181, 184, 191

Kedar, Benjamin   56, 89
Kingdom of Prussia   16
Klak, Harald   109
Knights Templar   1, 79, 95
Knuba   110
Kurs   128, 132
Kushite kingdom   98

labarum   63, 81, 122
laesae maiestatis (treason)   76
Langobard   130
Last Supper   85
lawful authority   80
LeBras, Gabriel   139–40
Lembit   129
Lent   11
Lenten fast   109
Leo IV, Pope   89
Letts   21, 100, 102, 126, 163–4
Levant   26
leyenda negra ("black legend")   184
libido dominandi ("lust to dominate")   83, 170
Licinius   110, 122, 144
Life of Charlemagne (Notker the Stammerer)   58
Life of St. Lebuin   92
Life of St. Liborius   70

lima ("threshold") 173
Lithuanians 128, 131, 136
Livonian Chronicle (Henry) 24, 30, 33, 36, 69, 79, 98, 101, 106, 120, 123, 131, 140, 143, 149, 158, 160, 168, 172
Livonian Crusade 28
Livonian Rhymed Chronicle (Henry) 36, 69, 118, 124, 126, 128, 136, 143, 158
Livs 21, 30, 33–4, 99
locus sanctorum (holy places) 35, 137, 144–5, 149–50, 152, 154–6
Lombards 89
Long, Edward LeRoy, Jr. 125
longue dureé 54, 188
Lotter, Friedrich 33, 116
Louis the Pious 109
Louis VII 13–14
Lübeck 19, 22, 30
Lupus of Ferrieres 90

Madden, Thomas F. 44, 174
The Magdeburg Appeal 151
magisterium 166
Main River 11
major palatii ("mayor of the palace") 91
manaich (lay clients) 90
Margraviate of Brandenburg 16
Marian triumphalism 136
Markus, R. A. 78
Martel, Charles 91–2
Martha (Morta) 167
Martin of Braga 101
Martin V 180
Marxian class oppression 29
matricularii pauperi ("matriculating poor") 176
mawla (sponsor) 103
Maximin 122
Mayer, Hans Eberhard 95
Mazeika, Rasa 100

Medard of Noyon 177
Meinhard of Uexküll 30, 33, 72, 98, 124, 159–60, 167
mesolithic era 63–4, 91, 107
meso-prehistory phase 81
militia ecclesiae 90, 93
militia sancti Petri ("army of St. Peter") 93, 95
Mindaugas 166
"missionary war" *(missionskrieg)* 31, 35–6, 38, 71–96
"mission creep" 89
"monastic banks" 177
Monism 190–1
Montezuma 186–7
Moors 153
Morton, Nicholas Edward 152
Muhammad 103
mulieres et parvulos 129, 134
Muslim East 12, 53
muthos (myth) 58

natio 133
naval support, for crusading 44
Neibuhr, Reinhold 181
Nelson, Janet 89, 93
neolithic era 63–4, 93
Nevertheless (Yoder) 86
New World 183–7, 193
Nicholas I, Pope 89
Nicholas II, Pope 50
Nielsen, Torben K. 113, 130
Niklot 22–3, 30
Nock, Arthur Darby 140
Nordmark 16, 19
Notker the Stammerer 58

Odin 117
Odo 90
Olaf Haraldson 117
Olaf Tryggvason 117
Old Testament 135, 138
ordo pugnatorum (order of warriors) 95

Origen   75
The Origin of the Idea of Crusade (Erdmann)   55, 60
Orthodox Church   161
Oselians   131, 178
Otto II   116
Otto of Freising (Otto I)   16–17, 86, 116, 126
Our Lady   136, 186
The Oxford Illustrated History of the Crusades (Bull)   58

pacifism   86
pacis firma (lasting peace)   100
Pact of Omar   103
"pagan Balts"   33
pagani ("pagans")   32, 166
pagus   138
paleolithic era   63–4, 91
Paul (apostle)   22, 75
Paul III, Pope   186
Pauline epistles   76
Paulinus of Nola   137
Paul the Deacon   130, 177
Peace of God movement   63, 94
Peace of Thorn   180
peregrinatio pro amore Christo (pilgrimage for the love of Christ)   146–8, 154, 157
peregrini ("pilgrims")   35, 142–57
per molestias eruditio (teaching by inconveniences)   172
Persecution Edict   104
Peter (apostle)   22
Peter the Venerable   16, 85
Philip (apostle)   98
Philip of Swabia   143
"pilgrim's year"   154
Pius II, Pope   181
pluralists   47
Polish-Lithuanian forces   124
polytheists   71
Poor Peoples' Crusade   47
popularists   47

post-Constantinian era   75
post-Roman barbarian kingdoms   81
potior peregrinatio ("the better pilgrimage")   146
Prawer, Joshua   55–6
pre-Carolingian wars   111
preliando quam predicando ("preaching and fighting")   69
Pribislav   30
Protestant Reformation   183
Prussian Crusade   28, 189
Pskov   134
Pudiviru   120, 163

Quantum praedecessores   13, 15
Queen of Heaven   135, 140
quondam peregrinatio et futurus (the once and future pilgrimage)   146

Ranke, Leopold von   53
Rashid, Harun al-   58
Reccared   114
regnum   108
reisens ("risings")   24, 60, 142, 154, 192
remissio peccatorum (the remission of sins)   145
Renaissance   59
Renaissance of the Twelfth Century (Haskins)   59
rex et sacerdos ("king and priest")   112
Rhine/Danube   82, 84
Rhineland   82
Richard I (Coeur de Lion)   1
Riley-Smith, Jonathan   48, 181
Robert of Rheims   13
Robert the Monk   171
Roman Christianity   101
Roman civil war   76
Roman Empire   78, 81, 83, 132, 143

Rosamond of the Gepids   130
Royal Frankish Annals   20
Rudolf of Stotle   80
Rudolph of Jerichow   165
Rugians   21
Russell, James C.   84

Saccalians   99–101, 129
sacramentum (military induction ceremony)   75
Saint Mary, help us to victory (song)   136
St. Ambrose   76, 84, 147
St. Augustine   76, 78, 80–1, 83–4, 101, 104–6, 137, 162, 170, 181, 184
St. Benedict   147
St. Bernard of Clairvaux   13–14, 16–18, 20–2, 34, 62, 95, 116, 132, 134, 155, 174
St. Denis   93
St. Hilary of Poitiers   138
St. James   153
St. Leocadia   114
St. Louis   1
St. Martin   114, 156
St. Patrick   92, 169–70
St. Radegund   130, 177
St. Remigius   113
Saladin   1
Salvatorkirche (Church of the Savior)   11, 15, 28
Samogitian Crusade   28
Samogitians   173
Saxon Wars   118
Scandinavian politics   117–18
Schenen River   136
Second Crusade   17, 19, 28–9, 37, 51, 55
Sedde River   126
Selones   99–100
Semgallians   21
Semgalls   128
seniores (tribal leaders)   130

Sepúlveda, Juan Ginés de   187
Serbs   161
Setton, Kenneth M.   55
Shaw, Brent D.   71, 132
Sisebut   107
Slavic Europe   70
Slavic Wilzi   134
Slavs   18, 20, 23, 25, 87–8, 112–13, 155, 168, 185, 190
sommer-reysa   24
Sorbs   20
sortes Biblicae   127
Speculum   56
Spinks, Bryan   105
stare decisis (settled situation)   61
Stark, Rodney   29
statutory tax   168
Stettin (Szczecin)   23, 168, 170
Stierland, Andreas von   69
Stoinef   126
Stone Age   63
Strousma, Guy   151
Sturluson, Snorri   116–17
Svantovit/Redigast   23, 33, 168–9, 185
Svelgate   128
Swedes   135, 160
Swift, Louis J.   75–6
Swordbrothers (*Fratres militiae Christi Livoniae*)   25–6, 120, 123, 129, 131, 135, 155, 163–5, 168–9, 174, 179
syncretism   124
Synod of Melfi   50
"syntality"   112
"Syrians" ("Turcopoles")   12
Syse, Henrik   83

Tabelin   163
Taghamon   90
Tanz mit den Heiden ("dance with the heathen")   25
Tarragona   49

tempus acceptibile ("acceptable time") 21, 134
Ten Books of History (Gregory of Tours) 170
Tertullian 56, 61, 75
Tetislav 115
Teutonic Knights 25–6, 36, 69, 100, 124, 126, 131–2, 135, 155, 166–7, 174, 179–81, 186–7
Teutonic Order 152
Thalibald 128–9
"thanes" 85
Theodoric/Theuderic 79–81
Theodosius I 111
Theodulf of Orleans 108
Theodwin 17
Third Council of Toledo 114
Third Crusade 46
Thoros 12
"Thundering Legion" 75
Tlascalan 187
topos 37, 80, 98
"traditional crusading" 54
traditors 104–6
Triglaus 168
Trinitarian view 114
tropaea 149
Truce of God movement 63, 94
tudun (Avar leader) 109
"Turcopoles" ("Syrians") 12
Tyerman, Christopher 1, 43, 45–6, 49, 79, 94, 166

ulciscuntur iniurias 83
unbaptism 107
Ungannians 100, 101, 120, 129, 134
Urban II, Pope 13, 49, 51, 54, 57, 61, 170–1
Urban, William 24, 29, 88, 130–1, 133, 142, 144, 148, 159, 167, 183, 185, 189, 192
urbs 138

Valdemar "the Great" 23, 115, 118, 159
verbum directum 81
vexillum sancti Petri 63
victoriam de gentibus apostatantibus 121
Vikings 90, 110
vim vi repellare ("force may repel force") 181
Vincent of Lerins 172
Virgin Mary 135–7, 139, 141, 151, 186
Visigothic Arians 111
Visigothic Spain 106, 170
Visigoths 82, 138
Vladimiri, Paul 180–2
Vladimir of Kiev 118, 134
Vladimir of Polozk 159–60

Wallace-Hadrill, J. M. 85, 108, 112, 171–2
Waltz, James 56
warfare, among Christians 169
Webb, Diana 142
Webster, Alexander F. C. 48
Welfs 14, 17
Weltgeschichte (Ranke) 53
Wendish Crusade 18–19, 21, 23, 28–30, 37, 62, 116, 128, 170, 174–5
Wends 18, 20, 23, 60, 88
Western church 165
West Saxons 82
"white martyrdom" 146
Wibald of Corvey 18
Widukind of Corvey 100, 126, 134
Wilfrid 177–8
William of Modena 158, 167–8, 178
Wills, Garry 105
Wilzes 20

Winroth, Anders   117
winter-reysa   25
Woischleg   167
Wood, Ian   173
Word of God   69

Yoder, John Howard   86

zehnte   167
Zengi, 'Imad ad-Din   11–12
zins   167

www.ingramcontent.com/pod-product-compliance
Lightning Source LLC
Chambersburg PA
CBHW050136240426
43673CB00043B/1688